PHYTOMORPHOLOGY, TAXONOMY AND ANATOMY-MCQs

SET, NET, NEET, JRF, GATE, MPSC, UPSC, PET Examinations

PHYTOMORPHOLOGY, TAXONOMY AND ANATOMY-MCQs

SET, NET, NEET, JRF, GATE MPSC, UPSC, PET Examinations

By

Dr. Sumia Fatima
M.Sc., Ph.D., F.S.Sc., F.S.L.Sc.
Professor and Head
Department of Botany
Dr. Rafiq Zakaria College for Women
Jubilee Park, Aurangabad - 431 001
Maharashtra (India)

&

Prof. Ravi Patil
M.Sc., Ph.D.,
Professor and Head
Department of Botany
Devgiri College Aurangabad - 431 001
Maharashtra (India)

DPH

DISCOVERY PUBLISHING HOUSE PVT. LTD.
INDIA

Published by:
Namit Wasan

DISCOVERY PUBLISHING HOUSE PVT. LTD.
4383/4B, Ansari Road, Darya Ganj
New Delhi-110 002 (India)
Phone : +91-11-23279245; 23253475; 43596065
E-mail : discoverybooksindia@gmail.com
discoverypublishinghouse@gmail.com
namitwasan9@gmail.com
web : www.discoverypublishinggroup.com

***First Edition:* 2021**

ISBN: 978-93-88854-65-8

Phytomorphology, Taxonomy and Anatomy-MCQs

Printed at:
Infinity Imaging Systems
Delhi

Preface

The book entitled "Phytomorphology, Taxonomy and Anatomy-MCQs" has been specially designed for the students of all the universities of the world appearing for competitive examinations for admission purpose in higher class or to get a job. The book is a condensed knowledge of complete Plant Morphology (External features of plant, root & its modification, stem & its modifications, leaf shape, leaf margin, apex, leaf base, leaf venation, Phyllotaxy, leaf surface, typical flower structure, calyx & its modification, corolla, forms of corolla, Androecium, Gynoecium, Aestivation, Placentation, ovule and seed), Taxonomy (History & Classification of taxonomy, Advanced discoveries in Taxonomy, Modern trends in Taxonomy, Origin of angiosperms, Taxonomic hierarchy, Dicot and Monocot, and Plant families) and Anatomy (Types of tissue, function of tissue, dicot and monocot, root, stem and leaf anatomy).

Sumia Fatima

Ravi Patil

Contents

CHAPTER - 1

Introduction

A variety of plants occur on earth. To know all the details of the plant it is very essential to know the details of growth, reproduction and external morphology of plant. The study of angiospermic plants is based on deep knowledge of all the morphological features of plants. To know the natural resources of the earth one requires vast understanding of plants is very essential. The Ayurvedic science and science of naturopathy medicine is entirely dependent on correct identification of plants. The book is designed as a guide to the systematic study of external features of plant (Phytomorphologylogy), Taxonomy and Anatomy.

Presently the flowering plants are most dominant members on the earth. There is a greatest biodiversity among plants. Morphologically the plants are variable in size, shape and structure. There are reports on the presence of 3,00000 flowering plants species on the earth, but the basic concept of construction of plant is similar to all the plants of the planet. The study of external features of plant is termed as external morphology. There are lakhs of flowering plant present on the earth, but the basic components & development of all the plants is the same. The basic requirement of all such a variably looking plants is same. The basic body components of a plant are roots, stem, leaves and flowers.

The root is the underground part which is geotropic in nature. It is branched spread several inches or several feet in length. All the roots of a plant together are known as root system. It consists of main branch and several secondary & tertiary branches. The root system of plant is a homogenous part of plant. The root grows, extend to a longer distance but it is the root only. The root system is positively geotropic in nature.

The stem is mostly aerial part except certain modified stems. The stem is highly branched system of plant. The stem is also termed as shoot which is heterogeneous because besides branches it also produces leaves & flowers, fruits and seeds. Any plant body of flowering plant consists of vegetative and reproductive parts. The leaves stem, branches, roots are the vegetative parts of plants. The reproductive part of plant is the flower. The flower consist of two types of organs i.e. the accessory organs such as calyx (sepals) & corolla (petals), and the sexual organs of flower are androecium (stamens) and gynoecium (carpels). Hence the androecium and gynoecium of flower are the reproductive part of flower.

Morphology is the study of external features of plant. It is a key unit for description of plant. Theophrastus (285B.C.) was pioneer to give detailed description of plant by using scientific taxonomical terminology. Study of morphology of plants is very important aspect which is useful in identification of plant. It is also known as of visible biology of plants. Morphology is the science that deals with structural description of plants i.e. the features which can be seen by necked eye. There are two important aspect of plant morphology.

There are various types of plant grow in a variety of habitat. The plant kingdom is consists of different forms which are scattered in greater or less abundance over most of the soil surface of earth as well as in water. The study of angiospermic plants is bases on deep knowledge and complete enculcating of external characteristics of plants. The plants are primary producers of food. Without plants life is not possible on the earth. Even the health of earth is directly concern with the existence of plants. To know the natural resources of the earth one requires vast understanding of plants.

On the earth in present days the flowering plants are more dominant members throughout the world. There is a great variation in plants. The plants are of variable size, shape and structure. The study of external features of flowering shoot of plant is termed as inflorescence. There are numerous of flowering plant present everywhere, but the basic components & development of all the plants is the same. The basic structures of plant body are roots, stem, and leaves, inflorescence, flowers and seeds. The root is the underground part which is geotropic in nature. It is branched spread several inches or several feet in length. It consists of main branch and several secondary & tertiary branches.

Plant anatomy is the study of internal structure of plants. Plant consists of different types tissue. Different types of cells in plant involved in different types of function.

CHAPTER - 2

Phytomorphology - I to XIX

PHYTOMORPHOLOGY - I

1. The plants adapted to grow on rocky surface of earth termed as
   (a) Epilithic (b) Epiphytic
   (c) Submerged (d) Epiphytic
2. Survival of plants for many years even after flowering & formation of seed are termed as
   (a) Parasitic (b) Monocarpic
   (c) Insectivorous (d) None of these
3. The plants which are adapted to a specific habitat are termed as
   (a) Ecad (b) Taxon
   (c) Both a and b (d) None of these
4. The plant having two different form of leaves are termed as
   (a) Polymorphic (b) Trimorphic
   (c) Dimorphic (d) None of these
5. The plant having well developed stem above ground level is termed as
   (a) Epiphytic (b) Caulescent
   (c) Gamotrophic (d) None of these
6. The plant grow on land which do not require very dry or wet soil is termed as
   (a) Mesophyte (b) Hydrophyte
   (c) Epiphytic (d) halophyte
7. The plants which grow in very dry habitat termed as
   (a) Xerophytes (b) Mesophyte
   (c) Hydrophyte (d) Epiphytic
8. Plants that absorb food from dead organic matter are termed as
   (a) Epiphytic (b) Mesophyte
   (c) Hydrophyte (d) Saprophytes

9. The salt tolerant plant are termed as
(a) Halophytes (b) Hydrophyte
(c) Epiphytic (d) None of these
10. Which of the following are antigeotropic root?
(a) Storage root (b) Tap root
(c) Fibrous root (d) Pneumatophore
11. The plant growing in water termed as
(a) Hydrophytes (b) Xerophytes
(c) Mesophyte (d) Epiphytic
12. The water storing plant develop from
(a) Submerged (b) Succulent
(c) Floating (d) None of these
13. Which of the following is a succulent plant?
(a) Aloe vera (b) Mangifera indica
(c) Santalum album (d) None of these
14. The plants which grow as bark at large trees termed as
(a) Epiphytic (b) Epiphloedic
(c) Endophytic (d) None of these
15. Which of the following is an epiphloedic plant?
(a) Orchids (b) Cereals
(c) Pulses (d) None of these
16. The plants that grow on grass land are described as
(a) Forbs (b) Epiphloedic
(c) Orchids (d) None of these
17. The nodes & internodes are absent in
(a) Roots (b) Root hair
(c) Radical (d) None of these
18. The very young stage of root is termed as
(a) Seedling (b) Plumule
(c) Bud (d) Radical
19. The root having main primary root with secondary& tertiary branches termed as
(a) Prop root (b) Adventitious roots
(c) Tap root (d) Stranglers
20. The tap root system develop from
(a) Radical (b) Lower node of stem
(c) Rhizome (d) None of these

21. Root which develop from any part of plant other than radical is termed as
    (a) Adventitious root (b) Tap root
    (c) Root cap (d) Root hairs
22. Which of the following plant consist of fibrous roots?
    (a) Gram (b) Bean
    (c) Groundnut (d) Maize
23. The root nodules occur in the plants of sub family
    (a) Papilionaceae (b) Annonaceae
    (c) Acanthaceae (d) Solanaceae
24. The spindle shaped food storing root is termed as
    (a) Adventitious root (b) Fusiform root
    (c) Napiform root (d) None of these
25. A spherical root with tail like apex is termed as
    (a) Napiform root (b) Fusiform root
    (c) Adventitious root (d) Tuberous root
26. The root with broad base & becomes narrow gradually termed as
    (a) Conical root (b) Fusiform root
    (c) Adventitious root (d) Napiform root
27. A thick, fleshy, irregular shaped root is termed as
    (a) Fusiform root (b) Tuberous root
    (c) Adventitious root (d) None of these
28. The respiratory roots of sea shore plants which grow above ground level termed as
    (a) Pneumatophore (b) Conical root
    (c) Fusiform root (d) Adventitious root
29. The negatively geotropic root are termed as
    (a) Pnematophores (b) Hanging roots
    (c) Fusiform root (d) None of these
30. The function of adventitious root is
    (a) Reproduction (b) Mechanical Support
    (c) Absorption (d) None of these
31. The roots that posses spiral thickenings on the surface is termed as
    (a) Fusiform root (b) Contractile root
    (c) Adventitious root (d) None of these
32. The peg like roots which absorb food from host plant termed as
    (a) Contractile root (b) Haustoria root
    (c) Adventitious root (d) None of these

33. Which of the following is food storage root?
    (a) Carrot (b) Pigeon pea
    (c) Bajra (d) Spinach
34. The hanging roots of *Ficus bengalensis* are termed as
    (a) Strangles (b) Pnematophores
    (c) Conical root (d) Fusiform root
35. The foliar roots occur in
    (a) *Bryophyllum* (b) *Aloe*
    (c) *Mentha* (d) None of these
36. Roots which absorb water from atmospheric moisture are termed as
    (a) Pnematophores (b) Strangles
    (c) Shallow root (d) Buttress root
37. Fungal hyphae associated with main root & resemble root herbs termed as
    (a) Mycorrhiza (b) Root hairs
    (c) Pnematophores (d) None of these
38. The roots have ability to absorb atmospheric water termed as
    (a) Strangles (b) Shallow root
    (c) Aerial roots (d) Conical root
39. Branched thalloid roots which penetrate the rock to fix the plant is termed as
    (a) Hepteron (b) Mycorrhiza
    (c) Root nodules (d) Nome of these
40. The cluster of tuberous roots occur in Asparagus are described as
    (a) Aerial roots (b) Fasciculate roots
    (c) Shallow root (d) Strangles
41. The roots which show swellings & appear like a beaded chain are described
    (a) Moniliform (b) Contractile
    (c) Fusiform root (d) adventitious root
42. When the root show several ring like thickenings on the root surface are termed as
    (a) Aerial roots (b) Fasciculate roots
    (c) Annulated root (d) None of these
43. The profusely branched coral shaped roots with typical dichotomy termed as
    (a) Coralloid roots (b) Fasciculate roots
    (c) Annulated root (d) None of these

44. The small sized roots produced by plants which grow in cracks of trees termed as
(a) Shallow root (b) Fasciculate roots
(c) Aerial roots (d) Clinging roots
45. In certain floating hydrophytes a cluster of roots found to maintain its position in particular place is termed as
(a) Ballasting root (b) Annulated root
(c) Fasciculate roots (d) None of these
46. The root of rhizome takes place by activation of
(a) Apical bud (b) Lateral bud
(c) Both a and b (d) None of these
47. Which of the following posses scaly leaves, eyes nodes & internodes
(a) Tubers (b) Creeper
(c) Corm (d) Stolon
48. Which of the following posses many buds on the surface
(a) Corm (b) Bulb
(c) Tunicated bulb (d) None of these
49. The plants which consist of creeping stem ins termed as
(a) Twinners (b) Creeper
(c) Runner (d) None of these
50. Which one is the modified aquatic stem?
(a) Offset (b) Stolon
(c) Runner (d) None of these

Answer key: PHYTOMORPHOLOGY - I

1. (a) 2. (b) 3. (a) 4. (c) 5. (b) 6. (a) 7. (a) 8. (d) 9. (a) 10. (d) 11. (a) 12. (b) 13. (a) 14. (b) 15. (a) 16. (a) 17. (a) 18. (d) 19. (c) 20. (a) 21. (a) 22. (d) 23. (a) 24. (b) 25. (a) 26. (a) 27. (b) 28. (a) 29. (a) 30. (b) 31. (b) 32. (b) 33. (a) 34. (a) 35. (a) 36. (c) 37. (a) 38. (c) 39. (a) 40. (b) 41. (a) 42. (c) 43. (a) 44. (b) 45. (a) 46. (b) 47. (a) 48. (a) 49. (c) 50. (a)

PHYTOMORPHOLOGY - II

1. The offset occur in
(a) Pistia (b) Wolfia
(c) Echornia (d) Hydrilla
2. Which of the following possesses a kind of wet land habitat?
(a) Sunflower (b) *Coriandrum sativum*
(c) Carrot (d) Fern

3. The main branch of a tree is termed as
(a) Bough (b) Caudex
(c) Bole (d) None of these
4. The unfertilized seed is termed as
(a) Cotyledon (b) Ovule
(c) Embryo (d) None of these
5. The type of stem occur in coconut or date is termed as
(a) Caudex (b) Bough
(c) Both a and b (d) None of these
6. Stem having nodes & internodes, where as internodes are hallow as in bamboo termed as
(a) Culm (b) Caudex
(c) Bough (d) None of these
7. Stem having pattern of branches in acropetal succession is termed as
(a) Decurrent (b) Excurrent
(c) Both a and b (d) None of these
8. Plant having non-woody stem is termed as
(a) Hollow (b) Herbaceous
(c) Solid (d) None of these
9. The stalk of individual flower is termed as
(a) Pedicel (b) Peduncle
(c) Petiole (d) Androphore
10. Stalk of inflorescence is termed as
(a) Peduncle (b) Pedicel
(c) Petiole (d) Androphore
11. When the stems grow in a confused masses are termed as
(a) Climbers (b) Shrub
(c) Caespitose type (d) None of these
12. The large woody climbing plants in the forest termed as
(a) Twinners (b) Runner
(c) Lianas (d) Creeper
13. Which of the following plant posses' fistular type of stem
(a) Wheat (b) Green gram
(c) Pea (d) Safflower
14. The Shoot of grass is termed as
(a) Tiller (b) Solid stem
(c) Both a and b (d) None of these

15. The stem having hollow centre termed as
    (a) Solid (b) Quadrangular
    (c) Triangular (d) Fistular
16. Plant stem grow horizontal on soil surface & roots arise at every nodal region termed as
    (a) Creepers or repent (b) Tendrillar
    (c) Runner (d) None of these
17. Plant stem grow horizontally on soil but no roots arise at nodal region termed as
    (a) Repent (b) Creeper
    (c) Trailers (d) None of these
18. The flattened stem that perform the function of leaf termed as
    (a) Cladode (b) Phylloclade
    (c) Tiller (d) Fistular
19. Which of the following is part of stem that serve to hold flowers?
    (a) Scape (b) Lateral branch
    (c) Petiole (d) Hanging branch
20. Horizontal stem which produces plantlets at nodal region is termed as
    (a) Stolen (b) Rhizome
    (c) Bulb (d) Tunicate bulb
21. Which of the term is used to describe stems of plants that appear to be stem less
    (a) Strait (b) Acaulescent
    (c) Unbranched (d) None of these
22. Which of the term is used if the basal region of stem is woody? and upper region may not be woody?
    (a) Suffrutescent (b) Herbaceous
    (c) Woody (d) Lianas
23. Which of the following is tendril climber?
    (a) *Pisum sativum* (b) Pigeon pea
    (c) *Gloriosa* (d) *Mentha*
24. When the plant takes support of other plant to climb over, by using sharp pointed spines or thick thorns termed as
    (a) Ramblers or Scramblers (b) Twinners
    (c) Runner (d) None of these
25. The underground runners are termed as
    (a) Runner (b) Scape
    (c) Bole (d) None of these

26. The function of prickles in plant is
(a) Protection (b) Reproduction
(c) Transpiration (d) Guttation
27. The underground runners are termed as
(a) Suckers (b) Offset
(c) Creeper (d) None of these
28. Which of the following is vegetatively propagation organ of plant ?
(a) Node (b) Sucker
(c) Shoot apex (d) Root nodule
29. The modified aquatic horizontal stem develops from axile of leaf is termed as
(a) Offset (b) Stolon
(c) Rhizome (d) Corm
30. Which one is the modified leaf?
(a) Offset (b) Pitcher
(c) Rhizome (d) Corm
31. The stem modified to a flat thick leaf like structure having several node & internode is termed as
(a) Phylloclade (b) Cladode
(c) Foliaceous stem (d) None of these
32. Which of the following consist of phylloclade?
(a) *Aloe* (b) *Asparagus*
(c) *Opuntia* (d) *Agave*
33. The unbranched, woody stem with a number of leaf scars is termed as
(a) Caudex (b) Fistular
(c) Hollow (d) None of these
34. Swollen underground stem posses scaly leaves , eyes, nodes & internodes is termed as
(a) Rhizome (b) Bulb
(c) Tunicated bulb (d) None of these
35. The underground horizontal stem made for storage of food is termed as
(a) Root (b) Rhizome
(c) Node (d) None of these
36. External protective layer of stem which is formed by secondary meristems is termed as
(a) Cortex (b) Epidermis
(c) Bark (d) Hypodermis

37. Which type of cells occur in barks
    (a) Sclerenchymatous (b) Parenchyma
    (c) Chlorenchyma (d) Collenchyma
38. Which of the following is function of bark?
    (a) Protection (b) Growth
    (c) Transpiration (d) Epidermis
39. Which of the following is highly condensed shoot?
    (a) Internode (b) Bud
    (c) Lower node (d) None of these
40. Way of folding type of an individual leaf in the bud is termed as
    (a) Ptyxis (b) Vestiture
    (c) Both a and b (d) None of these
41. Way of folding type of young leaves in the bud in relation to each other is termed as
    (a) Vernation (b) Curl
    (c) Ptyxis (d) None of these
42. Which of the following terms denotes the conveying of any plant? or part plant
    (a) Phyllotaxy (b) Vestiture
    (c) Aestivation (d) placentation
43. A non green thin dry leaf texture is termed as
    (a) Scarious (b) Smooth
    (c) Reticulate (d) None of these
44. When the leaf is covered with star shaped hairs termed as
    (a) Stellate (b) Hairy
    (c) Glabrous (d) woolly
45. When the plant surface consist of short stiff hairs in as ascending manner is termed as
    (a) Moniliform (b) Reticulate
    (c) Stellate (d) Strigose
46. When plant surface consist of multicellular hairs it is described as
    (a) Scarious (b) Soft
    (c) Silky (d) Moniliform
47. When the plant surface is covered with matted woody but curled hairs described as
    (a) Tomentose (b) Strigose
    (c) Scarious (d) None of these

48. When the plant surface consist of mucous exudates is termed as
    (a) Vicid (b) Waxy
    (c) Dry (d) None of these
49. Which of the following is main organ of plant for photosynthesis?
    (a) Leaf (b) Bud
    (c) Shoot apex (d) None of these
50. The base of leaf is also termed as
    (a) Petiole (b) Hypopodium
    (c) Lamina (d) None of these

Answer key: PHYTOMORPHOLOGY - II

1. (a) 2. (d) 3. (a) 4. (b) 5. (a) 6. (a) 7. (d) 8. (b) 9. (a) 10. (a) 11. (c) 12. (c) 13. (a), 14. (a) 15. (d) 16. (a) 17. (c) 18. (a) 19. (a) 20. (a) 21. (b) 22. (a) 23. (a) 24. (a) 25. (c) 26. (a) 27. (a) 28. (b) 29. (a) 30. (b) 31. (a) 32. (c) 33. (a) 34. (a) 35. (b) 36. (c) 37. (a) 38. (a) 39. (b) 40. (a) 41. (a) 42. (b) 43. (a) 44. (a) 45. (d) 46. (d) 47. (a) 48. (a) 49. (a) 50. (b)

PHYTOMORPHOLOGY - III

1. In absence of petiole the leaf is described as
    (a) Petioluate (b) Petiolate
    (c) Sessile (d) None of these
2. The compound leaf which consist of even number of leaf lets is described as
    (a) Paripinnate compound (b) Imparipinnate compound
    (c) Both a and b (d) None of these
3. When compound leaf consist of odd number of leaflets is described as
    (a) Imparipinnate compound
    (b) Paripinnate compound
    (c) Both a and b
    (d) None of these
4. Which of the following plant consist of decomposed leaves
    (a) *Cajanus cajan* (b) *Parthenium hyskriphorus*
    (c) *Arachis hypogea* (d) *Sorghum*
5. Small leafy structure which occur at the basal region of petiole of leaf is termed as
    (a) Stipule (b) Bract
    (c) Epicalyx (d) Leaflet

6. The central vein of the simple leaf blade is termed as
   (a) Midrib (b) Lamina
   (c) Rachis (d) None of these
7. The small leafy structure which occur on rachis of compound leaf is termed as
   (a) Leaflet (b) Bract
   (c) Scale (d) None of these
8. The swollen petiole occur in plant like
   (a) Wolfia (b) Hydrilla
   (c) Echornia (d) Azolla
9. The egg shaped leaf is termed as
   (a) Peltate (b) Obovate
   (c) Sagittate (d) Rhomboid
10. The spherical shaped of leaf is termed as
    (a) Falcate (b) Orbicular
    (c) Sagittate (d) None of these
11. The triangle wedge shaped leaf is described as
    (a) Cuneate (b) Obovate
    (c) Orbicular (d) Flabellate
12. A narrow long leaf is described as
    (a) Linear (b) Oblong
    (c) Ovate (d) Obovate
13. A pointed needle like leaves are described as
    (a) Acicular (b) Rhomboid
    (c) Fenestrate (d) truncate
14. Leaf with broad laminar with a very long tail like structure at apex is termed as
    (a) Sagittate (b) Caudate
    (c) Cochleate (d) None of these
15. When the shape of leaf resemble a shell of mollusca it is described as
    (a) Falcate (b) Orbicular
    (c) Cochleate (d) Sagittate
16. The wind blowing fan shaped leaf is described as
    (a) Cuneate (b) Flabellate
    (c) Falcate (d) caudate
17. An arrow shaped elongated triangle like leaf is described as
    (a) Sagittate (b) Orbicular
    (c) Falcate (d) Peltate

18. The sickle shaped leaf is termed as
    (a) Falcate (b) Flabellate
    (c) Cuneate (d) Falcate
19. The square shaped leaf with triangular apex is described as
    (a) Truncate (b) Peltate
    (c) Cuneate (d) Falcate
20. The round diamond shaped leaf is described as
    (a) Rhomboid (b) Flabellate
    (c) Falcate (d) None of these
21. When the leaf like lamina possesses natural holes of variable size it is described as
    (a) Truncate (b) Reniform
    (c) Fenestrate (d) None of these
22. The kidney shaped leaf is described as
    (a) Sagittate (b) Caudate
    (c) Reniform (d) Cochleate
23. The long tread like leaf is termed as
    (a) Filiform (b) Peltate
    (c) Sagittate (d) Cochleate
24. When the leaf apex end into a sharp pointed region it is described as
    (a) Peltate (b) Broad
    (c) Acute (d) None of these
25. The tail like long apex of leaf is termed as
    (a) Peltate (b) Acute
    (c) Broad (d) Caudate
26. When the apex of leaf is having deep notch is described as
    (a) Emerginate (b) Truncate
    (c) Caudate (d) None of these
27. The broad & flat apex of leaf described as
    (a) Caudate (b) Truncate
    (c) Acute (d) Broad
28. A very thin thread like apex of leaf is described as
    (a) Caudate (b) Cirrhoses
    (c) Acute (d) Emerginate
29. Rounded leaf apex with slight depression as
    (a) Retuse (b) Acuminate
    (c) Spatulate (d) None of these

30. A spoon shaped apex of leaf is described as
    (a) Spatulate (b) Cirrhoses
    (c) Caudate (d) Acute
31. When the leaf apex is tapering to a long pointed structure is termed as
    (a) Emerginate (b) Peltate
    (c) Acute (d) Acuminate
32. A blunt apex of leaf is described as
    (a) Cirrhoses (b) Truncate
    (c) Achilary (d) None of these
33. Presently which plants are most dominant on the earth?
    (a) Angiosperm (b) Gymnosperms
    (c) Pteridophytes (d) bryophytes
34. The study of external features of plant is termed as
    (a) Plant morphology (b) Plant anatomy
    (c) Taxonomy (d) None of these
35. Which part of plant is geotropic in nature?
    (a) Flower (b) Leaf
    (c) Branches (d) Root
36. Which of the following is vegetative part of plant?
    (a) Protection (b) Leaf
    (c) Reproduction (d) None of these
37. Which is the main function of leaf?
    (a) Photosynthesis (b) Pistil
    (c) Stigma (d) Stamen
38. Spiny leaf margin occurs in
    (a) Ocimum (b) Nerium
    (c) Argemone (d) Tamarind
39. Unifoliate compound leaf occurs in
    (a) Onion (b) Garlic
    (c) Ginger (d) Lemon
40. Which is the example of hook climber?
    (a) Bignonia (b) Santalum
    (c) Tectona (d) Shorea
41. Which one is the leaf medication?
    (a) Phyllode (b) Phylloclade
    (c) Cladode (d) All of these

42. In which plant vegetative reproduction takes place by bulbils?
(a) Mimosa (b) Luffa
(c) Cucumber (d) Arbotrys

43. What is the function of leaf vains?
(a) Transport of water, mineral and organic substances
(b) Transport of water, mineral
(c) Transport of mineral and organic substances
(d) None of these

44. Which one is the carnivorous plant?
(a) Radish (b) Mentha
(c) Coriandrum (d) Utricularia

45. Which one is the non-carnivorous plant?
(a) *Dischidia* (b) Pitcher plant
(c) Utricularia (d) None of these

46. The cactus spines are modification of
(a) Stipel (b) Stipule
(c) Epicalyx (d) Leaf

47. Which one is the insectivorous plant?
(a) Loranthus (b) Cuscuta
(c) Striga (d) Nepenthes

48. Which one is the parasitic plant?
(a) Cuscuta (b) Nepenthes
(c) Utricularia (d) Dalbergia

49. In which plant the bracts resemble petals?
(a) Hordeum (b) Musa
(c) Tectona (d) Bougainvillea

50. In which endosperm is absent
(a) Orchids (b) Groundnut
(c) Ricinus (d) Sunflower

Answer key: PHYTOMORPHOLOGY - III

1. (c) 2. (a) 3. (a) 4. (b) 5. (a) 6. (a) 7. (a) 8. (c) 9. (b), 10. b) 11. (a) 12. (a) 13. a) 14. (b) 15. (c) 16. (b) 17. (a) 18. (a) 19. (a) 20. (a) 21. (c) 22. (c) 23. (a) 24. (c) 25. (d) 26. (a) 27. (b) 28. (b) 29. (a) 30. (a) 31. (d) 32. (c) 33. (a) 34. (a) 35. (d) 36. (b) 37. (a) 38. (c) 39. (d) 40. (a) 41. (a) 42. (d) 43. (a) 44. (d) 45. (a) 46. (d) 47. (d) 48. (a) 49. (d) 50. (a)

PHYTOMORPHOLOGY - IV

1. Which plant is the source of blue dye?
   (a) Indigofera (b) Mentha
   (c) Caesalpinia (d) Butea
2. Which one is the Monocarpic perennial plant?
   (a) Oxalis (b) Loranthus
   (c) Lantana (d) Agave
3. What is the eye of potato?
   (a) Axillary bud (b) Lateral bud
   (c) Assessary bud (d) None of these
4. Which type of fruit occurs in *Ficus*?
   (a) Drup (b) Pome
   (c) Hesperidium (d) Syconous
5. Which one is the edible part of banana?
   (a) Mesocarp and less developed endocarp
   (b) Skin
   (c) Pericarp
   (d) None of these
6. In which family 9+1 arrangement of stamen occurs?
   (a) Rutaceae (b) Mimosaceae
   (c) Fabaceae (d) Sapotaceae
7. Which term is used for filament attached along the whole? length of anther?
   (a) Adnate (b) Acropetal
   (c) Versatile (d) Basipetal
8. In which family the ovary is obliquely placed?
   (a) Solanaceae (b) Myrtaceae
   (c) Rosaceae (d) Rutaceae
9. Which is the function of Pnematophores?
   (a) Photosynthesis (b) Respiration
   (c) Protection (d) Food preparation
10. Which term is used for arrangement of leaves in bud?
    (a) Phyllotaxy (b) Vernation
    (c) Aestivation (d) None of these
11. Which one is concerned with phylloclade?
    (a) Dalbergia (b) Tectona
    (c) Bamboo (d) Acacia

12. A mechanical rupturing of seed dormancy is termed as
    (a) Scarification (b) Dormancy
    (c) Both a and b (d) None of these
13. The aleurone layer of maize is made up of
    (a) Protein (b) Lipid
    (c) Carbohydrate (d) Cellulose
14. In which family Capitulum type of inflorescence occurs?
    (a) Malvaceae (b) Asteraceae
    (c) Papilionaceae (d) Acanthaceae
15. Pappus is the modification of
    (a) Corolla (b) Calyx
    (c) Androecium (d) Gynoecium
16. Which is the edible part of apple?
    (a) Thalamus (b) Gynophore
    (c) Androphore (d) Involucre
17. Which is the edible part in sorosis type of fruit?
    (a) Exocarp (b) Endocarp
    (c) Seed (d) None of these
18. A Spadix type of inflorescence occurs in
    (a) Colocasia (b) Garlic
    (c) Pea (d) Tamarind
19. Which term is used for bracts associated with spikelet inflorescence of grasses?
    (a) Verticelaster (b) Catkin
    (c) Spathe (d) Spike
20. Axile placentation occurs in
    (a) Jowar (b) Cucumber
    (c) Citrus (d) Carrot
21. The seeds of which plant consists of endosperm, perisperm and caruncle.
    (a) Castor (b) Maize
    (c) Jowar (d) Rice
22. In which of the following testa and cotyledons are edible?
    (a) Groundnut (b) *Lantana*
    (c) *Datura* (d) None of these
23. Which type of placentation occurs in unilocular ovary with single ovule?
    (a) Basal (b) Marginal
    (c) Both a and b (d) None of these

24. Which type of inflorescence occurs in tomato?
    (a) Parietal (b) Marginal
    (c) Basal (d) Axile
25. Which of the following is a bulb?
    (a) Ginger (b) Onion
    (c) *Colocasia* (d) Pea
26. Pineapple is a
    (a) Composite fruit (b) Berry
    (c) Siliqua (d) Pome
27. Which is the characteristic feature of family fabaceae?
    (a) Presence of vexillary type of inflorescence
    (b) Presence of vexillary type of inflorescence
    (c) Presence of vexillary type of inflorescence
    (d) Presence of vexillary type of inflorescence
28. The pseudocarps are usually bear by plants having
    (a) Superior ovary (b) Inferior ovary
    (c) Semi-inferior ovary (d) None of these
29. The maturation zone of root produces
    (a) Root hairs (b) Root cap
    (c) Both a and b (d) None of these
30. Which is the example of winged petiole?
    (a) Pear (b) Banana
    (c) Papaya (d) *Citrus*
31. In which plant stipule is modified to tendril
    (a) *Smilax* (b) *Oxalis*
    (c) *Hibiscus* (d) None of these
32. Which one is the highly evolved Recemose Inflorescence?
    (a) Spadix (b) Capitulum
    (c) Spike (d) Verticelaster
33. Which one is the accessory organ of flower?
    (a) Calyx (b) Stigma
    (c) Anther (d) Ovary
34. A Phenomenon of study of morphology of vegetative parts of plant is termed as
    (a) Vegetative biology (b) Reproductive biology
    (c) Both a and b (d) None of these

35. Who is the author of flora of Marathwada?
(a) V.N. Naik (b) L.V. Gangawane
(c) D.S. Mukadam (d) None of these
36. Which one is the reproductive part of plant?
(a) Leaf (b) Young branches
(c) Flowers (d) None of these
37. Which part of plant does not require light to grow & develop?
(a) Flower (b) Leaf
(c) Root (d) None of these
38. The tip of root consists of a pad of highly dividing tissue which is termed as
(a) Apical meristems (b) Lateral meristems
(c) Internodal meristems (d) None of these
39. The descending axis of plant is termed as
(a) Root system (b) Shoot system
(c) Lateral branches (d) Adventitious roots
40. The ascending axis of plant is termed as
(a) Shoot system (b) Root system
(c) Lateral branches (d) None of these
41. Which of the following are characteristic features of shoot axis?
(a) Internode (b) Petal
(c) Epicalyx (d) Leaves
42. The following is the modified epidermal cell
(a) Nodal bud (b)Trichomes
(c) Both a and b (d) None of these
43. Which one is essential organs of flower
(a) Calyx and corolla (b) Sepals and petals
(c) Androecium & Gynoecium (d) None of these
44. In absence of distinct whorls of calyx & corolla in flower, the whorl is termed as
(a) Epicalyx (b) Perianth
(c) Bracteoles (d) None of these
45. All the stamens together is known as
(a) Androecium (b) Staminode
(c) Gynoecium (d) Style
46. All the sepals together known as
(a) Petals (b) Corolla
(c) Epicalyx (d) Calyx

47. All the petals of flower together known as
    (a) Epicalyx (b) Calyx
    (c) Corolla (d) None of these
48. The ovary, style & Stigma together is known as
    (a) Gynoecium (b) Androecium
    (c) Staminode (d) Androphore
49. The stalk of flower known as
    (a) Pedicel (b) Petiole
    (c) Peduncle (d) style
50. The stalk of inflorescence is termed as
    (a) Pedicel (b) Peduncle
    (c) Petiole (d) None of these

Answer key: PHYTOMORPHOLOGY - IV

1. (a) 2. (d) 3. (a) 4. (d) 5. (a) 6. (c) 7. (a) 8. (a) 9. (b) 10. (b) 11. (d) 12. (a) 13. (a) 14. (b) 15. (a) 16. (a) 17. (b) 18. (a) 19. (c) 20. (c) 21. (a) 22. (a) 23. (a) 24. (d) 25. (b) 26. (a) 27. (a) 28. (b) 29. (a) 30. (d) 31. (a) 32. (b) 33. (a) 34. (a) 35. (a) 36. (c) 37. (c) 38. (a) 39. (a) 40. (a) 41. (d) 42. (b) 43. (c) 44. (b) 45. (a) 46. (b) 47. (c) 48. (a) 49. (a) 50. (b)

PHYTOMORPHOLOGY - V

1. The stalk of the leaf in termed as
   (a) Petiole (b) Pedicel
   (c) Peduncle (d) None of these
2. The stamen in the fertile part of
   (a) Gynoecium (b) Androecium
   (c) Staminode (d) None of these
3. The pollen grain producing part of flower is
   (a) Anther (b) Androphore
   (c) Filament (d) Stigma
4. All the stamens of flower together termed as
   (a) Androecium (b) Gynoecium
   (c) Staminode (d) None of these
5. A stalk like structure supported to the anther termed as
   (a) Filament (b) Style
   (c) Tendril (d) Pedicel
6. In the absence of filament, the anther is described as
   (a) Sterile (b) Sessile
   (c) Staminode (d) None of these

7. A unit of Gynoecium is termed as
(a) Stigma (b) Carpel
(c) Style (d) None of these
8. The gynoecium with free carpels termed as
(a) Syncarpus (b) Apocarpus
(c) Both a and b (d) None of these
9. When carpels are united, that are described as
(a) Syncarpus (b) Apocarpus
(c) Both a and b (d) None of these
10. The ovary, style & Stigma together known as
(a) Gynophore (b) Androphore
(c) Carpel (d) None of these
11. Which of the following portion of pistil connects the ovary with stigma
(a) Style (b) Filament
(c) Anther (d) None of these
12. The swollen basal portion of carpel is known as
(a) Ovary (b) Embryo
(c) Androecium (d) Stigma
13. Which of the following is stalk of ovule
(a) Chalaza (b) Micropile
(c) Funiculus (d) None of these
14. The region of attachment of funicle to placenta is termed as
(a) Funiculus (b) Hilum
(c) Micropile (d) Chalaza
15. Which part of flower get converted into seed
(a) Ovule (b) Style
(c) Stigma (d) Filament
16. The opened region of ovule is termed as
(a) Micropile (b) Hilum
(c) Funiculus (d) None of these
17. The opposite end of micropile of ovule is termed as
(a) Funiculus (b) Micropile
(c) Chalaza (d) None of these
18. The fully mature and ripen ovary is termed as
(a) Fruit (b) Seed
(c) Thalamus (d) None of these
19. Which of the following is smallest angiospermic plant
(a) Pistia (b) Hydrilla
(c) Wolfia (d) Echornia

20. Which plant is the latest herb?
    (a) Banana (b) Ocimum
    (c) Coriandrum (d) Fenugreek
21. The medium sized tree in termed as
    (a) Shrub (b) Herb
    (c) Tree (d) None of these
22. The weak stemmed plant which require support of other plant to extend termed as
    (a) Monocot (b) Herb
    (c) Shrub (d) Climber
23. A large sized woody climber is termed as
    (a) Twinners (b) Creeper
    (c) Lianas (d) None of these
24. The plant which capture and digest insects termed as
    (a) Parasitic (b) Insectivores
    (c) Herbaceous (d) None of these
25. Which of the following is a parasitic angiospermic plant
    (a) Loranthus (b) Sesbania
    (c) Acacia (d) Wolfia
26. Plant which grow on branches of large trees termed as
    (a) Epiphytes (b) Halophytes
    (c) Terrestrial (d) None of these
27. The plants which are highly branched but does not raise much are termed as
    (a) Creeper (b) Bole
    (c) Runner (d) Bush
28. The plant which grow in metal containing soil termed as
    (a) Accumulator plant (b) Lithophytes
    (c) Terrestrial (d) None of these
29. The plant which do not shed off leaves institute or summer season called as
    (a) Deciduous (b) Evergreen
    (c) Cespitous (d) None of these
30. Those plants shed off their leaves after maturity during winter are called as
    (a) Cespitous (b) Evergreen
    (c) Deciduous (d) None of these

31. Plants that are intermediate between herbaceous & shrub plant termed as
(a) Suffrutescent (b) Acaulescent
(c) Both a and b (d) None of these
32. The stem less or the plant with very short story are termed as
(a) Suffrutescent (b) Acaulescent
(c) Both a and b (d) None of these
33. The tufted from of plants is termed as
(a) Caespitose (b) Suffrutescent
(c) Acaulescent (d) None of these
34. The plant with many upright branches which are parallel to main stem termed as
(a) Acaulescent (b) Caespitose
(c) Suffrutescent (d) Fastigiated
35. Entire stem including all branches creeping on ground but not rooting at nodes is termed as
(a) Prostrate or procumbent trailer's
(b) Caespitose
(c) Suffrutescent
(d) None of these
36. Plant grow horizontally on soil surface producing root at every nodal region is termed as
(a) Bole (b) Twinners
(c) Runner (d) Creepers
37. Plant with a single woody stem which grow like a tree termed as
(a) Arborescent (b) Caespitose
(c) Suffrutescent (d) None of these
38. Which part of plant is the factory of food preparation?
(a) Bud (b) Root nodules
(c) Petals (d) Leaf
39. The lateral outgrowth of base of leaf is termed as
(a) Stipule (b) Bract
(c) Stipel (d) Epicalyx
40. The stipules are absent in
(a) Monocots (b) Dicot
(c) Algae (d) Gymnosperm
41. When the stipule fell off just after unfolding of lamina is termed as
(a) Convolute (b) Caducous
(c) Persistent (d) Deciduous

42. When the stipule fall down just before unfolding of lamina is termed as
    (a) Winged (b) Foliaceous
    (c) Persistent (d) Caducous
43. When stipules remain even after formation of fruit is termed as
    (a) Persistent (b) Opposite
    (c) Free lateral (d) Photosynthetic
44. The tendrillar stipule occur in
    (a) *Smilax* (b) *Mentha*
    (c) Fenugreek (d) Radish
45. The Crotalaria plant, which type of stipules is present ?
    (a) Winged stipule (b) Foliaceous stipule
    (c) Ochraceous stipule (d) Sheathing stipule
46. In case of *Ziziphus*, the stipule is modified to a
    (a) Broad leaf (b) Spine
    (c) Tendril (d) Scale
47. A large leaf like stipule occur in Pisum sativum is called as
    (a) Foliaceous stipule (b) Scale like stipule
    (c) Convolute stipule (d) Median stipule
48. Hairy growth formed by modification of epidermal cells of leaf or stem is termed as
    (a) Tendril (b) Trichomes
    (c) Stipule (d) Bract
49. The thin hair like trichomes are termed as
    (a) Glochidiate (b) Plumose
    (c) Unicinate (d) Dendric
50. The leather like trichomes are termed as
    (a) Dendric (b) Glochidiate
    (c) Unicinate (d) Plumose

Answer key: PHYTOMORPHOLOGY - V

1. (a) 2. (b) 3. (a) 4. (a) 5. (a) 6. (b) 7. (b) 8. (b) 9. (a) 10. (c) 11. (a) 12. (a) 13. (c) 14. (b) 15. (a) 16. (a) 17. (c) 18. (a) 19. (c) 20. (a) 21. (a) 22. (d) 23. (c) 24. (b) 25. (a) 26. (a) 27. (d) 28. (a) 29. (b) 30. (c) 31. (a) 32. (b) 33. (a) 34. (d) 35. (a) 36. (d) 37. (a) 38. (d) 39. (a) 40. (a) 41. (d) 42. (a) 43. (a) 44. (a) 45. (a) 46. (b) 47. (a) 48. (b) 49. (a) 50. (d)

PHYTOMORPHOLOGY - VI

1. The much branched trichomes are termed as
   (a) Dendric (b) Plumose
   (c) Glochidiate (d) Unicinate
2. The hook shaped Trichomes is termed as
   (a) Plumose (b) Glochidiate
   (b) Unicinate (c) None of these
3. The cup shaped trichome termed as
   (a) Paleate (b) Dendric
   (c) Glochidiate (d) Plumose
4. The club shaped trichome is termed as
   (a) Clavate (b) Plumose
   (c) Dendric (d) Paleate
5. The sickle shaped trichome is termed as
   (a) Plumose (b) Unicinate
   (c) Glochidiate (d) Falcate
6. When the upper region of trichome divided into two, it is termed as
   (a) Forked (b) Glochidiate
   (c) Unicinate (d) Loriform
7. The trichomes with long pointed ends as are termed as
   (a) Unicinate (b) Plumose
   (c) Glochidiate (d)Echinate
8. The strap shape trichome is termed as
   (a) Loriform (b) Glochidiate
   (c) Unicinate (d) Dendric
9. The triangular shaped trichome is termed as
   (a) Deltoid (b) Echinate
   (c) Falcate (d) Unicinate
10. The bristle shape trichome is termed as
    (a) Setose (b) Loriform
    (c) Glochidiate (d) Unicinate
11. When the tip of trichome in like a round plate is termed as
    (a) Unicinate (b) Falcate
    (c) Peltate (d) Deltoid
12. The "T" Shaped trichomes are termed as
    (a) Setose (b) Unicinate
    (c) Loriform (d) Malphigian

13. When the tip of trichome is bent or covered, the trichome is termed as
    (a) Setose (b) Hooked
    (c) Loriform (d) Glochidiate
14. When trichomes are finely, minute, soft, wooly are termed as
    (a) Tomentose (b) Loriform
    (c) Glochidiate (d) Unicinate
15. The membranous scaly trichomes are termed as
    (a) Echinate (b) Deltoid
    (c) Paleaceous (d) Falcate
16. When trichomes resemble beaded chain are termed as
    (a) Moniliform (b) Tomentose
    (c) Loriform (d) Paleaceous
17. The trichome with much broad base and pointed end is termed as
    (a) Conical (b) Tomentose
    (c) Loriform (d) Glochidiate
18. The simple multicellular trichomes are termed as
    (a) Articulate (b) Tomentose
    (c) Loriform (d) None of these
19. When the trichomes are slit outgrowth with blunt end termed as
    (a) Tomentose (b) Paleaceous
    (c) Moniliform (d) Papillate
20. The star shaped trichomes are termed as
    (a) Stellate (b) Echinate
    (c) Falcate (d) Conical
21. When a trichome tip is like a small head is termed as
    (a) Capitate (b) Deltoid
    (c) Echinate (d) Falcate
22. Which of the following structure produced by plants of weak stems
    (a) Buds (b) Tendril
    (c) Branches (d) Trichomes
23. The flower producing shoot of plant is termed as
    (a) Inflorescence (b) Shoot
    (c) Floral formula (d) None of these
24. If a single flower is produced on peduncle the inflorescence is termed as
    (a) Complete (b) Unbranched
    (c) Perfect (d) Solitary

25. When the mature flowers are present at the basal region and younger buds situated at upper region of axis the inflorescence is termed as
    (a) Racemes (b) Cymose
    (c) Verticelaster (d) Spike
26. Which of the following is compound inflorescence?
    (a) Cymose (b) Spikelet
    (c) Racemes (d) None of these
27. The spikelet type of inflorescence occur in plants of family
    (a) Graminae (b) Compositae
    (c) Solanaceae (d) Asclepidiaceace
28. When inflorescence consists of a massive flowering axis which is enclosed by a large sized one of two bracts formed as
    (a) Scorpiod (b) Spike
    (c) Spadix (d) Head
29. The large sized bract enclose flower in Spadix type of inflorescence termed as
    (a) Spathe (b) Verticelaster
    (c) Spike (d) Spadix
30. Which of the following is largest herb of plants?
    (a) *Musa paradiscicca* (b) *Mentha piperata*
    (c) *Daccus carota* (d) *Coccus nucifera*
31. Inflorescence having long axis of unisexual flowers is termed as
    (a) Verticelaster (b) Catkin
    (c) Spadix (b) Spike
32. When the main reproductive shoot is highly reduced which resemble a flat disc as in sunflower, the inflorescence is termed as
    (a) Capitulum or Head or Anthopodium
    (b) Racemes
    (c) Cymose
    (d) Spike
33. In which type of inflorescence the floret and disc floret occur in –
    (a) Capitulum type (b) Solitary
    (c) Spadix (d) Perfect
34. Which of the following is specialized modified leaf ?
    (a) Filament (b) Stamen
    (c) Bract (d) Stigma

35. What is the function of bract?
   (a) Support (b) Reproduction
   (c) Asexual reproduction (d) Absorption
36. In absence of bract the flower is described as
   (a) Bracteate (b) Ebractiate
   (c) Scaly (d) None of these
37. A calyx like lobes which occur below the main calyx is termed as
   (a) Epicalyx (b) Sepal
   (c) Bract (d) Trichome
38. A whorl of leaf bracts which occur below the flowering axis is termed as
   (a) Trichome (b) Involucre
   (c) Thalamus (d) Staminode
39. In case of monocot inflorescence, a thin bract structure occurs at the base of spikelet, which is termed as
   (a) Glum (b) Stipule
   (c) Spine (d) Hook
40. The hard woody large persistent bracteoles remain surrounded to fruit is termed as
   (a) Cupule (b) Stipule
   (c) Stipule (d) Spine
41. Which of the following is reproductive part of angiosperms?
   (a) Fruit (b) Leaf
   (c) Flower (d) Bark
42. In absence of distinct whorl of calyx and corolla, the whorl is termed as
   (a) Calyx (b) Perianth
   (c) Corolla (d) Androecium
43. The essential whorl of flower consists of
   (a) Androecium and gynoecium (b) Sepal and petals
   (c) Calyx and corolla (d) Epicalyx and calyx
44. The highly condensed reproductive shoot of plant is termed as
   (a) Flower (b) Fruit
   (c) Leaf (d) Apical shoot
45. All the sepals together called as
   (a) Androecium (b) Corolla
   (c) Calyx (d) Gynoecium
46. All the petals together termed as
   (a) Corolla (b) Calyx
   (c) Androecium (d) Gynoecium

47. When the sepals are united to each other are described as
    (a) Polysepalous (b) Gamosepalous
    (c) Apo-sepaloid (d) None of these
48. When petals are united, they are described as
    (a) Gamopetalous (b) Polysepalous
    (c) Apo-sepaloid (d) None of these
49. Which of the following is main function of flower?
    (a) Branching (b) Growth
    (c) Reproduction (d) None of these
50. All the stamens together known as
    (a) Androecium (b) Gynoecium
    (c) Placentation (d) Aggregation

Answer key: PHYTOMORPHOLOGY - VI

1. (a) 2. (b) 3. (a) 4. (a) 5. (d) 6. (a) 7. (d) 8. (a) 9. (a) 10. (a) 11. (c) 12. (d) 13. (b) 14. (a) 15. (c) 16. (a) 17. (a) 18. (a) 19. (d) 20. (a) 21. (a) 22. (b) 23. (a) 24. (d) 25. (a) 26. (b) 27. (a) 28. (c) 29. (a) 30. (a) 31. (b) 32. (a) 33. (a) 34. (c) 35. (a) 36. (b) 37. (a) 38. (b) 39. (a) 40. (a) 41. (c) 42. (b) 43. (a) 44. (a) 45. (c) 46. (a) 47. (b) 48. (a) 49. (c) 50. (a)

PHYTOMORPHOLOGY - VII

1. The slender stalk of stamen is termed as
   (a) Filament (b) Style
   (c) Connective (d) Stigma
2. The pollen bearing region of flower is termed as
   (a) Stigma (b) Pistil
   (c) Bract (d) Anther
3. Which of the following is female part of flower ?
   (a) Gynoecium (b) Androecium
   (c) Stamen (d) Staminode
4. The ovary, style and stigma together known as
   (a) Staminode (b) Androecium
   (c) Stamen d) Gynoecium
5. The seed bearing part of flower is termed as
   (a) Petal (b) Pistil
   (c) Sepal (d) Filament
6. If the flower consists of androecium as well as gynoecium is termed as
   (a) Bisexual (b) unisexual
   (c) Sterile (d) None of these

7. If the flower consists of either androecium or gynoecium it is termed as
   (a) Unisexual (b) Bisexual
   (c) Sterile (d) Fertile
8. Which of the following term used for the flower which does not close up after having once opened
   (a) Agamotropic flower (b) Eutrophic
   (c) Gamotrophic (d) None of these
9. The stalk less flower is termed as
   (a) Sessile (b) Petiolate
   (c) Bracteate (d) Pedicilate
10. The flower having stalk is termed as
   (a) Bracteate (b) Sessile
   (c) Petiolate (d) Pedicellate
11. When the flower consists of only gynoecium is termed as
   (a) Pistillate flower (b) Staminate
   (c) Bisexual (d) None of these
12. When the flower consists of only gynoecium, it is termed as
   (a) Pistillate flower (b) Staminate
   (c) Bisexual (d) None of these
13. When a flower is having only one whorl of perianth that either calyx or corolla is termed as
   (a) Monochlamydous flower (b) Heterochlamydous
   (c) Dichlamydous (d) None of these
14. A radially symmetric flower is termed as
   (a) Zygomorphic (b) Irregular
   (c) Regular flower (d) All of these
15. When the flower can be divided in two equal parts is termed as
   (a) Actinomorphic (b) Irregular
   (c) Zygomorphic (d) All of these
16. When the flower does not divided in two equal parts is described as
   (a) Actinomorphic (b) Zygomorphic
   (c) Both a and b (d) None of these
17. A small flower having a flat strap shaped corolla is termed as
   (a) Ray floret (b) Disc floret
   (c) Both a and b (d) None of these
18. When the flower consists of five sepals and five petals are termed as
   (a) Tetramerous (b) Polymerous
   (c) Pentamerous (d) None of these

19. A boat shaped pair of petals of papilionacious flower is termed as
    (a) Keel petals (b) Standard petals
    (c) Wings (d) None of these
20. Which of the following is first whorl of flower ?
    (a) Corolla (b) Calyx
    (c) Androecium (d) Gynoecium
21. If calyx remains even after formation of fruit as in brinjal it is termed as
    (a) Persistent calyx (b) Hard calyx
    (c) Non-persistent calyx (d) None of these
22. The second whorl of flower is termed as
    (a) Epicalyx (b) Calyx
    (c) Corolla (d) None of these
23. The funnel shaped corolla is termed
    (a) Infundibuliform (b) Cruciform
    (c) Papilionacious (d) Tubular
24. A bell shaped corolla is termed as
    (a) Campanulate (b) Infundibuliform
    (c) Cruciform (d) Papilionacious
25. When a corolla consists of a slandered petal, two wing petals and one pair of boat shaped petals is termed as
    (a) Cruciform (b) Rotate
    (b) Papilionacious (d) Tubular
26. The corolla having two tip like structures is termed as
    (a) Simple (b) Tubular
    (c) Cruciform (d) Bilabiate
27. When the corolla of flower resemble a wheel is termed as
    (a) Rotate (b) Infundibuliform
    (c) Cruciform (d) Tubular
28. Which type of corolla occurs in "Radish"
    (a) Rotate (b) Carianate
    (c) Papilionacious (d) Cruciform
29. When the shaped of corolla resembles a pitcher or an urn is termed as
    (a) Urceolate (b) Bilabiate
    (b) Tubular (d) Cruciform
30. A boat shaped corolla is termed as
    (a) Carianate (b) Campanulate
    (c) Infundibuliform (d) Cruciform

31. The pauch like shape of corolla is termed as
    (a) Carianate (b) Papilionacious
    (c) Saccate (d) Rotate
32. A single unit of perianth is termed as
    (a) Tepals (b) Sepal
    (c) Petal (d) Bract
33. The way of arrangement of sepals in a flower is termed as
    (a) Placentation (b) Aestivation
    (c) Vernation (d) None of these
34. When one edge of petal or sepal overlap to other and another edge remain inside for all petals or sepals, such type of aestivation is termed as
    (a) Twisted or contorted (b) Imbricate
    (c) Quincuncial (d) Vexillary
35. What type of aestivation occur in China rose
    (a) Imbricate (b) Twisted
    (c) Quincuncial (d) Vexillary
36. When both the edges of one petal or sepal remain outside and other are petal may have one edge outside and one inside is termed as
    (a) Imbricate aestivation (b) Twisted or contorted
    (c) Quincuncial (d) Vexillary
37. Which type of aestivation occurs in plants of family Papilionaceae
    (a) Quincuncial (b) Twisted or contorted
    (b) Imbricate (c) Vexillary
38. When the arrangement of sepals or petals in a flower appears coiled like a shell of mollusk the aestivation is termed as
    (a) Cochleate (b) Crumpled
    (c) Dochleate (d) None of these
39. When the arrangement of sepals or petals in a way showing a ridged surface, it is termed as
    (a) Ascending (b) Crumpled aestivation
    (c) Descending (d) Twisted
40. When the arrangement of sepals or petals in a flower situated right angle to each, the aestivation is termed as
    (a) Decussate (b) Opposite
    (c) Alternate (d) None of these
41. All the stamens together are termed as
    (a) Filaments (b) Gynoecium
    (c) Androecium (d) None of these

42. When the flower is having only one stamen, it is termed as
(a) Monandrous (b) Diandrous
(c) Polyandrous (d) None of these
43. The flower with two stamens is termed as
(a) Monandrous (b) Diandrous
(c) Polyandrous (d) None of these
44. The flower with four stamens is termed as
(a) Tetrandrous (b) Diandrous
(c) Monandrous (d) Polyandrous
45. The flower with many stamens are termed as
(a) Monandrous (b) Tetrandrous
(c) Diandrous (d) Polyandrous
46. The example of Monandrous condition occur in
(a) *Zingiber officinale* (b) *Caesalpinia pulcherima*
(c) *Withania somnifera* (d) *Daccus carota*
47. The diandrous flower occur in
(a) *Ricinus communis* (b) *Annona squimosa*
(c) *Catharanthus roseus* (d) *Adhatoda vasica*
48. The triandrous condition occur in
(a) Wheat (b) Groundnut
(c) Sunflower (d) Brassica
49. The hexandrous flower occur in
(a) *Santalum album* (b) *Coriandrum sativum*
(c) *Arachis hypogea* (d) *Oryza sativa*
50. The polyandrous condition occur in
(a) *Rosa domestica* (b) *Hibiscus esculentus*
(c) Mentha piperata (d) *Saraca indica*

Answer key: PHYTOMORPHOLOGY - VII

1. (a) 2. (d) 3. (a) 4. (d) 5. (b) 6. (a) 7. (c) 8. (a) 9. (a) 10. (d) 11. (a) 12. (b) 13. (a) 14. (c) 15. (a) 16. (b) 17. (a) 18. (c) 19. (a) 20. (b) 21. (a) 22. (c) 23. (a) 24. (a) 25. (b) 26. (d) 27. (a) 28. (d) 29. (a) 30. (a) 31. (c) 32. (a) 33. (b) 34. (a) 35. (b) 36. (a) 37. (c) 38. (a) 39. (b) 40. (a) 41. (c) 42. (a) 43. (b) 44. (a) 45. (d) 46. (a) 47. (d) 48. (a) 49. (d) 50. (a)

PHYTOMORPHOLOGY - VIII

1. Which of following is male reproductive part of plant ?
   (a) Stamen (b) Pistil
   (c) Carpel (d) None of these
2. The stamen consists of
   (a) Ovule (b) Pistil
   (c) Carpel (d) Anther and filament
3. When the entire filament occur free in flower, it is termed as
   (a) Hexandrous (b) Polyandrous
   (c) Diandrous (d) None of these
4. When the filament are attached to petals are termed as
   (a) Epipetalous (b) Episepalous
   (c) Monandrous (d) Epitepalous
5. When all the stamens occur in a single bundle , the condition is termed as
   (a) Didelphous (b) Monodelphous
   (c) Polydelphous (d) None of these
6. In a flower, when two bundles of stamen occur, the condition is termed as
   (a) Diadelphous (b) Monodelphous
   (c) Polydelphous (d) None of these
7. In certain cases, two short stamen occur in outer whorl and four longer stamen occur in inner whorl the condition is termed as
   (a) Monodelphous (b) Didynamous
   (c) Didelphous (d) Tetradynamous
8. When in flower two short stamen occur in outer whorl and two longer stamen occur in inner whorl , the condition is termed as
   (a) Didynamous (b) Tetradynamous
   (c) Didelphous (d) Monodelphous
9. The scientific name for anther lobe in
   (a) Filament (b) Connective
   (c) Anther (d) Theca
10. The anther lobe enclosed pollen bearing sac which is known as
    (a) Microsporangium (b) Macrosporangium
    (c) Megasporangium (d) None of these
11. A pad of tissue which helps in joining the anther to the filament termed as
    (a) Filament (b) Theca
    (c) Anther (d) Connective

12. Which of the following is pollen bearing part of stamen?
   (a) Stigma (b) Filament
   (c) Style (d) Anther
13. When the petals and stamens are equal in number, and stamens situated alternate to petal, the condition is termed as
   (a) Antipetalous (b) Epipetalous
   (c) Antisepalous (d) None of these
14. When the stamen is having sterile anther, it is termed as
   (a) Staminode (b) Stamen
   (c) Pistil (d) None of these
15. The petal like shape of stamen is termed as
   (a) Tepaloid (b) Sepaloid
   (c) Petaloid (d) None of these
16. When the anther resemble a leaf lamina it is described as
   (a) Laminar (b) Margin
   (c) Lobed (d) None of these
17. The concept of fusion of the stamens involves filaments is termed as
   (a) Theca (b) Adelphy
   (c) Staminode (d) None of these
18. Fused bundle of filament is termed as
   (a) Monodelphous (b) Didelphous
   (c) Polydelphous d) None of these
19. The concept of fusion stamens involves anther only and filament remain free is termed as
   (a) Apogeny (b) Progeny
   (c) Syngeny (d) None of these
20. The concept of union of stamens involves both filament and anther is termed as
   (a) Synandry or synandrous (b) Apoandry
   (c) Gamoandry (d) None of these
21. When the stamens are arranged in two whorls it is termed as
   (a) Diplostemonous (b) Monodelphous
   (c) Polydelphous (d) None of these
22. When the stamens show complete union of filament as well as anthers is termed as
   (a) Gamoandrous (b) Synandrous stamens
   (c) Polydelphous (d) None of these

23. In which of the following plant, synandrous condition of stamens occurs ?
    (a) Cucurbita (b) Solanum
    (c) Withania (d) None of these
24. Phenomenon of attachment of stamen with any one of its flower part is termed as
    (a) Adhesion (b) Cohesion
    (c) Gynostemenous (d) None of these
25. When the stamens are attached to sepals it is described as
    (a) Epipetalous (b) Epitepalous
    (c) Episepalous (d) None of these
26. When the stamens are attached to the perianth lobe that are described as
    (a) Epiphyllous (b) Episepalous
    (b) Epitepalous (c) Epipetalous
27. When the stamens show fusion with style and stigma the condition is termed as
    (a) Gynostegium (b) Gynostemenous
    (c) Gynophorous d) None of these
28. Which of the following term is used to described presence of many free stamens in a flower
    (a) Diplostemanous (b) Apostemenous or Adelphy
    (c) Gynostemanous (d) None of these
29. When the stamens extending beyond the corolla of flower is termed as
    (a) Exerted (b) Inserted
    (c) Both a and b (d) None of these
30. When the stamens are not extending beyond the corolla of flower is termed as
    (a) Extrorse (b) Exerted
    (c) Introrse (d) Inserted
31. When the anthers are fused in the same whorl that are termed as
    (a) Basifixed (b) Adnate
    (c) Dorsifixed (d) Connate
32. When the anther are fused in more than one whorl that are termed as
    (a) Adnate (b) Connate
    (c) Dorsifixed (d) Basifixed
33. The connective, locule, pollen sac, theca and pollen grain are the part of
    (a) Pistil (b) Carpel
    (c) Anther (d) All of above

34. Predominant stage in life cycle of moss is
(a) Gametophyte (b) Sporophyte
(c) Zygote (d) None of these
35. Which one of the following are considered as soil binders
(a) Hydrophytes (b) Pteridophytes
(c) Orchids (d) None of these
36. Plant body of which group differentiated into true root, stem & leaves
(a) Pteridophytes (b) Algae
(c) Fungi (d) Bryophytes
37. In Angiosperms, each cell of an embryo sac is
(a) Polyploidy (b) Diploid
(c) Triploid (d) Haploid
38. How many cells occur in egg apparatus of embryo sac of phanerograms?
(a) 2 (b) 3
(c) 4 (d) Many
39. Whorled arrangement of leaves occur in
(a) Alstonia (b) Calotropis
(c) Guava (d) Allium
40. Palmately compound leaves occur in
(a) Silk cotton (b) China rose
(c) Banana (d) Wheat
41. Thalamus is a
(a) Swollen end of pedicel (b) Over growth of style
(c) End region of stigma (d) Swollen end of filament
42. Which type of bud gives rise to leafy shoots
(a) Adventitious buds (b) Radical buds
(c) Reproductive bud (d) Vegetative buds
43. Which is the location of buds occurring on the nodes? outside the leaf bases are ?
(a) Apical (b) Extra axillary
(c) Extraordinary (d) None of these
44. From which one of the following axillary buds develop
(a) Pericycle (b) Cuticle
(c) Cortex (d) Hypodermis
45. In which of the following largest bud occurs
(a) Ginger (b) Cabbage
(c) Onion (d) Brinjal

46. Which is the function of epiphyllous buds?
    (a) Terminal grow (b) Respiration
    (c) Reproduction (d) Respiration
47. In which of the following bulbils occur
    (a) Oxalis (b) Agave
    (c) Lily (d) All the above
48. Mostly the buds occur at
    (a) Lateral root (b) Root apex
    (c) Internal region (d) Tips of branches and leaf
49. Which of the following buds produces monopodial stem?
    (a) Reproductive bud (b) Accessory bud
    (c) Apical bud (d) Extra axillary bud
50. Which type of leaves produced by reduced stem?
    (a) Peltate (b) Radical
    (c) Cladode (d) Compound

Answer key: PHYTOMORPHOLOGY - VIII

1. (a) 2. (d) 3. (b) 4. (a) 5. (b) 6. (a) 7. (d) 8. (a) 9. (d) 10. (a) 11. (d) 12. (d) 13. (a) 14. (a), 15. (c) 16. (a) 17. (b) 18. (a) 19. (c) 20. (a) 21. (a) 22. (a) 23. (a) 24. (a) 25. (c) 26. (a) 27. (b) 28. (b) 29. (a) 30. (d) 31. (d) 32. (a) 33. (c) 34. (a) 35. (b) 36. (a) 37. (d) 38. (a) 39. (a) 40. (a) 41. (a) 42. (d) 43. (b) 44. (c) 45. (b) 46. (c) 47. (d) 48. (d) 49. (c) 50. (b)

PHYTOMORPHOLOGY - IX

1. A weak Stemed plants which coils around any type of support are termed as
   (a) Twiner (b) Creeper
   (c) Spirillar (d) Erect
2. Which term is used for bulb of garlic ?
   (a) Nontunicated (b) Non-layered
   (c) Compound tunicated (d) Decompound tunicated
3. Study of external features of plant is termed as
   (a) Morphology (b) Anatomy
   (c) Angiosperms (d) Physiology
4. Modified tendrils occur in
   (a) Aloe (b) Garlic
   (c) Gram (d) Luffa

5. Which one is the modification of Luffa tendril?
   (a) Extra axillary bud (b) Bract
   (c) Adventitious bud (d) Leaf lamina
6. Climbers climb with the help of spines, prickles & thorns are termed as
   (a) Horizontal (b) Creeper
   (c) Scramblers (d) Tendrillar
7. Each areole of Opuntia represents
   (a) A node (b) Apical meristems
   (c) Axillary bud (d) An accessory bud
8. In which of the following culm occur
   (a) Garlic (b) Bamboo
   (c) Onion (d) Santalum
9. Which one is the twining structure in twinners?
   (a) Leaf tendril (b) Hook
   (c) Stolon (d) Sensitive stem
10. Potato is considered as underground stem because
    (a) It bears buds on nodes
    (b) It bears abundant fat globules
    (c) Pnematophores
    (d) Bears roots
11. Which is the primary function of underground stems?
    (a) Asexual reproduction
    (b) Perennation
    (c) Protection from water deficiency
    (d) Transpiration
12. Why the thorn is considered as stem because it is
    (a) Axillary (b) Like a bud
    (c) Terminal (d) Underground
13. In which of the following stem is modified into tendril
    (a) Cucurbita (b) Calotropis
    (c) Coriander (d) Rice
14. Which stem function as photosynthetic organ ?
    (a) Ginger (b) Underground buds
    (c) Potato (d) Phylloclade
15. Which one is concern with offset?
    (a) Pistia (b) Triticum
    (c) Chaenopodium (d) Allium

16. Sucker is a
    (a) Apical meristems (b) Vertical branch
    (c) Horizontal branch (d) Underground root
17. In which plant sucker occurs
    (a) Chrysanthemum (b) Radish
    (c) Santalum (d) Lily
18. From which epiphyllous buds develops
    (a) Leaf apex (b) Leaf margin
    (c) Petiole (d) Leaf axils
19. Which of the following can perennate & store food?
    (a) Ginger (b) Triticum
    (c) Groundnut (d) Maize
20. The stem of colocasia is a
    (a) Tuber (b) Corm
    (c) Bulb (d) None of these
21. Sucker producing plant is
    (a) Mint (b) Fenugreek
    (c) Spinach (d) Rhubarb
22. Which climber use hooks for climbing purpose ?
    (a) Gram (b) Lotus
    (c) Artabotrys (d) None of these
23. Certain plants produces thorn, spines prickles for
    (a) Defense (b) Reproduction
    (c) Respiration (d) Transpiration
24. Potato's are cultivated by using
    (a) Seeds (b) Aerial stem grafting
    (c) Tubers (d) Slices of potato
25. The rose prickles are
    (a) Exogenous (b) Endogenous
    (c) Highly branched (d) None of these
26. In which plant stem is modified to thorn
    (a) Guava (b) Citrus
    (c) Melia (d) Asparagus
27. The modified stem corm is a
    (a) Underground compressed stem (b) Elongated stem
    (c) Horizontal aerial stem (d) Aerial Stem

28. Which is the characteristic feature of corm?
(a) Absence of nodes (b) Presence of long internodes
(c) Presence of circular nodes (d) Absence of buds
29. In which plant cladode occurs
(a) Asparagus (b) Ginger
(c) Agave (d) Aloe
30. Stem with hollow internodes is
(a) Corn (b) Culms
(c) Tuber (d) Lythrus
31. Which is the example of hollow stem?
(a) Bamboo (b) Dalbergia
(c) Sugarcane (d) Ricinus
32. A highly reduced stem occurs in
(a) Culm (b) Onion
(c) Arachis (d) Helianthus
33. Which part of plant modified to phylloclade in Opuntia
(a) Stem (b) Petiole
(c) Root (d) Peduncle
34. The location of accessory bud is
(a) Axillary (b) Extra axillary
(c) Lateral (d) Apical
35. Fruit is a
(a) Ripened ovary (b) Region of food preparation
(c) Both a and b (d) None of these
36. When a ovary of flower develop into fruit it is a
(a) Parthenocarpic fruit (b) False fruit
(c) True fruit (d) None of these
37. Apple is a
(a) Drup (b) Berry
(c) Legume (d) Aggregate type of fruit
38. Which type of fruit occur in pea
(a) Capsule (b) Hesperidium
(c) Legume (d) None of these
39. A fleshy edible part of mango is termed as
(a) Mesocarp (b) Exocarp
(c) Endocarp (d) Pericarp
40. Coconut water is a
(a) Exosperm (b) Liquid endosperm
(c) Periderm (d) Fruit wall

41. The ovary walls develop into
(a) Fruit Wall (b) Periderm
(c) Seed (d) Seed wall
42. Coconut water is a
(a) Exosperm (b) Liquid Endosperm
(c) Germ tube (d) Fruit fiber
43. Which is the fruit type of rice ?
(a) Caryopsis (b) Parthenocarpic
(c) Pome (d) Hesperidium
44. A type of tomato fruit is
(a) Hesperidium (b) Stone fruit
(c) Drupe (d) Berry
45. Which is the example of unisexual flower?
(a) Papaya (b) Daccus
(c) Sorghum (d) China rose
46. Which type of inflorescences occur in garlic
(a) Verticelaster (b) Catkin
(c) Head (d) Umbel
47. Inflorescence in banana plant is of
(a) Spadix (b) Umbel
(c) Recemose (d) Catkin
48. Hypanthodium type of inflorescence occurs in
(a) Papaya (b) Ficus
(c) Strawberry (d) Sugarcane
49. In which of the following dichasial cyme occurs
(a) Ixora (b) Wheat
(c) Grape (d) Sunflower
50. Cyathium type of inflorescence occurs
(a) Gram (b) Mango
(c) Bean (d) Acacia

Answer key: PHYTOMORPHOLOGY - IX

1. (a) 2. (c) 3. (a) 4. (d) 5. (a) 6. (c) 7. (a) 8. (b) 9. (a) 10. (a) 11. (b) 12. (a) 13. (a) 14. (d) 15. (a) 16. (c) 17. (a) 18. (d) 19. (a) 20. (b) 21. (a) 22. (c) 23. (a) 24. (c) 25. (a) 26. (b) 27. (a) 28. (c) 29. (a) 30. (b) 31. (a) 32. (b) 33. (a) 34. (a) 35. (a) 36.(c) 37. (a) 38. (c) 39. (a) 40. (b) 41. (a) 42. (b) 43. (a) 44. (d) 45. (a) 46. (d) 47. (a) 48. (b) 49. (a) 50. (d)

PHYTOMORPHOLOGY - X

1. In which plant helicoid cyme type of inflorescence occurs
   (a) *Begonia* (b) *Dalbergia*
   (c) *Musa* (d) *Longifolia*
2. Inflorescence of family asteraceae
   (a) Catkin (b) Verticelaster
   (c) Spike (d) Head
3. A main function of inflorescence is
   (a) To show beauty of flowers (b) To produce beautiful flowers
   (c) Both a and b (d) None of these
4. When stamens united in several bundles, the phenomenon is termed as
   (a) Monodelphous (b) Polydelphous
   (c) Adelphous (d) None of these
5. Deeply bifid petals occur is
   (a) *Moringa* (b) Groundnut
   (c) *Tamarind* (d) *Stellaria*
6. Which family is more primitive than others?
   (a) Magnoliaceae (b) Caesalpinaceae
   (c) Annonaceae (d) Papilionaceae
7. Which is the Botanical name of kari patta?
   (a) *Murraya koenigii* (b) *Mentha piperata*
   (c) *Daccus carota* (d) *Mangifera indica*
8. Obdiplostemous condition of stamen occur
   (a) *Datura* (b) *Daccus*
   (c) *Dianthus* (d) *Dalbergia*
9. Which family belongs to series disciflorae according to Bentham and Hooker
   (a) Malvaceae (b) Malvaceae
   (c) Asteraceae (d) Rutaceae
10. Which is the botanical name of bael?
    (a) *Aegle marmelos* (b) *Sorghum vulgare*
    (c) *Aloe vera* (d) *Musa paradiscica*
11. Which is the botanical name of strawberry?
    (a) *Fragaria ananasa* (b) *Caesalpinia pulcherima*
    (c) *Mangifera indica* (d) *Vinca rosea*
12. Which family is commonly called as milkweed family?
    (a) Poaceae (b) Solanaceae
    (c) Malvaceae (d) Asclepiadaceace

13. In which plant pollinia occurs
    (a) *Calotropis gigantea* (b) *Daccus carota*
    (c) *Tamarindus indica* (d) *Cajanus cajan*
14. Which is the family of tobacco
    (a) Caesalpinaceae (b) Rutaceae
    (c) Solanaceae (d) Myrtaceae
15. Milky sap occur in
    (a) *Calotropis* (b) *Coriandrum*
    (c) Striga (d) Fenugreek
16. Stony hard endocarp occurs in
    (a) Tomato (b) Sweet pea
    (c) Mango (d) Wheat
17. Which type of fruits occur Pisum sativum
    (a) Silicle (b) Legume
    (c) Siliqua (d) Berry
18. Development of simple fruit takes place from
    (a) A single carpel of single ovary
    (b) A single stamen of a single flower
    (c) A many carpel of a single flower
    (d) All of these
19. The fruit of *Abelmoschus esculentus* describe as
    (a) Loculicidal (b) Drup
    (c) Pome (d) Legume
20. Which of the following influences also called as pendulous?
    (a) Catkin (b) Corymb
    (c) Spike (d) Catkin
21. In which city the National Orchidaria is situated
    (a) Australia (b) Germany
    (c) India (d) Shillong
22. Which is the source of serpentine?
    (a) Ocimum (b) Mentha
    (c) Acacia (d) Rauwolfia
23. Which is the source of atropine?
    (a) Belladonna (b) Indigofera
    (c) Lantana (d) Fenugreek
24. Which tree is considered as tree of 21st century?
    (a) Neem (b) *Terminalia*
    (c) Bamboo (d) *Tectona*

25. Type of root occur in monocots are
(a) Tap root system (b) Fibrous root
(c) Pnematophores (d) Reproduction root
26. Which is concern with the tap root system?
(a) Positively geotropic (b) Non geotropic
(c) Negatively geotropic (d) All of these
27. In which of the following secondary growth is absent
(a) *Dalbergia* (b) *Pinus*
(c) *Melia* (d) *Lycopodium*
28. Study of external features of plant is termed as
(a) Morphology (b) Physiology
(c) Anatomy (d) Taxonomy
29. The bud occur at tip of plant stem is termed as
(a) Terminal bud (b) Axile bud
(c) Secondary bud (d) Proximal bud
30. In which plant nodes and inter nodes are absent
(a) Sugarcane (b) Santalum
(c) Bamboo (d) Sorghum
31. Epiphytic roots occur in
(a) Orchids (b) Cereals
(c) Pulses (d) None of these
32. In which of the following Napiform type of root occurs
(a) *Daccus carota* (b) *Beta vulgaris*
(c) *Raphanus sativus* (d) None of these
33. The edible part of jackfruit is
(a) Fleshy pod cover of seed (b) Dry cover of fruit
(c) Seed embryo (d) None of these
34. In which of the following all floral parts of inflorescence unit to form
(a) Simple dry fruit (b) Dry deciduous fruit
(c) Simple fleshy fruit (d) Composite fruit
35. Which is the one seeded fleshy fruit?
(a) Mango (b) Tomato
(c) Banana (d) Pea
36. In which of the following fruit lets are observed
(a) Aggregate fruit (b) Dry indehiscent fruit
(c) Dry dehiscent fruit (d) None of these

37. Which is the example of sorosis type of fruit?
    (a) Moringa (b) Mango
    (c) Dalbergia (d) Jackfruit
38. Which fruit develop from polycarpellary apocarpus gynoecium is
    (a) Wheat (b) Gram
    (c) Jack fruit (d) Polyalthia
39. Legume type of fruit is an example of
    (a) Simple fleshy fruit (b) Dry dehiscence fruit
    (c) Simple dry fruit (d) Multiple fruit
40. Which is the parthenocarpic fruit?
    (a) Banana (b) Sunflower
    (c) Groundnut (d) Rice
41. Development of pericarp takes place from
    (a) Micropile (b) Chalaza end
    (c) Ovule (d) Ovary wall
42. Horticulture is the study of
    (a) Fruit, vegetable and flower
    (b) Fruit diseases
    (c) Horticulture diseases management
    (d) Study of vegetable
43. Shoot that arise from the roots to form new plant is termed as
    (a) Tendril (b) Branch sucker
    (c) Stolon (d) Root sucker
44. Which technique is used for seed saving?
    (a) Tissue culture (b) Cryopreservation
    (c) Both a and b (d) None of these
45. Which is not the plant growth regulator
    (a) Acetic acid (b) Gibberellins
    (c) Auxin (d) None of these
46. Which one is used to check soil pH?
    (a) Silica (b) Lime
    (c) Phosphorous (d) Urea
47. Which of the following is a corm?
    (a) Musa (b) Sesbania
    (c) Opuntia (d) Gloriosa

48. For which of the following external agencies are not required
    (a) Natural vegetative propagation
    (b) Asexual reproduction
    (c) Sexual reproduction
    (d) All of these
49. Plants of which of the following crop is used by farmers as green manure
    (a) Rosaceae (b) Cactaceae
    (c) Malvaceae (d) Leguminosae
50. Why water logging makes soil physiologically dry because
    (a) It does not allow oxygen to enter
    (b) It allow more respiration
    (c) Allow more transpiration
    (d) Allow to grow internodes faster

Answer key: PHYTOMORPHOLOGY - X

1. (a) 2. (d) 3. (d) 4. (b) 5. (d) 6. (a) 7. (a) 8. (c) 9. (d) 10. (a) 11. (a) 12. (d) 13. (a) 14. (c) 15. (a) 16. (c) 17. (b) 18. (a) 19. (a) 20. (a) 21. (d) 22. (d) 23. (a) 24. (a) 25. (b) 26. (a) 27. (d) 28. (a) 29. (a) 30. (b) 31. (a) 32. (b) 33. (a) 34. (d) 35. (a) 36. (a) 37. (d) 38. (c) 39. (c) 40. (a) 41. (d) 42. (a) 43. (d) 44. (b) 45. (a) 46. (b) 47. (d) 48. (a) 49. (d) 50. (a)

PHYTOMORPHOLOGY - XI

1. The seeds of monocot are mostly
    (a) Albuminous (b) Exalbuminous
    (c) Both a and b (d) None of these
2. Which term is used for a scar left by stalk of ovule attached to ovary wall?
    (a) Micropile (b) Hilum
    (c) Scutellum (d) Pericarp
3. Which one is monocot albiminious seed?
    (a) Rice (b) Castor
    (c) Orchid (d) Pea
4. Which one is monocot exalbuminous seed
    (a) Barley (b) Gram
    (c) Raphanus sativus (d) Pea
5. Which term is used for seed without endosperm or perisperm?
    (a) Albiminious (b) Exalbuminous
    (c) Angiosperm (d) Gymnosperm

6. Which are in dicot albuminous seed?
   (a) Bean (b) Groundnut
   (c) Cotton (d) Gram
7. Which one is absent in gymnosperm
   (a) Trachids (b) Cotyledon
   (c) Trachids (d) Fruits
8. Which type of root develop from any part of plant except roots
   (a) Adventitious roots (b) Tap root
   (c) Pnematophores (d) Stolons
9. The term used for arrangement of leaves is
   (a) Placentation (b) Phyllotaxy
   (c) Aestivation (d) Foliage leaves
10. Origin of branches of stem is
   (a) Exogenous (b) Endogenous
   (c) Internal (d) None of these
11. Which term is used to onion stem which bear flowers
   (a) Bract (b) Scape
   (c) Pedicel (d) Peduncle
12. Phyllode is concern with
   (a) Xerophytes (b) Halophytes
   (c) Epiphytes (d) Hydrophytes
13. Woody large thick climbers are termed as
   (a) Climber (b) Linnaeus
   (c) Scramblers (d) Twinners
14. In which parallel venation occurs
   (a) Monocot (b) Dicot
   (c) Both a and b (d) None of these
15. How the angiosperm differ from gymnosperm
   (a) In having ovule enclosed with ovary
   (b) Ovules open
   (c) Seed open
   (d) None of these
16. The distinct features of monocot is
   (a) Broad leaves (b) Presence of petiole
   (c) Parallel venation (d) Tap root system

17. The axillary buds arise from
    (a) Exogenously from the inner cortical layer
    (b) Exogenously from the outer cortical layer
    (c) Endogenously from the inner cortical layer
    (d) None of these
18. Onion bulb is a modification of
    (a) Stem (b) Root
    (c) Petiole (d) Peduncle
19. The natural insecticide is
    (a) Pyrethrum (b) Captan
    (c) Bavistin (d) Zineb
20. Which of the following is a polycarpic plant?
    (a) Pear (c) Mango
    (b) Bamboo (d) None of these
21. When a plant produce fruits only once in its life time is termed as
    (a) Polycarpic (c) Monocarpic
    (b) Multicarpic (d) None of these
22. Presence of tap root is characteristics feature of
    (a) Gymnosperm (b) Bryophyte
    (c) Pteridophytes (d) None of these
23. Maize produces fibrous roots which initiate from
    (a) Upper node (c) Lower node
    (b) Middle node (d) None of these
24. The roots develop from any part of plant except radical termed as
    (a) Parasitic root (c) Tap root
    (b) Adventitious roots (d) None of these
25. The prop roots are the
    (a) Adventitious roots (c) Buttress root
    (b) Conical root (d) None of these
26. The hanging roots of banyan tree are termed as
    (a) Prop roots (b) Parasitic root
    (c) Adventitious roots (d) Hanging root
27. The roots originated from branches of Ficus bengalensis are
    (a) Negatively geotropic (b) Positively phototrophic
    (c) Positively geotropic (d) None of these
28. The food sucking roots found in
    (a) Cuscuta (b) Mangroves
    (c) Ficus (d) None of these

29. The roots which occur in Cuscuta are termed as
    (a) Prop roots (b) Adventitious roots
    (c) Parasitic root (d) Hanging root
30. The respiratory roots are occurs in
    (a) Pnematophores (b) Adventitious roots
    (c) Prop roots (d) None of these
31. Which of the following produces Pnematophores?
    (a) Ficus (c) Cuscuta
    (b) Avicennia (d) None of these
32. The *Ipomoea batatas* is a
    (a) Corm (b) Rhizome
    (c) Underground stem (d) Underground root
33. Which part of sweet potato is edible?
    (a) Adventitious tuberous roots (b) Prop roots
    (c) Pnematophores (d) Adventitious roots
34. Which of the following is plant have climbing roots
    (a) Ficus (b) Avicennia
    (c) Betel (d) None of these
35. In which plants epiphytic roots are found
    (a) Ficus (b) Orchids
    (c) Cuscuta (d) None of these
36. Which type of roots form velamen tissue?
    (a) Hanging root (b) Adventitious roots
    (c) Prop roots (d) Hanging root
37. In which plant contractile root are present
    (a) Adventitious root (b) Tuberous root
    (c) Bulb (d) None of these
38. The photosynthetic roots are found in
    (a) Taeniophyllum (b) Avicennia
    (c) Cuscuta (d) None of these
39. The stem of banana is a
    (a) True stem (b) Both a and b
    (c) False stem (d) None of these
40. The bud which gives rise to leafy shoot is termed as
    (a) Vegetative bud (b) Both a and b
    (c) Axillary bud (d) None of these

41. The accessory buds develop at the side of
    (a) Radial bud (b) Axillary bud
    (c) Apical bud (d) None of these
42. The origin of branches of stem is
    (a) Exogenous (b) Mesogenous
    (c) Endogenous (d) None of these
43. The main reason of underground modification of stem is
    (a) Perennation (b) Procumbence
    (c) Creeping (d) None of these
44. Which of the following is characteristic feature of underground modified stem?
    (a) Stolon (b) Both a and b
    (c) Nodes and internodes (d) None of these
45. The underground swollen edible portion of onion is called as
    (a) Bulb (b) Corm
    (c) Underground rhizome (d) None of these
46. In which plant the stem performs the functions of food storage and perennation
    (a) Radish (b) Ginger
    (c) Carrot (d) None of these
47. The function of eyes of potato is
    (a) Vegetative propagation (b) Both a and b
    (c) Grafting (d) None of these
48. Which of the following in sub aerial modified stem?
    (a) Stolon (b) Rhizome
    (c) Corm (d) None of these
49. The corm is
    (a) Bulb (b) Rhizome
    (c) An underground vertical stem (d) None of these
50. Which plant propagates by offset is?
    (a) Agave (b) Coconut
    (c) Cuscuta (d) None of these

Answer key: PHYTOMORPHOLOGY - XI

1. (a) 2. (b) 3. (c) 4. (a) 5. (b) 6. (a) 7. (d) 8. (a) 9. (b) 10. (a) 11. (b) 12. (a) 13. (b) 14. (a) 15. (a) 16. (c) 17. (a) 18. (a) 19. (a) 20. (a) 21. (c) 22. (a) 23. (c) 24. (b) 25. (a) 26. (a) 27. (c) 28. (a) 29. (c) 30. (a) 31. (b) 32. (d) 33. (a) 34. (c) 35. (b) 36. (a) 37. (c) 38. (a) 39. (c) 40. (a) 41. (b) 42. (a) 43. (a) 44. (c) 45. (a) 46. (b) 47. (a) 48. (a) 49. (c) 50. (a)

PHYTOMORPHOLOGY - XII

1. Why the ginger is called stem not a root because
   (a) It consists of nodes and internodes
   (b) It consists of leaves
   (c) It consists of chlorophyll
   (d) None of these
2. Why the thorn is called as modified branch
   (a) Because it originate from the axil of leaf
   (b) Hard like stem
   (c) Woody
   (d) None of these
3. The pickles which occur in rose are
   (a) Endogenous in origin (b) Both a and b
   (c) Exogenous in origin (d) None of these
4. In Opuntia the photosynthesis takes place in
   (a) Phylloplane (b) Phyllosphere
   (c) Phylloclade (d) None of these
5. Phylloclade is a
   (a) Modified stem (b) Modified bract b.
   (c) Modified root (d) Modified scale
6. The disc like stem occur in
   (a) Maize (b) Onion
   (c) Sunflower (d) None of these
7. Which of the following produces stolon?
   (a) Mint (b) Ginger
   (c) Ocimum (d) Onion
8. Which one is the example of phylloclade?
   (a) Bamboo (b) Asparagus
   (c) Cuscuta (d) Opuntia
9. The main function of leaf is
   (a) Photosynthesis (b) Both a and b
   (c) Reproduction (d) None of these
10. The petiole less leaf is termed as
    (a) Scaly leaf (b) Sessile
    (c) Petiolate (d) Succulent

11. The term vernation is used for
    (a) Arrangement of leaves in bud
    (b) Arrangement of sepals
    (c) Arrangement of petals
    (d) None of these
12. The leaf has parallel vernation in
    (a) Santalum (b) Gram
    (c) Caesalpinia (d) Grass
13. In which plant leaf lamina is highly reduced
    (a) Halophyte (b) Mesophyte
    (c) Hygrophyte (d) Xerophytes
14. Which plant store food in leaves?
    (a) Onion (b) Ginger
    (c) Carrot (d) None of these
15. The phyllotaxy is the
    (a) Arrangement of leaves in stem
    (b) Arrangement of sepals
    (c) Arrangement of petals
    (d) Arrangement of ovules
16. The mode of arrangement of leaves in bud is termed as
    (a) Germination (b) Vernation
    (c) Pollination (d) None of these
17. The margin of which plant is spiney
    (a) *Aloe vera* (b) *Citrus*
    (c) *Ficus* (d) *Withania*
18. In case of Nepenthes, the pitchers are developed from
    (a) Midrib (b) Veins
    (c) Lamina (d) None of these
19. The bipinnate leaf is characteristic feature of family
    (a) Mimosaceae (b) Meliaceae
    (c) Malvaceae (d) Acanthaceae
20. The simple leaf occur in
    (a) Annona (b) Acacia
    (c) Tamarind (d) Caesalpinia
21. The imparipinnate leaves occur in
    (a) Annona (b) Ficus
    (c) Rose (d) None of these

22. The adnate type of stipule occur in
    (a) Rose (b) *Mentha*
    (c) Neem (d) *Ocimum*
23. Which plant consists of interpetiolar stipule?
    (a) *Ixora* (b) *Nelumbo*
    (c) Rose (d) None of these
24. The onion bulb is a modified
    (a) Leaf (b) Root
    (c) Stem (d) Rhizome
25. The tendril of sweet pea is a modified
    (a) Stem (b) Leaflet
    (c) Petiole (d) None of these
26. The spine, thorns, pickles in plant function as
    (a) Defensive organs (b) Both a and b
    (c) Ornamental organ (d) None of these
27. The vegetative reproduction by bulbils takes place in
    (a) Tectona (b) Agave
    (c) Coconut (d) Santalum
28. The hooks present in Artabotrys is a modified
    (a) Inflorescence axis (b) Root
    (c) Leaf (d) Bract
29. The black pepper plant is a
    (a) Runner (b) Creeper
    (c) Climber (d) None of these
30. The function of leaf veins is
    (a) Transport of water, minerals (b) Transpiration
    (c) Photosynthesis (d) None of these
31. In Ficus, the bud scales represent
    (a) Trichomes (b) Both a and b
    (c) Stipules (d) None of these
32. The tendrillar petiole occur in
    (a) Clematis (b) Mangifera
    (c) Gossipium (d) None of these
33. Folding of young leaves itself in the bud is called
    (a) Ptyxis (b) Epicalyx
    (c) Scaly leaf (d) Calyx

34. The stalk of leaflet is known as
 (a) Receptacle (b) Petiolule
 (c) Petiole (d) Androphore
35. The tubular hollow long petioles occur in
 (a) *Carica papaya* (b) *Ficus religiosa*
 (c) *Delonix regia* (d) None of these
36. The winged petiole occurs in
 (a) Mango (b) Papaya
 (c) Banana (d) Citrus
37. The time taken for the development of two adjacent leaves is called
 (a) Plastochron Index (b) *Phytochron*
 (c) Cystochrone (d) None of these
38. Which of the following helps in counting age of plants?
 (a) Cystochrone (b) Phytochron
 (c) Plastochron Index (d) None of these
39. Which of the following produces a compound leaf but looks like simple leaf?
 (a) *Solanum* (b) *Citrus*
 (c) *Ficus* (d) None of these
40. The root develops from
 (a) Radical (c) Stem
 (b) Node (d) None of these
41. The stem develops from
 (a) Radical (b) Node
 (c) Plumule (d) None of these
42. The rhizome differs from root because it consists of
 (a) Scale leaves and buds (b) Both a and b
 (c) Absence of root leaves (d) None of these
43. Which of the following is a root?
 (a) Brinjal (b) Potato
 (c) Ginger (d) Carrot
44. The function of adventitious roots of Pistia is
 (a) Balancing the plant (b) Both a and b
 (c) Photosynthesis (d) None of these
45. The garlic and onion bulbs consists of
 (a) Well developed stem (b) Elongated stem
 (c) Greatly reduced stem (d) None of these

46. The potatoes are borne as
    (a) Stolons (b) Runner
    (c) Creeper (d) Twinners
47. When the petiole is modified to a green leafy structure it is known as
    (a) Cladode (b) Both a and b
    (c) Phyllode (d) None of these
48. The spines of citrus are morphologically
    (a) Terminal leaf of a terminal branch
    (b) Stipule of lower branch
    (c) Axillary
    (d) None of these
49. The leaf lamina of Calotropis is
    (a) Obtuse (b) Auricular
    (c) Oblique (d) None of these
50. Which of the following in the non-carnivorous pitcher plant
    (a) Dischida (b) Drocera
    (c) Nepenthes (d) None of these

Answer key: PHYTOMORPHOLOGY - XII

1. (a) 2. (a) 3. (c) 4. (c) 5. (a) 6. (b) 7. (a) 8. (d) 9. (a) 10. (b) 11. (a) 12. (d) 13. (d) 14. (a) 15. (a) 16. (b) 17. (a) 18. (c) 19. (a) 20. (a) 21. (c) 22 (a) 23. (a) 24. (a) 25. (c) 26. (a) 27. (b) 28. (a) 29. (c) 30. (a) 31. (c) 32. (a) 33. (a) 34. (b) 35. (a) 36. (d) 37. (a) 38. (c) 39. (b) 40. (a) 41. (c) 42. (a) 43. (d) 44. (a) 45. (c) 46. (a) 47. (c) 48. (a) 49. (b) 50. (a)

PHYTOMORPHOLOGY - XIII

1. The petiole modified into tendrils are found in
    (a) Clematis (b) Solanum
    (c) Ipomoea (d) None of these
2. When the stem modify to a thick leafy structure it is termed as
    (a) Cladode (b) Both a and b
    (c) Phylloclade (d) None of these
3. Parallel venation, fibrous root, trimerous flower and one cotyledon occurs in
    (a) Monocot (b) Dicot
    (c) Alga (d) None of these
4. The buttress type of roots are found in
    (a) *Ficus bengalensis* (b) *Polyanthia indica*
    (c) Mangifera indica (d) None of these

5. The underground runner in called
   (a) Creeper (b) Roots
   (c) Sobole (d) None of these
6. The leaf margins are wavy in
   (a) *Polyanthia* (b) *Calotropis*
   (c) *Citrus* (d) None of these
7. The maturity of cotton plant can be identified on the basic of
   (a) Shape of leaves (b) Branching system
   (c) Growth pattern (d) None of these
8. The leaf of cladophyllum consists of
   (a) Cross venulation (b) Parallel veinatation
   (c) Reticulate venation (d) None of these
9. The function of hanging root of banyan tree is
   (a) Mechanical support (b) Photosynthesis
   (c) Respiration (d) Transpiration
10. Which plant consists of tuberous root?
    (a) Ipomoea batata (b) Both a and b
    (c) Solanum tuberosum (d) None of these
11. Which is the example of the stilt root?
    (a) Mango (b) Citrus
    (c) Ficus (d) Sugarcane
12. Mostly the buds are found
    (a) At the apex or axil of the leaves (b) On short roots
    (c) Internodes (d) None of these
13. The obliquely growing lateral branch form underground stems in called
    (a) Pistil (b) Receptacle
    (c) Placenta (d) Sucker
14. The presence of well developed vessel is a characteristic feature of
    (a) Angiosperms (b) Bryophytes
    (c) Algae (d) Fungi
15. The companion cell present in
    (a) Gymnosperms (b) Pteridophytes
    (c) Angiosperms (d) none of these
16. The closed seed is the feature of
    (a) Angiosperms (b) Pteridophytes
    (c) Gymnosperms (d) None of these

17. Which of the following is unique feature of angiosperms?
    (a) Double fertilization and triple fusion
    (b) Gymnosperms
    (c) Pteridophytes
    (d) Bryophytes
18. Which type of pollination is common in angiosperms?
    (a) Water pollination (b) Insect pollination
    (c) Wind pollination (d) None of these
19. In the angiosperms female gametophyte or endosperm in post fertilization stages remain
    (a) Triploid (b) Diploid
    (c) Monoploid (d) None of these
20. Presence of ovary and true fruits are the characteristic features of
    (a) Gymnosperms (b) Pteridophytes
    (c) Angiosperms (d) None of these
21. All the cereal and pulses are
    (a) Angiosperms (b) Pteridophytes
    (c) Gymnosperms (d) None of these
22. If the central portion of stem in hollow the stem in described as
    (a) Solid (b) Both a and b
    (c) Fistular (d) None of these
23. The corn is modification of
    (a) Stem (b) Leaf
    (c) root (d) None of these
24. Which of the following is runner?
    (a) Acanthus (b) Aster
    (c) Oxalis (d) None of these
25. The stolon in present
    (a) Fragaria (b) Aster
    (c) Acanthus (d) None of these
26. The cladodes occur in
    (a) Asparagus (b) Cucumis
    (c) Ginger (d) None of these
27. A jointed stem with hollow internode in known as
    (a) Phylloclade (b) Culm
    (c) Cladode (d) None of these

28. The tendrils occur in
(a) Passiflora (b) Arachis
(c) Helianthus (d) None of these

29. The function of offset is
(a) Vegetative propagation (b) Micropropogation
(c) Sexual reproduction (d) None of these

30. Presence phylloclade or cladode is the characteristic feature of
(a) Mesophyte (b) Xerophytic plant
(c) Hydrophyte (d) Halophyte

31. The decussate phyllotaxy occur in
(a) Calotropis (c) Azadiracta
(b) Annona (d) Citrus

32. The stipule occur at the base of
(a) Leaf (b) Inflorescence
(c) Root (d) None of these

33. The rachis is the part of
(a) Simple leaf (b) Inflorescence
(c) Compound leaf (d) None of these

34. A secondary leaf let in a pinnately compound leaf is termed as
(a) Pinnule (b) Rachilla
(c) Petiole (d) None of these

35. The carpel is the part of
(a) Seed (c) Fruit
(b) Flower (d) None of these

36. The flower without perianth occur in
(a) Magnolia (b) Solanum
(c) Ipomea (d) None of these

37. The maturation of gynoecium before androecium in termed as
(a) Eugyny (b) Protoandrae
(c) Protogyny (d) None of these

38. The thalamus occur in
(a) *Annona squimosa* (b) Coriander
(c) Apium (d) None of these

39. The example of dense umbel type of inflorescence is
(a) *Polyalthia longifolia* (b) Arachis hypogeal
(c) Citrus sinensis (d) None of these

40. Which of the following in medicinal plant
    (a) *Argemone mexicana* (b) *Saccharum officinalis*
    (c) *Sorghum vulgare* (d) None of these
41. The leaf margin of *Capparis spinosa* is
    (a) Dissected (b) Spinus
    (c) Entire (d) None of these
42. All the pulse crops are angiosperms and are
    (a) Dicotyledons (b) Both a and b
    (c) Monocots (d) None of these
43. The habitat of aquatic plants is described as
    (a) Hydrophytic (b) Halophytic
    (c) Xerophytic (d) None of these
44. The plants growing in scanty of water are considered as
    (a) Halophytic (b) Xerophytes
    (c) Hydrophytic (d) None of these
45. Plants growing on branches of large trees are termed as
    (a) Halophytic (b) Hydrophytic
    (c) Xerophytes (d) Epiphytes
46. Which of the following is an epiphyte?
    (a) Orchids (b) Both a and b
    (c) Cuscuta (d) None of these
47. Which of the angiospermic plant is a plant parasite?
    (a) Loranthus (c) Mentha
    (c) Catharanthus (d) Daccus
48. The angiosperms grow an land are termed as
    (a) Submerged (b) Terrestrial
    (c) Aquatic (d) None of these
49. The wing petals and standard petals occur in flowers of family
    (a) Annonaceae (b) Mimosaceae
    (c) Caesalpinaceae (d) Papilionaceae
50. A boat shaped petal is termed as
    (a) Keel petal (b) Wings
    (c) Standard petal (d) None of these

Answer key: PHYTOMORPHOLOGY - XIII

1. (a) 2. (c) 3. (a) 4. (a) 5. (c) 6. (a) 7. (a) 8. (b) 9. (a) 10. (a) 11. (d) 12. (a) 13. (d) 14. (a) 15. (c) 16. (a) 17. (a) 18. (b) 19. (c) 20. (c) 21. (a) 22. (c) 23. (a) 24. (c) 25. (a) 26. (a) 27. (b) 28. (a) 29. (a) 30. (b) 31. (a) 32. (a) 33. (c) 34. (a) 35. (b) 36. (a) 37. (c) 38. (a) 39. (a) 40. (a) 41. (c) 42. (a) 43. (a) 44. (b) 45. (d) 46. (a) 47. (a) 48. (b) 49. (d) 50. (a)

PHYTOMORPHOLOGY - XIV

1. The cruciform type of corolla occur in
   (a) Radish (b) Carrot
   (c) Brinjal (d) Asparagus
2. Which of the following in dicot plant
   (a) Grasses (b) Gram
   (c) Cereals (d) None of these
3. The tetradynamous condition occur in
   (a) *Brassica nigra* (b) *Datura stramonium*
   (c) Hibiscus rosa sinensis (d) None of these
4. The unilocular ovary looks like bilocular because of false septum in
   (a) *Raphanus sativus* (b) *Coriandrum sativum*
   (c) *Helianthus annuus* (d) None of these
5. The false septum occur in ovary in known as
   (a) Rostellum (b) Labellum
   (c) Replum (d) None of these
6. Family of *Hibiscus rosa sinensis* is
   (a) Malvaceae (b) Magnoliaceae
   (c) Meliaceae (d) Apiaceae
7. The schizocarpic fruit consists of many indehiscent mericarps in
   (a) *Abutilon indicum* (c) *Cajanua cajan*
   (b) *Acacia nilotica* (d) None of these
8. The reticulate venation and taproot system in the characteristic feature of
   (a) Monocot plants (b) Both a and b
   (c) Dicot plants (d) None of these
9. Jowar and bamboo are examples of
   (a) Monocot plants (b) Both a and b
   (c) Dicot plants (d) None of these
10. Which family of angiosperm consists of large number of plants?
    (a) Malvaceae (b) Caesalpinaceae
    (c) Fabaeceae (d) Compositae
11. Which angiosperm in an aromatic plant
    (a) Mint and Ocimum (b) Ricinus
    (c) Solanum (d) Triticum
12. The reproductive organ of angiosperms is
    (a) Bract (b) Calyx
    (c) Fruit (d) Flower

13. The sterile stamens in the flower are termed as
    (a) Staminode (b) Carpel
    (c) stamens (d) None of these
14. A following is the example of one seeded drupe
    (a) *Triticum vulgarae* (b) *Ricinus communis*
    (c) *Calotropis gigantea* (d) *Melia azadirachta*
15. Which of the following plant have prickles?
    (a) *Rose indica* (b) *Solanum tuberosum*
    (c) *Melia azadirachta* (d) None of these
16. Quincuncial type of aestivation occur in
    (a) *Raphanus* (b) *Daccus*
    (c) *Hibiscus* (d) Rose
17. Which one is the plant of family Papilionaceae?
    (a) Trigonella (b) Sugarcane
    (c) Potato (d) Tamarind
18. The *Crotalaria juncea* (Papilionaceae) is a
    (a) Shrub (b) Creeper
    (c) Tree (d) Herb
19. The terminal leaflet of compound leaf modified to a tendril in
    (a) *Pisum sativum* (b) *Cassia tora*
    (c) *Caesalpinia pulcherima* (d) None of these
20. The plant bears aerial flowers and fruits mature in soil in
    (a) *Cassia tora* (b) *Arachis hypogea*
    (c) *Delonix regia* (d) None of these
21. Diadelphous condition occur in
    (a) *Pisum sativum* (b) *Cassia tora*
    (c) *Delonix regia* (d) None of these
22. Descending imbricate aestivation occur in
    (a) *Lythrus odoratus* (b) *Cassia tora*
    (c) *Delonix regia* (d) None of these
23. Which plant consists of zygomorphic flower?
    (a) *Dalbergia sisso* (b) *Cassia tora*
    (c) *Delonix regia* (d) None of these
24. The marginal placentation occur in
    (a) Sunflower (b) Solanum
    (c) Cucumis (d) Pea

25. The sheathing leaf base occurs in plants of family
    (a) Graminae (b) Meliaceae
    (c) Orchidaceae (d) None of these
26. The paripinnate compound leaf occur in
    (a) *Cajanus cajan* (b) *Ricinus communis*
    (c) *Cassia tora* (d) None of these
27. Tamarindus indica is a
    (a) Large tree (b) Herb
    (c) Shrub (d) Climber
28. The leaf of *Caesalpinia pulcherima* is
    (a) Bipinnate compound (b) Tripinnate
    (c) Unipinnate (d) None of these
29. A globose head type of inflorescence occur in
    (a) *Cassia tora* (b) *Abutilon indica*
    (c) *Mimosa pudica* (d) None of these
30. The *Mimosa pudica* stipules are modified to
    (a) Spine (b) Involucres
    (c) Bracts (d) Tendril
31. Which one is called as touch me not plants?
    (a) *Mimosa pudica* (b) *Delonix regia*
    (c) *Daccus carota* (d) None of these
32. Which plant yield gum of commercial value?
    (a) *Terminalia indica* (b) *Acacia nilotica*
    (c) *Mentha piperata* (d) *Caesalpinia pulcherima*
33. The fruit type of *Acacia nilotica* is
    (a) Lomentum (b) Legume
    (c) Drupe (d) Pod
34. Which of the following in a deciduous tree growing in dry places?
    (a) *Alstonia scolaris* (b) *Murraya paniculata*
    (c) *Albizzia lebbek* (d) None of these
35. Monodelphous condition of stamen occur in
    (a) *Hibiscus rosa sinensis* (b) *Acacia nilotica*
    (c) *Cassia tora* (d) *Raphanus sativus*
36. Which one is a tall tree with non endospermic seeds?
    (a) *Polyanthia longifolia* (b) Both a and b
    (c) *Eucalyptus lanceolatus* (d) None of these

37. The family of *Psidum guajava* is
    (a) Magnoliaceae (b) Myrtaceae
    (c) Meliaceae (d) None of these
38. Fruit of guava is a
    (a) Many seeded berry (b) Drupe
    (c) Capsule (d) None of these
39. The fruit of *Ficus carica* is a
    (a) Hesperidium (b) Follicle
    (c) Hypanthodium (d) None of these
40. The leaf of Perithecium grass in an example of
    (a) Decompound leaf (b) Simple
    (c) Compound (d) None of these
41. The sorosis of pineapple is a type of
    (a) Multiple fruit (b) Etaerio of berries
    (c) Simple fruit (d) None of these
42. A single seeded dehiscent fruit with thin wall in described as
    (a) Drupe (b) Capsule
    (c) Legume (d) Utricle
43. The one seeded dry indehiscent fruit with bony shell derived from compound syconium is termed as
    (a) Nut (b) Berry
    (c) Capsule (d) Achene
44. The petals are absent in flower of
    (a) *Cassia tora* (b) *Terminalia bellerica*
    (c) *Hibiscus rosa-sinensis* (d) *Cucumis sativus*
45. A five angled achene type of fruit occur in
    (a) *Quiqualis indica* (b) *Aegle marmelos*
    (c) *Cucumis sativus* (d) *Mangifera indica*
46. Which one is the climbing herb?
    (a) *Cucurbita maxima* (b) *Ficus religiosa*
    (c) *Annona squimosa* (d) *Tamarindus indica*
47. The *Cucurbita maxima* is a
    (a) Monoecious and dicot plant
    (b) Dioecious and dicot plant
    (c) Monoecious and monocot plant
    (d) None of these

48. The type of fruit occur in *Luffa cylindrica* is a
    (a) Capsule (b) Pepo
    (c) Legume (d) Drupe
49. The flowers without petiole termed as
    (a) Sessile (b) Stalked
    (c) Petiolate (d) Androgynous
50. The ovules are attached to ovary wall with the help of
    (a) Receptacle (b) Gynophore
    (c) Placenta (d) None of these

Answer key: PHYTOMORPHOLOGY - XIV

1. (a) 2. (b) 3. (a) 4. (a) 5. (c) 6. (a) 7. (a) 8. (c) 9. (a) 10. (d) 11. (a) 12. (d) 13. (a) 14. (d) 15. (a) 16. (d) 17. (a) 18. (d) 19. (a) 20. (b) 21. (a) 22. (a) 23. (a) 24. (d) 25. (a) 26. (c) 27. (a) 28. (a) 29. (c) 30. (a) 31. (a) 32. (b) 33. (a) 34. (c) 35. (a) 36. (c) 37. (b) 38. (a) 39. (c) 40. (a) 41. (a) 42. (d) 43. (a) 44. (b) 45. (a) 46. (a) 47. (a) 48. (b) 49. (a) 50. (c)

PHYTOMORPHOLOGY - XV

1. The roots of *Momordica charantia* appear like a chain of beads which is described as
    (a) Moniliform (b) Scalariform
    (c) Polyads (d) None of these
2. The *Coriandrum sativum* is member of family
    (a) Euphorbiaceae (b) Solanaceae
    (c) Solanaceae (d) Apiaceae
3. Which of the following is a cultivated plant?
    (a) *Cucumis sativus* (b) *Tephrosia purpurea*
    (c) *Cassia tora* (d) None of these
4. A cremocarp type of fruit occur in
    (a) *Cucumis sativus* (b) *Cassia tora*
    (c) *Coriandrum sativum* (d) *Terminalia chebula*
5. Which type of inflorescence occur in *Foeniculum vulgare*
    (a) Compound umbel (b) Cymose
    (c) Recemose (d) None of these
6. A disc like stylopodium occur at the base of the style in
    (a) *Foeniculum vulgare* (b) *Allium cepa*
    (c) *Cassia tora* (d) *Aegle marmelos*

7. Which of the following is a ornamental plant
   (a) *Coriandrum sativum* (b) *Ixora parviflora*
   (c) *Cassia angustifolia* (d) None of these
8. The family of *Eclipta alba* is
   (a) Compositae (b) Malvaceae
   (c) Malvaceae (d) Asclepidiaceace
9. Botanical name of sunflower is
   (a) *Annona squimosa* (b) *Withania somnifera*
   (c) *Catharanthus roseus* (d) *Helianthus annuus*
10. Presence of ray and disc florets is a characteristic feature of family
    (a) Compositae (b) Mimosaceae
    (c) Meliaceae (d) Apiaceae
11. Ray floret are the
    (a) Male flowers (b) Both a and b
    (c) Female flower (d) None of these
12. The involucres of bract is a characteristic feature of family
    (a) Papaveraceae (b) Caesalpinaceae
    (c) Malvaceae (d) Compositae
13. Which plant consists of decumbent type of stem
    (a) *Tridax procumbence* (b) *Rosa indica*
    (c) *Helianthus annuus* (d) None of these
14. The family of *Manilkara zapotsa* is
    (a) Sapotaceae (b) Magnoliaceae
    (c) Anacardiaceae (d) None of these
15. The fruit of *Manilkara zapotsa* is a
    (a) Drupe (b) Capsule
    (c) Nut (d) Fleshy berry
16. The *Madhuca india* is a mesophyte occur in
    (a) Deciduous forest (b) Alpine forest
    (c) evergreen forest (d) None of these
17. The botanical name of Sadabahar is
    (a) *Nerium indicum* (b) *Tamarindus indica*
    (c) *Vinca rosea* (d) none of these
18. Which of the following require dry soil for growth?
    (a) Calotropis gigantea (b) *Saccharum officinarum*
    (c) *Zingiber officinale* (d) None of these

19. The presence of a pair of caudicle (pollinium) is a characteristics feature of
    (a) *Acacia nilotica* (b) *Mimosa pudica*
    (c) *Cassia angustifolia* (d) *Calotropis gigantea*
20. Which of the following is an ornamental climbing shrub?
    (a) *Curcuma longa* (b) *Cryptostegia grandiflora*
    (c) *Catharanthus roseus* (d) None of these
21. The family of *Ipomoea palmata* is
    (a) Convolvulaceae (b) Cucurbitaceae
    (c) Asclepiadaceace (d) None of these
22. The leaves are absent in
    (a) *Cuscuta reflexa* (c) *Alstonia scholaria*
    (b) *Vinca rosea* (d) None of these
23. The roots are absent but haustoria are present in plant like
    (a) *Asparagus* (b) *Curcuma*
    (c) *Ipomoea* (d) *Cuscuta*
24. Which of the following in wild plant growing on waste land?
    (a) *Solanum nigrum* (b) *Helianthus annuus*
    (c) Curcuma longa (d) None of these
25. The thorns on the leaf occur in
    (a) *Daccus carrota* (b) *Raphanus sativus*
    (c) *Solanum tuberosum* (d) *Solanum nigrum*
26. Family of *Withania somnifera* is
    (a) Solanaceae (b) Malvaceae
    (c) Convolvulaceae (d) None of these
27. Which is the plant used as medicine
    (a) *Solanum tuberosum* (b) *Withania somnifera*
    (c) *Solanum melongiana* (d) None of these
28. Which plant grow in wet or marshy places
    (a) *Bacopa monnieri* (b) *Mangifera indica*
    (c) *Annona squimosa* (d) *Alstonia scolaris*
29. The persistent style occurs in
    (a) *Cassia tora* (b) *Musa paradiscicca*
    (c) *Bacopa monnieri* (d) None of these
30. Family of *Bacopa monnieri* is
    (a) Scrophulariaceae (b) Myrtaceae
    (c) Annonaceae (d) Anacardiaceae

31. The *Justicia adhatoda* is a member of family
    (a) Mimosaceae (b) Solanaceae
    (c) Papilionaceae (d) Acanthaceae
32. The *Justicia adhatoda* is a
    (a) Perennial shrub (b) Climber
    (c) Annual herb (d) Annual Shrub
33. The best wood yielding plant is
    (a) *Tectona grandis* (b) *Annona squimosa*
    (c) *Cassia angustifolia* (d) None of these
34. The *Vitex nigundo* is a member of family
    (a) Myrtaceae (b) Verbenaceae
    (c) Apocynaceae (d) None of these
35. The cymose panicle type of inflorescence occur in
    (a) *Vitex nigundo* (b) *Mentha piperata*
    (c) *Daccus carota* (d) *Delonix regia*
36. Carcerulus type of fruit occurs in
    (a) *Ocimum sanctum* (b) *Coriander sativum*
    (c) *Mimosa pudica* (d) None of these
37. The gland dotted aromatic leaves occur in
    (a) *Sorghum vulgarae* (b) Sugarcane
    (c) *Ocimum sanctum* (d) All of these
38. Persistent perianth and spiny bracteoles occur in
    (a) *Achyranthes aspera* (b) *Mimosa pudica*
    (c) *Cassia tora* (d) None of these
39. Which of the following angiosperm used as vegetable
    (a) *Curcuma longa* (b) *Amaranthus spinosus*
    (c) *Citrus aurantifolia* (d) None of these
40. The tapels are present in
    (a) *Chenopodium album* (b) China rose
    (c) *Mirabilis jalapa* (d) None of these
41. The plant *Euphorbia hirta* is a
    (a) Dioecious (b) Both a and b
    (c) Monoecious (d) None of these
42. A three coccoid schizocarpic capsule occur in
    (a) *Ricinus communis* (b) *Hibiscus rosa-sinensis*
    (c) *Cucumis sativus* (d) None of these

43. Presence of milk latex in the characteristic feature of family
    (a) Nyctaginaceae (b) Annonaceae
    (c) Malvaceae (d) Euphorbiaceae
44. The family of *Ficus glomarata* is
    (a) Caesalpinaceae (b) Papilionaceae
    (c) Moraceae (d) Anacardiaceae
45. The fruit of which plant are edible
    (a) *Ficus glomarata* (b) *Ricinus communis*
    (c) *Gossipium herbacium* (d) None of these
46. The *Phoenix* is a member of family
    (a) Annonaceae (b) Orchidaceae
    (c) Palmae (d) None of these
47. Which of the following angiosperm possesses prominent leaf? bases on stem
    (a) *Cocos nucifera* (b) *Ricinus communis*
    (c) *Jatropha curcus* (d) *None of these*
48. A fibrous drup occur in
    (a) *Annona squimosa* (b) *Ricinus communis*
    (c) *Cocos nucifera* (d) None of these
49. An aromatic herb perennating trough underground rhizome is
    (a) *Raphanus sativus* (b) *Zingiber officiale*
    (c) *Daccus carrota* (d) None of these
50. Which of the following plant grow in canal banks?
    (a) *Zeuxine sulcata* (b) *Alocasia indica*
    (c) *Vanda roxburghii* (d) None of these

Answer key: PHYTOMORPHOLOGY - XV

1. (a) 2. (d) 3. (a) 4. (c) 5. (a) 6. (a) 7. (b) 8. (a) 9. (d) 10. (a) 11. (a) 12. (d) 13. (a) 14. (a) 15. (d) 16. (a) 17. (c) 18. (a) 19. (d) 20. (b) 21. (a) 22. (a) 23. (d) 24. (a) 25. (d) 26. (a) 27. (b) 28. (a) 29. (c), 30. (a) 31. (d) 32. (a) 33. (a) 34. (b) 35. (a) 36. (a) 37. (c) 38. (a) 39. (b) 40. (a) 41. (c) 42. (a) 43. (d) 44. (c) 45. (a) 46. (c) 47. (a) 48. (c) 49. (b) 50. (a)

PHYTOMORPHOLOGY - XVI

1. Which of the following in a orchid?
   (a) *Vanda roxburghii* (b) *Pistia stratiotes*
   (c) *Allium cepa* (d) None of these
2. Which is the member of family Liliaceae?
   (a) *Tamarindus indica* (b) *Terminalia chebula*
   (c) *Cajanus cajan* (d) *Asparagus officinalis*
3. The rhizome of which plant are edible
   (a) *Alocasia indica* (b) *Pistia shatiotes*
   (c) *Vanda roxburghii* (d) None of these
4. The family of *Alocasia indica* is
   (a) Apocynaceae (b) Graminae
   (c) Palmae (d) Araceae
5. Which of the following is floating stolon bearing herb?
   (a) *Pistia stratiotes* (b) *Alocasia indica*
   (c) *Vanda roxburghii* (d) None of these
6. The wheat (*Triticum aestivum*) is the member of family
   (a) Orchidaceae (b) Araceae
   (c) Palmae (d) Poaceae
7. The inflorescence of wheat plant is
   (a) Spike (b) Cymose
   (c) Recemose (d) None of these
8. The *Zea mays* is a
   (a) Aromatic plant (b) Pulse
   (c) spice (d) Cereal
9. A pad of sterile tissue which helps to connect anther lobes to the stamen is termed as
   (a) Connective (b) Corpusculum
   (c) Pollinia (d) None of these
10. The sac like structure in which pollen grains are present
    (a) Pollinia (b) Locule
    (c) Tapetum (d) Connective
11. The anther with only one pollen sac is termed as
    (a) Monothecous (b) Dithecous
    (c) Both a & b (d) None of these
12. The anther with two pollen sac is termed as
    (a) Monothecous (b) Dithecous
    (c) None of these (d) Both a & b

13. The lengthwise dehiscence of mature anther is termed as
    (a) Longitudinal (b) Transverse
    (c) Horizontal (d) None of these
14. The dehiscence of anther by forming a small pare is termed as
    (a) Poricidal (b) Longitudinal
    (c) Transverse (d) Horizontal
15. When the dehiscence of anther takes place by forming two parts is termed as
    (a) Transverse (b) Poricidal
    (c) Longitudinal (d) Valvular
16. When the anther lobe opening away from the center of the flower is termed as
    (a) Extrorse (b) Introrse
    (c) Latrorse (d) Basifixed
17. In which of the following plant epicalyx is present
    (a) Malvaceae (b) Poaceae
    (c) Rutaceae (d) Myrtaceae
18. Which type of fruit occur in family solanaceae
    (a) Capsule (b) Siliqua
    (c) Drupe (d) Legume
19. Which type of inflorescence occur in family Lamiaceae
    (a) Racemes (b) Verticillaster
    (c) Solitary (d) Capitulum
20. The flower of which family are not actinomorphic
    (a) Lamiaceae (b) Anacardiaceae
    (c) Annonacece (d) Rubiaceae
21. Which type of fruit occur in family Lamiaceae
    (a) Carcerulus (b) Pome
    (c) Drup (d) Hesperidium
22. Which type of inflorescence occur in family Asteraceae
    (a) Catkin (b) Verticelaster
    (c) Spadix (d) Capitulum
23. Number of stamens occurs in flower of family Asteraceae
    (a) 7 (b) 6
    (c) 8 (d) 5
24. Which type of leaves occur in family Liliaceae
    (a) Radical (b) Ramal
    (c) Simple (d) Compound

25. How many perianth occur in flower of family Liliaceae
    (a) 2 (b) 6
    (c) 4 (d) 1
26. Which type of fruit occur in family Liliaceae
    (a) Capsule (b) Carcerulus
    (c) Legume (d) Pome
27. Carpel's are absent in family
    (a) Ranunculaceae (b) Malvaceae
    (c) Rosaceae (d) Poaceae
28. Which one is not concerned with family Rutaceae?
    (a) Perigynous nature (b) Exstipulate
    (c) Syncarpus (d) Pedicilated
29. How many carpels occur in family Rutaceae?
    (a) 5 (b) 2
    (c) 1 (d) 3
30. Which type of fruit occur in family Rutaceae
    (a) Berry (b) Hesperidium
    (c) Drupe (d) Aggregate
31. How many perianth occurs in family Moraceae
    (a) 5 (b) 2
    (c) 3 (d) 4
32. Which type of fruit occur in Moraceae
    (a) Legume (b) Nut
    (c) Pome (d) Drupe
33. Which is incorrect for family Chaenopodiaceae?
    (a) Bracteate (b) Ebractiate
    (c) Branched Shoot (d) None of these
34. How many perianth occur in family chaenopodiaceae
    (a) 2 (b) 3
    (c) 4 (d) 5
35. Which type of fruit occur in family Chaenopodiaceae
    (a) Berry (b) Siliqua
    (c) Legume (d) Nut
36. Inflorescence of Cucurbitaceae is
    (a) Solitary (b) Verticelaster
    (c) Catkin (d) Spadix

37. How many sepals occur in flower of Cucurbitaceae?
    (a) 2 (b) 4
    (c) 3 (d) 5
38. Fruit of family cucurbitaceae are described as
    (a) Drupe (b) Pome
    (c) Berry (d) Aggregate fruit
39. How many sepals occur in family solanaceae?
    (a) 3 (b) 4
    (c) 5 (d) 2
40. When the anther lobe opening towards the center of the flower is termed as
    (a) Introrse (b) Orbicular
    (c) Latrorse (d) Basifixed
41. An anther lobe directed towards the central side of the flower is termed as
    (a) Introrse (b) Peltate
    (c) Latrorse (d) None of these
42. When the anther is joined to the filament by its base is described as
    (a) Basifixed (b) Extrorse
    (c) Introrse (d) None of these
43. If the filament in attached the dorsal region of anther, the attachment is described as
    (a) Introrse (b) Linear
    (c) Adnate (d) None of these
44. When the filament is attached at the optical region of the anther it is termed as
    (a) Apicifixed (b) Sagittate
    (c) Introrse (d) None of these
45. When the filament is attached to the dorsal region of anther but appear free from filament is termed as
    (a) Versatile (b) Extrorse
    (c) Introrse (d) Latrorse
46. A slightly elongated anther with narrow tip is term of anther described as
    (a) Cadcus (b) Caudate
    (c) Introrse (d) Linear
47. When the anther lobes resemble kidney that form in described as
    (a) Reni form (b) Sagittate
    (c) Linear (d) None of these

48. Arrow shaped elongated triangular anther is termed as
    (a) Sagittate (b) Reniform
    (c) Caudate (d) Linear
49. When the anther lobe in rolled up in the form of capital "S" this form is described as
    (a) Sinuous (b) Versatile
    (c) Reniform (d) None of these
50. The triangular heart shaped form of anther is described as
    (a) Reniform (b) Sagittate
    (c) Cordate (d) Linear
51. When a pollen grain occur in a group of two is termed as
    (a) Diads (b) Monad
    (c) Polyads (d) Tetrads
52. When the pollen grain does not occur in a group is termed as
    (a) Polyads (b) Diads
    (c) Monad (d) Monad
53. When a pollen grains occur in group of more than four or termed as
    (a) Polyads (b) Monad
    (c) Diads (d) Monad
54. When pollen grain occur in a group of four it is termed as
    (a) Diads (b) Tetrads
    (c) Monad (d) Polyads
55. The thread like long anther is described as
    (a) Filiterus (b) Pollinia
    (c) Reniform (d) None of these
56. An uniform masses of pollen grains is termed as
    (a) Anther lobe (b) Pollinia
    (c) Anther chamber (d) None of these
57. The single unit of gynoecium is called as
    (a) Carpel (b) Stamen
    (c) Tepals (d) None of these
58. Collectively all the carpel's together is termed as
    (a) Gynoecium (b) Androecium
    (c) Male gametophyte (d) Anther
59. The style stigma and ovary are three important parts of
    (a) Male gametophyte (b) Stamen
    (c) Anther (d) Carpel

60. The upper most region of carpel is termed as
(a) Stigma (b) Style
(c) Ovary (d) None of these
61. A pin head shaped stigma is described as
(a) Clarate (b) Cristate
(c) Discoid (d) Plumose
62. An elongated stigma but slightly bent downward is described as
(a) Discoid (b) Knob shaped
(c) Decurrent (d) None of these
63. The stigma with a distinct ridge is termed as
(a) Cristate (b) Discoid
(c) Plumose (d) None of these
64. The disc shaped stigma in termed as
(a) Discoid (b) Cristate
(c) Plumose (d) None of these
65. When the stigma resemble a birds feather is termed as
(a) Cristate (b) Plumose
(c) Discoid (d) None of these
66. A cylindrical shaped stigma in described as
(a) Terate (b) Cristate
(c) Discoid (d) None of these
67. When shape of stigma is fringed cylindrical it is described as
(a) Fimbriate (b) Discoid
(c) Cristate (d) Plumose
68. When the stigma are fused to form a compound undifferentiated structure, it is described as
(a) Plumose (b) Cristate
(c) Capitates (d) None of these
69. When the stigma is divided into many narrow lobes of equal length this type of term is described as
(a) Laciniate (b) Cristate
(c) Discoid (d) None of these
70. A feathery form of stigma described as
(a) Discoid (b) Plumose
(c) Terate (d) Fimbriate

Answer key: PHYTOMORPHOLOGY - XVI

1. (a) 2. (d) 3. (a) 4. (d) 5. (a) 6. (d) 7. (a) 8. (d) 9. (a) 10. (b) 11. (a) 12. (b)
13. (a) 14. (a), 15. (d) 16. (a) 17. (a) 18. (a) 19. (b) 20. (a) 21. (a) 22. (d)
23. (d) 24. (a) 25. (b) 26. (a) 27. (d) 28. (a) 29. (a) 30. (a) 31. (d) 32. (b)
33. (a) 34. (b) 35. (d) 36. (a) 37. (d) 38. (c) 39. (c) 40. (a) 41. (c) 42. (a)
43. (c) 44. (a) 45. (a) 46. (d) 47. (a) 48. (a) 49. (a) 50. (c) 51. (a) 52. (d)
53. (a) 54. (b) 55. (a) 56. (b) 57. (a) 58. (a) 59. (d) 60. (a) 61. (a) 62. (c)
63. (a) 64. (a) 65. (b) 66. (a) 67. (a) 68. (c) 69. (a) 70. (b)

PHYTOMORPHOLOGY - XVII

1. Which portion of pistil connects the ovary with stigma?
(a) Style (b) Filament
(c) Gynophore (d) None of these
2. Which of the taxonomic term used to style with no well developed stigma
(a) Knob shaped (b) Filiform
(c) Acephalous (d) None of these
3. The thread like style is termed as
(a) Filiform (b) Discoid
(c) Bifid (d) None of these
4. The petal like style is termed as
(a) Petoloid (b) Sepaloid
(c) Tepaloid (d) None of these
5. The swollen portion of carpel is termed as
(a) Stigma (b) Style
(c) Ovary (d) None of these
6. The stalk of ovule is termed as
(a) Funicle (b) Chalaza
(c) Micropile (d) None of these
7. The ovules are attacked to ovary wall with the help of
(a) Placenta (b) Style
(c) Stigma (d) None of these
8. The region of attachment of Funicle is termed as
(a) Style (b) Hilum
(c) Micropile (d) All of these
9. The opposite end of micropile of ovule in termed as
(a) Chalazas (b) Antipodal
(c) Integuments (d) None of these

10. If all the floral parts originated from base of ovary, the ovary is described as
(a) Superior (b) Inferior
(c) Half inferior (d) Half superior
11. If all the floral parts originated from top region of ovary, the position of ovary is described as
(a) Half superior (b) Superior
(c) Half inferior (d) Inferior
12. The taxonomic term used for united carpels is
(a) Syncarpus (b) Apocarpus
(c) Both of these (d) None of these
13. The taxonomic term used for free carpels is
(a) Syncarpus (b) Apocarpus
(c) Monoocarpus (d) None of these
14. The unfertilized seed is termed as
(a) Propagules (b) Parthenocarpic
(c) Ovule (d) None of these
15. When the Funicle chalaza micro pile is situate on vertical line, it is described as
(a) Orthotropus (b) Apocarpus
(c) Hemianatropus (d) None of these
16. The phenomenon of arrangement of placenta within ovary is termed as
(a) Androphore (b) Placentation
(c) Gynophore (d) None of these
17. When the ovules are attached to margin of pod, the arrangement of ovule described as
(a) Marginal Placentation (b) Axile placentation
(c) Parietal placentation (d) Central placentation
18. When the placenta are attached to the central axis it is described as
(a) Central placentation (b) Marginal Placentation
(c) Parietal placentation (d) Axile placentation
19. When the ovules are attached to the inner side of the ovary wall where the margins of the carpous meet, such placentation is termed as
(a) Parietal placentation (b) Axile placentation
(c) Marginal Placentation (d) Central placentation

20. When the ovules are scattered over the entire inner surface of ovary wall, the placentation is termed as
    (a) Lamellate or Superficial placentation
    (b) Marginal Placentation
    (c) Central placentation
    (d) None of these
21. When the placenta is attached to the basal region of locule, the placentation is termed as
    (a) Parietal placentation (b) Basal placentation
    (c) Axile placentation (d) Marginal Placentation
22. When the placenta is attached it apical region of the inner wall of ovary, it is termed as
    (a) Apical placentation (b) Parietal placentation
    (c) Axile placentation (d) Marginal placentation
23. The fully mature ovary is termed as
    (a) Ovule (b) Fruit
    (c) Both of these (d) None of these
24. The pericarp and the seeds are the two important parts of
    (a) Fruit (b) Embryo
    (c) Ovule (d) None of these
25. The fertilized ovule is termed as
    (a) Ovary (b) Seed
    (c) Stamen (d) None of these
26. In certain plants developed without fertilization of ovary is termed as
    (a) Parthenocarpic Fruit (b) Parthenocarpic Fruit
    (c) Both a and b (d) None of these
27. Which of the following is outermost layer of fruit?
    (a) Epicarp (b) Pericarp
    (c) Mesocarp (d) Endocarp
28. The endocarp on the middle layer of
    (a) Endocarp (b) Epicarp
    (c) Mesocarp (d) Pericarp
29. A persistent septum which remains after dehiscence of fruit is termed as
    (a) Replum (b) Septa
    (c) Wall (d) None of these
30. A persistent hook like funiculus occurs in the fruits of Acanthaceae plants is termed as
    (a) Retinaculum or Echma (b) Gynophore
    (c) Androphore (d) None of these

31. A slender stalk of floral axis that supports each half of dehisced fruit is termed as
    (a) Carpophore (b) Retinaculum
    (c) Echma (d) Gynophore
32. Which of the following term used for natural line along which the fruit split open?
    (a) Septa (b) Suture
    (c) Replum (d) None of these
33. The extended floral axis occur between adjacent carpel's is termed as
    (a) Carpophore (b) Gynophore
    (c) Androphore (d) None of these
34. The outermost layer of Pericarp is termed as
    (a) Exocarp (b) Endocarp
    (c) Mesocarp (d) Integument
35. The innermost layer of pericarp is termed as
    (a) Exocarp (b) Endocarp
    (c) Endocarp (d) None of these
36. Which of the following is stalk of seed?
    (a) Funiculus (b) Gynophore
    (c) Receptacle (d) None of these
37. The middle layer of pericarp is known as
    (a) Endocarp (b) Exocarp
    (c) Pericarp (d) Mesocarp
38. The wall of the fruit known as
    (a) Pericarp (b) Mesocarp
    (c) Exocarp (d) Endocarp
39. The region of attachment of seed on the inner surface of fruit known as
    (a) Replum (b) Placenta
    (c) Carpophore (d) None of these
40. In certain plants, a persistent septum is seen after dehiscence of fruit is termed as
    (a) Replum (b) Placenta
    (c) Replum (d) Carpophore
41. The persistent hook like funiculus occur in fruit is known as
    (a) Carpophore (b) Gynophore
    (c) Replum (d) Retinaculum or Jaculator
42. The stylar base on fruit looks like heart in termed as
    (a) Rostellum (b) Jaculator
    (c) Gynophore (d) Replum

43. The matured fertilized ovule is termed as
    (a) Fruit (b) Pollen
    (c) Seed (d) None of these
44. The fruit which in derived from a ovary of single solitary pistil known as
    (a) Simple fruit (b) Compound fruit
    (c) Aggregate (d) None of these
45. A one seeded dry indehiscent fruit derived from one locule superior ovary termed as
    (a) Calybium (b) Blastula
    (c) Caryopsis (d) None of these
46. A many seeded many loculed dry fruit having tough leathery pericarp termed as
    (a) Caryopsis (b) Calybium
    (c) Blastula (d) None of these
47. A single seeded dry on dehiscent fruit derived from one locule superior ovary termed as
    (a) Caryopsis or grain (b) Blastula
    (c) Calybium (d) None of these
48. Which of the following fruit developed from a one loculed inferior ovary?
    (a) Cypsela (b) Caryopsis or grain
    (c) Blastula (d) Calybium
49. In which family Capitulum type of inflorescence occurs
    (a) Myrtaceae (b) Malvaceae
    (c) Rubiaceae (d) Compositae
50. The Papilionaceous form of corolla consists of
    (a) A standard petal, a pair of wing petals and a pair of keel petals
    (b) A standard petal, and two pair of keel petals
    (c) A standard petal three wing petals and a pair of keel petals
    (d) None of these

Answer key: PHYTOMORPHOLOGY - XVII

1. (a) 2. (c) 3. (a) 4. (a) 5. (c) 6. (a) 7. (a) 8. (b) 9. (a) 10. (a) 11. (d) 12. (a) 13. (b) 14. (c) 15. (a) 16. (b) 17. (a) 18. (d) 19. (a) 20. (a) 21. (b) 22. (a) 23. (b) 24. (a) 25. (b) 26. (a) 27.(a) 28. (d) 29. (a) 30. (a) 31. (a) 32. (b) 33. (a) 34. (a) 35. (b) 36. (a) 37. (d) 38. (a) 39. (b) 40. (a) 41. (d) 42. (a) 43. (c) 44. (a) 45. (a) 46. (c) 47. (a) 48. (a) 49. (d) 50. (a)

PHYTOMORPHOLOGY - XVIII

1. An androecium with united anthers and free filaments is termed as
   (a) Syngenesious (b) Epipetalous
   (c) Monodelphous (d) Didelphous
2. The Syngenesious condition occurs in family
   (a) Compositae (b) Asclepiadaceace
   (c) Mimosaceae (d) Myrtaceae
3. The term used for the condition of stamen where filaments and anthers are united
   (a) Epipetalous (b) Synandrous
   (c) Didynamous (d) None of these
4. Which type of fruit occur in maize
   (a) Capsule (b) Aggregate fruit
   (c) Sorosis (d) Caryopsis
5. Which is the reason to call maize grain as fruit?
   (a) Because grain develops from ovary
   (b) Because grain develops from ovary wall
   (c) Both a and b
   (d) None of these
6. Why ginger is considered as stem
   (a) Because it consists of nodes and internodes as in stem
   (b) Because it consists of buds
   (c) Because it resemble the stem
   (d) None of these
7. The reason of different phyllotaxy is to provide
   (a) Shade (b) Light
   (c) Aerial water (d) None of these
8. Alternate phyllotaxy occurs in
   (a) China rose (b) Mustard
   (c) Sunflower (d) All of these
9. In which type of fruit pericarp and testa are fused together
   (a) Caryopsis (b) Capsule
   (c) Drupe (d) Hesperidium
10. A simple fruit, indehiscent, throughout product of single pistil termed as
    (a) Hesperidium (b) Capsule
    (c) Drupe (d) Berry

11. The fruit exterior or firm, hard or leathery rind, several too many septate in termed as
(a) Hesperidium (b) Berry
(c) Capsule (d) Drupe
12. The fruit exterior or firm, soft, septa absent is termed as
(a) Capsule (b) Berry
(c) Pepo (d) Hesperidium
13. Which type of fruit occur in mango?
(a) Drupe (b) Achene
(c) Berry (d) Samara
14. The fruit exterior soft is with a paper or cartilaginous carpel at the center is described as
(a) Pome (b) Berry
(c) Pepo (d) Hesperidium
15. The dry is indehiscent simple fruit with are a two seed and winged is described as
(a) Hesperidium (b) Berry
(c) Drupe (d) Samara
16. A day indehiscent simple fruit wingless with thin pericarp termed as
(a) Achene (b) Pepo
(c) Berry (d) capsule
17. A small bladder like thin walled fruit is termed as
(a) Berry (b) Utricles
(c) Samara (d) Hesperidium
18. The dry indehiscent simple fruit, with inedible hard shell in which seed remain unattached to ovary wall is termed as
(a) Achene (b) Pome
(c) Drupe (d) Nut
19. The dehiscent fruit, are too many seeded, develop from unicarpellate ovary, dehisce by ventral suture is described as
(a) Follicle (b) Drupe
(c) Achene (d) Berry
20. The dehiscent fruit, one to many seeded develop from unicarpellate ovary, dehisce by longitudinal sutures is termed as
(a) Achene (b) Berry
(c) Legume (d) Pepo
21. The dehiscent fruit, one to many seeded, developed from unicarpellate. ovary, dehisce by transverse sutures is termed as
(a) Loment (b) Achene
(c) Pepo (d) Pome

22. The dehiscent fruit, one to many seeded, developed from bi or multicarpellate ovary, fruit split into one seeded halve termed as
(a) Schizocarp (b) Berry
(c) Legume (d) Nut
23. The dehiscent fruit, one or many seeded, develop from bi or multicarpellate. ovary, dehiscence circumscissile is termed as
(a) Pyxis (b) Nut
(c) Pome (d) Berry
24. The dehiscent fruit, one or many seeded, develop from bi or multicarpellate. ovary, dehiscence longitudinal is termed as
(a) Berry (b) Capsule
(c) Loment (d) Achene
25. Which of the following is specialized type of capsule and is characteristic of the cruciferae
(a) Silicle (b) Achene
(c) Pepo (d) Legume
26. The fruit which is developed from two or more pistils is termed as
(a) Compound fruit (b) Loment
(c) Hesperidium (d) Pod
27. The Compound fruit, product of several pistils of single gynoecium, connate and usually fleshy is termed as
(a) Lomentum (b) Aggregate fruit
(c) Achene (d) Pepo
28. The compound fruit formed of several gynoecia aggregated in one mass is termed as
(a) Multiple fruit (b) Berry
(c) Legume (d) Nut
29. Which of the following is a pure type of fruit-?
(a) Apple (b) Capsule
(c) Berry (d) Loment
30. The citrus is a
(a) Hesperidium type of fruit (b) Legume
(c) Berry (d) Pepo
31. Which of the following is a product of one carpelled unilocular ovary-?
(a) Berry (b) Follicle
(c) Achene (d) Multiple fruit
32. The fertilized mature ovules are termed as
(a) Ovules (b) Pollinia
(c) Synergid (d) None of these

33. The cladodes occur in
    (a) Asparagus (b) Cucumis
    (c) Ginger (d) None of these
34. A jointed stem with hollow internode in known as
    (a) Cladode (b) Phylloclade
    (c) Culm (d) None of these
35. The tendrils occur in
    (a) Passiflora (b) Arachis
    (c) Helianthus (d) None of these
36. The function of offset is
    (a) Micropropogation (b) Vegetative propagation
    (c) Sexual reproduction (d) None of these
37. Presence phylloclade or cladode is the characteristic feature of
    (a) Xerophytic plant (b) Mesophyte
    (c) Hydrophyte (d) Halophyte
38. The decussate phyllotaxy occur in
    (a) Calotropis (b) Annona
    (c) Azadiracta (d) Citrus
39. The stipule occur at the base of
    (a) Root (b) Inflorescence
    (c) Leaf (d) None of these
40. The rachis is the part of
    (a) Compound leaf (b) Inflorescence
    (c) Simple leaf c. (d) None of these
41. A secondary leaf let in a pinnately compound leaf is termed as
    (a) Rachilla (b) Pinnule
    (c) Petiole (d) None of these
42. The carpel is the part of
    (a) Flower (b) Seed
    (c) Fruit (d) None of these
43. The flower without perianth occur in
    (a) Ipomea (b) Solanum
    (c) Magnolia (d) None of these
44. The maturation of gynoecium before androecium in termed as
    (a) Protogyny (b) Protoandrae
    (c) Eugyny (d) None of these

45. The thalamus occur in
    (a) *Apium poppy* (b) Coriander
    (c) *Annona squimosa* (d) None of these
46. The example of dense umbel type of inflorescence is
    (a) *Polyalthia longifolia* (b) *Arachis hypogea*
    (c) *Citrus sinensis* (d) None of these
47. Which of the following in medicinal plant
    (a) *Saccharum officinalis* (b) *Argemone mexicana*
    (c) *Sorghum vulgare* (d) None of these
48. The leaf margin of *Capparis spinosa* is
    (a) Dissected (b) Spinus
    (c) Entire (d) None of these
49. All the pulse crops are angiosperms and are
    (a) Dicotyledons (b) Both a and b
    (c) Monocots d) None of these
50. The habitat of aquatic plants is described as
    (a) Xerophytic (b) Halophytic
    (c) Hydrophytic (d) None of these
51. The plants growing in scanty of water are considered as
    (a) Xerophytes (b) Halophytic
    (c) Hydrophytic (d) None of these
52. Plants growing on branches of large trees are termed as
    (a) Halophytic (b) Hydrophytic
    (c) Xerophytes (d) Epiphytes
53. Which of the following is an epiphyte?
    (a) Orchids (b) Both a and b
    (c) Cuscuta (d) None of these
54. Which of the angiospermic plant is a plant parasite?
    (a) Daccus (b) Mentha
    (c) Catharanthus (d) Loranthus
55. The angiosperms grow an land are termed as
    (a) Terrestrial (b) Submerged
    (c) Aquatic (d) None of these
56. The wing petals and standard petals occur in flowers of family
    (a) Papilionaceae (b) Mimosaceae
    (c) Caesalpinaceae (d) Annonaceae

57. A boat shaped petal of papilionacious form of corolla is termed as
(a) Wings (b) Standard petal
(c) Keel petal (d) None of these
58. The cruciform type of corolla occur in
(a) Radish (b) Carrot
(c) Brinjal (d) Asparagus
59. Which of the following in dicot plant
(a) Grasses (b) Gram
(c) Cereals (d) None of these
60. The tetradynamous condition occur in
(a) *Brassica nigra* (b) *Datura stramonium*
(c) *Hibiscus rosa sinensis* (d) None of these
61. The unilocular ovary looks like bilocular because of false septum in
(a) *Coriandrum sativum* (b) *Raphanus sativus*
(c) *Calotropis procera* (d) None of these
62. The false septum occur in ovary in known as
(a) Rostellum (b) Labellum
(c) Replum (d) None of these
63. Family of Hibiscus *Rosa sinensis* is
(a) Apiaceae (b) Magnoliaceae
(c) Meliaceae (d) Malvaceae
64. The schizocarpic fruit consists of many indehiscent mericarps in
(a) *Abutilon indicum* (b) *Acacia nilotica*
(c) *Cajanua cajan* (d) None of these
65. The reticulate venation and taproot system in the characteristic feature of
(a) Monocot plants (b) Both a and b
(c) Dicot plants (d) None of these
66. Sorghum and bamboo are the examples of
(a) Monocot plants (b) Both a and b
(c) Dicot plants (d) None of these
67. Which family of angiosperm consists of large number of plants?
(a) Compositae (b) Caesalpinaceae
(c) Fabaeceae (d) Malvaceae
68. Which angiosperm in an aromatic plant
(a) Triticum (b) Ricinus
(c) Solanum (d) Mint and Ocimum

69. The reproductive organ of angiosperms is
    (a) Flower (b) Calyx
    (c) Fruit (d) Bract
70. The sterile stamens in the flower are termed as
    (a) Staminode (b) Carpel
    (c) Stamens (d) None of these

Answer key: PHYTOMORPHOLOGY - XVIII

1. (a) 2. (a) 3. (b) 4. (d) 5. (a) 6. (a) 7. (b) 8. (d) 9. (a) 10. (d) 11. (a) 12. (c) 13. (a) 14. (a) 15. (d) 16. (a) 17. (b) 18. (d) 19. (a) 20. (c) 21. (a) 22. (a) 23. (a) 24. (b) 25. (a) 26. (a) 27. (b) 28. (a) 29. (a) 30. (a) 31. (b) 32. (a) 33. (a) 34. (c) 35. (a) 36. (b) 37. (a) 38. (a) 39. (c) 40. (a) 41. (b) 42. (a) 43. (c) 44. (c) 45. (c) 46. (a) 47. (b) 48. (c) 49. (a) 50. (c) 51. (a) 52. (d) 53. (a) 54. (d) 55. (a) 56. (a) 57. (c) 58. (a) 59. (b) 60. (a) 61. (b) 62. (c) 63. (d) 64. (a) 65. (c) 66. (a) 67. (a) 68. (d) 69. (a) 70. (a)

PHYTOMORPHOLOGY - XIX

1. A following is the example of one seeded drupe
   (a) *Triticum vulgarae* (b) *Ricinus communis*
   (c) *Calotropis gigantea* (d) *Melia azadirachta*
2. Which of the following plant have prickles?
   (a) *Rosa indica* (b) *Solanum tuberosum*
   (c) *Melia azadirachta* (d) None of these
3. Quincuncial type of aestivation occur in
   (a) Rose (b) Daccus
   (c) Hibiscus (d) Raphanus
4. Which one is the plant of family Papilionaceae?
   (a) Tamarind (b) Sugarcane
   (c) Potato (d) Trigonella
5. The *Crotalaria juncea* (Papilionaceae) is a
   (a) Herb (b) Creeper
   (c) Tree (d) Shrub
6. The terminal leaflet of compound leaf modified to a tendril in
   (a) *Dalbergia sisso* (b) *Cassia tora*
   (c) *Pisum sativum* (d) None of these
7. The plant bears aerial flowers and fruits mature in soil in
   (a) *Arachis hypogea* (b) *Cassia tora*
   (c) *Daccus carota* (d) None of these

8. Diadelphous condition occur in
   (a) *Cassia tora* (b) *Pisum sativum*
   (c) *Cajanus cajan* (d) None of these
9. Descendingly imbricate aestivation occur in
   (a) *Lythrus odoratus* (b) *Cassia tora*
   (c) *Delonix regia* (d) None of these
10. Which plant consists of zygomorphic flower?
   (a) *Raphanus sativus* (b) *Cassia tora*
   (c) *Dalbergia sisso* (d) None of these
11. The marginal placentation occur in
   (a) Pea (b) Solanum
   (c) Cucumis (d) Sunflower
12. The sheathing leaf base occurs in plants of family
   (a) Graminae (b) Meliaceae
   (c) Orchidaceae (d) None of these
13. The paripinnate compound leaf occur in
   (a) *Cajanus cajan* (b) *Ricinus communis*
   (c) *Cassia tora* (d) None of these
14. Tamarindus indica is a
   (a) Herb (b) Large tree
   (c) Shrub (d) Climber
15. The leaf of *Caesalpinia pulcherima* is
   (a) Bipinnate compound (b) Tripinnate
   (c) Unipinnate (d) None of these
16. A globose head type of inflorescence occur in
   (a) *Abutilon indica* (b) *Mimosa pudica*
   (c) *Cassia tora* (d) None of these
17. The *Mimosa pudica* stipules are modified to
   (a) Spine (b) Involucres
   (c) Bracts (d) Tendril
18. Which one is called as touch me not plants?
   (a) *Mimosa pudica* (b) *Delonix regia*
   (c) *Daccus carota* (d) None of these
19. Which plant yield gum of commercial value?
   (a) *Caesalpinia pulcherima* (b) *Terminalia indica*
   (c) *Mentha piperata* (d) *Acacia nilotica*

20. The fruit type of *Acacia nilotica* is
    (a) Lomentum (b) Legume
    (c) Drupe (d) Pod
21. Which of the following in a deciduous tree growing in dry places?
    (a) *Alstonia scolaris* (b) *Muraya paniculata*
    (c) *Albizzia lebbek* (d) None of these
22. Monodelphous condition of stamen occur in
    (a) *Raphanus sativus* (b) *Acacia nilotica*
    (c) *Cassia tora* (d) *Hibiscus rosa sinensis*
23. Which one is a tall tree with non endospermic seeds?
    (a) *Eucalyptus lanceolatus* (b) Both a and b
    (c) *Polyanthia longifolia* (d) None of these
24. The family of *Psidum guajava* is
    (a) Magnoliaceae (b) Myrtaceae
    (c) Meliaceae (d) None of these
25. Fruit of guava is a
    (a) Many seeded berry (b) Drupe
    (c) Capsule (d) None of these
26. The fruit of *Ficus carica* is a
    (a) Hypanthodium (b) Follicle
    (c) Hesperidium (d) None of these
27. The leaf of Perithecium grass in an example of
    (a) Compound leaf (b) Simple leaf
    (c) Decompound leaf (d) None of these
28. The sorosis of pineapple is a type of
    (a) Multiple fruit (b) Etaerio of berries
    (c) Simple fruit (d) None of these
29. A single seeded dehiscent fruit with thin wall in described as
    (a) Drupe (b) Capsule
    (c) Legume (d) Utricle
30. The one seeded dry indehiscent fruit with bony shell derived from compound syconium is termed as
    (a) Nut (b) Berry
    (c) Capsule (d) Achene
31. The petals are absent in flower of
    (a) *Cucumis sativus* (b) *Cassia tora*
    (c) *Hibiscus rosa-sinensis* (d) *Terminalia bellerica*

32. A five angled achene type of fruit occur in
    (a) *Quiqualis indica* (b) *Aegle marmelos*
    (c) *Cucumis sativus* (d) *Mangifera indica*
33. Which one is the climbing herb?
    (a) *Cucurbita maxima* (b) *Ficus religiosa*
    (c) *Annona squimosa* (d) *Tamarindus indica*
34. The *Cucurbita maxima* is a
    (a) Monoecious and dicot plant
    (b) Monoecious and monocot plant
    (c) Dioecious and dicot plant
    (d) None of these
35. The type of fruit occur in *Luffa cylindrica* is a
    (a) Legume (b) Capsule
    (c) Pepo (d) Drupe
36. The flowers without petiole termed as
    (a) Sessile (b) Stalked
    (c) Petiolate (d) Androgynous
37. The ovules are attached to ovary wall with the help of
    (a) Receptacle (b) Gynophore
    (c) Placenta (d) None of these
38. The roots of *Momordica charantia* appear like a chain of beads which is described as
    (a) Moniliform (b) Scalariform
    (c) Polyads (d) None of these
39. When the stem modify to a thick leafy structure it is termed as
    (a) Cladode (b) Both a and b
    (c) Phylloclade (d) None of these
40. The main features of family's monocot are
    (a) Parallel venation, fibrous root, trimerous flower and one Cotyledon.
    (b) Parallel venation, fibrous root, pentamerous flower and one Cotyledon.
    (c) Reticulate venation, fibrous root, trimerous flower and one Cotyledon.
    (d) Parallel venation, tap root, trimerous flower.
41. The buttress type of roots are found in
    (a) *Ficus bengalensis* (b) *Tectona grandis*
    (c) *Santalum album* (d) None of these

42. The underground runner in called
(a) Twinners (b) Stem
(c) Sobole (d) None of these
43. The leaf margins are wavy in
(a) Polyanthia (b) Calotropis
(c) Cactus (d) None of these
44. The maturity of cotton plant can be identified on the basic of
(a) Growth pattern (b) Branching system
(c) Shape of leaves (d) None of these
45. The leaf of cladophyllum consists of
(a) Parallel venation (b) Cross venulation
(c) Reticulate venation (d) None of these
46. The function of hanging root of banyan tree is
(a) Mechanical support (b) Photosynthesis
(c) Respiration (d) Transpiration
47. Which plant consists of tuberous root
(a) *Solanum tuberosum* (b) Both a and b
(c) *Ipomoea batata* (d) None of these
48. Which is the example of the stilt root?
(a) Sugarcane (b) Citrus
(c) Ficus (d) Mango
49. Mostly the buds are found
(a) At the apex or axil of the leaves (b) On short roots
(c) Internodes (d) None of these
50. The obliquely growing lateral branch form underground stems in called
(a) Pistil (b) Receptacle
(c) Placenta (d) Sucker
51. The presence of well developed vessel is a characteristic feature of
(a) Angiosperms (b) Bryophytes
(c) Algae (d) Fungi
52. The companion cell present in
(a) Algae (b) Pteridophytes
(c) Angiosperms (d) None of these
53. The closed seeds is the feature of
(a) Angiosperms (b) Pteridophytes
(c) Gymnosperms (d) None of these

54. Which of the following is unique feature of angiosperms?
    (a) Double fertilization and triple fusion
    (b) Pteridophytes
    (c) Gymnosperms
    (d) Bryophytes
55. Which type of pollination is common in angiosperms?
    (a) Water pollination (b) Insect pollination
    (c) Wind pollination (d) None of these
56. In the angiosperms female gametophyte or endosperm in post fertilization stages remain
    (a) Triploid (b) Diploid
    (c) Monoploid (d) None of these
57. Presence of ovary and true fruits are the characteristic features of
    (a) Pteridophytes (b) Angiosperms
    (c) Bryophyte (d) None of these
58. All the cereal and pulses are
    (a) Angiosperms (b) Pteridophytes
    (c) Gymnosperms (d) None of these
59. If the central portion of stem in hollow the stem in described as
    (a) Solid (b) Both a and b
    (c) Fistular (d) None of these
60. The corn is modification of
    (a) Leaf (b) Stem
    (c) Root (d) None of these
61. Which of the following is runner?
    (a) Oxalis (b) Aster
    (c) Acanthus (d) None of these
62. The stolon in present
    (a) Aster (b) Fragaria
    (c) Acanthus (d) None of these

Answer key: PHYTOMORPHOLOGY - XIX

1. (d) 2. (a) 3. (a) 4. (d) 5. (a) 6. (c) 7. (a) 8. (b) 9. (a) 10. (c) 11. (a) 12. (a) 13. (c) 14. (b) 15. (a) 16. (b) 17. (a) 18. (a) 19. (d) 20. (a) 21. (c) 22. (d) 23. (a) 24. (b) 25. (a) 26. (a) 27. (c) 28. (a) 29. (d) 30. (a) 31. (b) 32. (a) 33. (a) 34. (a) 35. (c) 36. (a) 37. (c) 38. (a) 39. (c) 40. (a) 41. (a) 42. (c) 43. (a) 44. (c) 45. (a) 46. (a) 47. (c) 48. (a) 49. (a) 50. (d) 51. (a) 52. (c) 53. (a) 54. (a) 55. (b) 56. (a) 57. (b) 58. (a) 59. (c) 60. (b) 61. (a) 62. (b)

CHAPTER – 3

Taxonomy - I to XIII

TAXONOMY - I

1. Study of flowering plant is termed as
   (a) Angiosperms (b) Bryophytes
   (c) Gymnosperms (d) Pteridophytes
2. Sporophyte is a dominant part of life cycle of
   (a) Equisetum (b) Algal plants
   (c) Flowering plant (d) Funaria
3. Phenomenon of double fertilization occur in plants of
   (a) Pteridophytes (b) Angiosperms
   (c) Bryophytes (d) Gymnosperms
4. The Bentham & Hookers system of classification of plants is a
   (a) Artificial system (b) Phylogenetic system
   (c) Natural system (d) None of these
5. Who is the author of Flora of Marathwada?
   (a) D.S. Mukadam (b) Arvind Dhabe
   (c) V.N. Naik (d) None of these
6. Which system of plant classification does not indicate the position of gymnosperms?
   (a) Englar & Prantl system
   (b) Bentham & Hookers system
   (c) Takhtajan system
   (d) Hutchinson system
7. In which year Carolus Linnaeus firstly proposed classification of plants?
   (a) 1775 (b) 1735
   (c) 1820 (d) 1753
8. Who introduced the Binomial nomenclature of plants
   (a) Englar (b) Bentham
   (c) Linnaeus (d) Hutchinson

9. Which of the following helps to understand basic arrangement of different parts of flower?
   (a) Habit of plant (b) Floral diagram
   (c) Flower morphology (d) Flower arrangement
10. Which term is used for system of classification of plants?
   (a) Phanerograms (b) Nomenclature
   (c) Taxonomy (d) Binomial nomenclature
11. The flower having androecium & gynoecium is termed as
   (a) Unisexual (b) Both a and b
   (c) Bisexual (d) None of these
12. The leaf with parallel venation is the distinguishing feature of
   (a) Gymnosperms (b) Dicot
   (c) Monocot (d) None of these
13. The part of leaf 'rachis 'occur in
   (a) Simple leaf (b) Compound leaf
   (c) Sessile leaf (d) Petiolate leaf
14. When all the petals united in the flower, the corolla is termed as
   (a) Gamopetalous (b) Papilionacious
   (c) Polypetalous (d) None of these
15. Which is the lowest and basic unit of classification of plants?
   (a) Taxa (b) Species
   (c) Genus (d) Specific name
16. The black spot in the floral diagram indicates
   (a) Position of ovule (b) Position of ovary
   (c) Nature of flower (d) Mother axis
17. Which language is used to write botanical name of plant?
   (a) German (b) English
   (c) French (d) Italics
18. If the flower consists of only stamens it in termed as
   (a) Flower (b) Basic flower
   (c) Female flower (d) Male flower
19. Which characters are selected by Engler and Prantl for f classification of plants?
   (a) Phylogenetic characters (b) Floral characters
   (c) Habit of plants (d) Natural characters
20. Which name is common to all the species of particular genus?
   (a) Genus name (b) Specific name
   (c) Species name (d) Latin name

21. The non-symmetrical nature of flower is termed as
(a) Actinomorphic (b) Unisexual
(c) Zygomorphic (d) Bisexual

22. The symbol of bisexual flower noted as
(a) ♂ (b) ♀
(c) ⚥ (d) None of these

23. Pea, gram, and groundnut are the plants of the family
(a) Malvaceae (b) Caesalpinaceae
(c) Papilionaceae (d) Meliaceae

24. The corolla of *Datura* sp. Is termed as
(a) Infundibuliform (b) Papilionacious
(c) Cruciform (d) None of these

25. The very important characteristic feature of angiosperms is
(a) Presence of seed (b) Triploid endosperm
(c) Coloured petals (d) Seed enclosed in fruit

26. The two lobed anther is termed as
(a) Monothecous (b) Tetrathecous
(c) Dithecous (d) None of these

27. The ovary, style & stigma are the parts of
(a) Androecium (b) Calyx
(c) Gynoecium (d) Corolla

28. The arrangement of ovules in the ovary is termed as
(a) Placentation (b) Ovulation
(c) Aestivation (d) None of these

29. Which type of corolla consists of keel petals?
(a) Cruciform (b) Tubular
(c) Papilionaceous (d) Infundibuliform

30. Which type of arrangement of stamens occurs in family Papilionaceae?
(a) Tetradelphous (b) Monodelphous
(c) Didynamous (d) Didelphous

31. Who worked as a director of Kew Botanic garden?
(a) Hooker (b) Linnaeus
(c) Bentham (d) None of these

32. What is the Botanical name of carrot?
(a) *Daccus carota* (b) *Ricinus communis*
(c) *Argemone Mexicana* (d) None of these

33. Which term is used for collection of dried and pressed plants?
    (a) Museum specimen (c) Herbarium
    (c) Preservation (d) None of these
34. Herbaria are generally associated with
    (a) DST
    (b) ICRISAT
    (c) CSIR
    (d) Educational Research Organization
35. Conservatory material & data of plants is also termed as
    (a) Museum specimen (b) Transparency
    (c) Herbarium (d) None of these
36. Verticelaster type of inflorescence in a characteristic features of family
    (a) Labiatae (b) Apiaceae
    (c) Malvaceae (d) Acanthaceae
37. Which of the following represents most of the characteristic features of a particular plant
    (a) Floral formula and floral diagram
    (b) Androecium and gynoecium
    (c) Calyx and corolla
    (d) None of these
38. Which of the following is the member of family amaranthaceae?
    (a) *Achyranthes aspera* (b) *Melia azadiracta*
    (c) Justiciea *adathoda* (d) *Azadiracta indica*
39. What is the Botanical name of butterfly tree?
    (a) *Melia azadiracta* (b) *Lantana camera*
    (c) *Clitoria ternatea* (d) None of these
40. The widely accepted classification of plants given by
    (a) Bessey (b) Engler & Prantl
    (c) Hutchinson (d) Bentham & Hooker
41. Which is the largest family of Dicotyledons?
    (a) Compositae (b) Cucurbitaceae
    (c) Rubiaceae (d) Rosaceae
42. The four – o – clock plant is a
    (a) Large perennial herb (b) Shrub
    (c) Large tree (d) Small tree
43. Which type of inflorescence occurs in family Nyctaginaceae?
    (a) Cymose (b) Solitary
    (c) Dichasial cyme (d) Verticelaster

44. Which type of fruit occurs in family of fabaceae?
 (a) Legume (b) Samara
 (c) Drupe (d) None of these
45. The fruit of *solanum nigrum* is a
 (a) Berry (b) Hesperidium
 (c) Pepo (d) Pome
46. In which family a gamopetalous funnel shaped corolla with rotate aestivation occurs?
 (a) Malvaceae (b) Cruciferae
 (c) Solanaceae (d) Papilionaceae
47. In which of the following seed is closed?
 (a) Pteridophytes (b) Bryophytes
 (c) Angiosperms (d) None of above
48. Which term is used for plants which requires only one year for completing its life cycle?
 (a) Annual (b) Perennial
 (c) Biennial (d) None of these
49. Which is the reproductive part of plant?
 (a) Root (b) Node
 (c) Stem (d) Flower
50. Angiosperms are divided into
 (a) Monocot & dicot (b) Monocot & Pteridophytes
 (c) Dicot & bryophytes (d) None of above
51. When the plants grow in water, the habit of plant in described as
 (a) Xerophytic (b) Terrestrial
 (c) Aquatic (d) None of these
52. When the stem modify to a thick leafy structure it is termed as
 (a) Phylloclade (b) Both a and b
 (c) Cladode (d) None of these
53. The buttress type of roots are found in
 (a) *Ficus bengalensis* (b) *Polyanthia indica*
 (c) *Mangifera indica* (d) None of these
54. The underground runner in called
 (a) Twinners (b) Roots
 (c) Sobole (d) None of these
55. The leaf margins are wavy in
 (a) Polyanthia (b) Calotropis
 (c) Citrus (d) None of these

56. The maturity of cotton plant can be identified on the basic of
    (a) Shape of leaves (b) Branching system
    (c) Growth pattern (d) None of these
57. The leaf of cladophyllum consists of
    (a) Cross venulation (b) Parallel veinatation
    (c) Reticulate venation (d) None of these
58. The function of hanging root of banyan tree is
    (a) Mechanical support (b) Photosynthesis
    (c) Respiration (d) Transpiration
59. Which plant consists of tuberous root
    (a) *Solanum tuberosum* (b) Both a and b
    (c) *Ipomoea batatas* (d) None of these
60. Which is the example of the stilt root
    (a) Citrus (b) Sugarcane
    (c) Ficus (d) Banana

Answer key: TAXONOMY - I

1. (a) 2. (c) 3. (b) 4. (c) 5. (c) 6. (c) 7. (b) 8. (c) 9. (b) 10. (c) 11. (c) 12. (c) 13. (b) 14. (a) 15. (b) 16. (d) 17. (d) 18. (d) 19. (a) 20. (b) 21. (c) 22. (b) 23. (c) 24. (a) 25. (d) 26. (c) 27. (c) 28. (a) 29. (c) 30. (d) 31. (a) 32. (a) 33. (c) 34. (d) 35. (c) 36. (a) 37. (a) 38. (a) 39. (b) 40. (d) 41. (b) 42. (a) 43. (c) 44. (a) 45. (a) 46. (c) 47. (c) 48. (a) 49. (d) 50. (a) 51. (c) 52. (a) 53. (a) 54. (c) 55. (a) 56. (a) 57. (b) 58. (a) 59. (c) 60. (b)

TAXONOMY - II

1. Mostly the buds are found
    (a) At the apex or axile of the leaves
    (b) On short roots
    (c) Internodes
    (d) None of these
2. The obliquely growing lateral branch form underground stems in called
    (a) Pistil (b) Receptacle
    (c) Placenta (d) Sucker
3. Which type of pollination is common in angiosperms?
    (a) Insect pollination (b) Water pollination
    (c) Wind pollination (d) None of these

4. In the angiosperms female gametophyte or endosperm in post fertilization stages remain
(a) Monoploid (b) Diploid
(c) Triploid (d) None of these
5. Presence of ovary and true fruits are the characteristic features of
(a) Algae (b) Angiosperms
(c) Gymnosperms (d) None of these
6. All the cereal and pulses are
(a) Angiosperms (b) Pteridophytes
(c) Bryophyte (d) None of these
7. If the central portion of stem is hollow, the stem in described as
(a) Solid (b) Both a and b
(c) Fistular (d) None of these
8. The corn is modification of
(a) Stem (b) Leaf
(c) Root (d) None of these
9. Which of the following is a runner?
(a) Aster (b) Oxalis
(c) Acanthus (d) None of these
10. The stolon in present
(a) Fragaria (b) Aster
(c) Acanthus (d) None of these
11. The cladodes occur in
(a) *Asparagus* (b) *Cucumis*
(c) Ginger (d) None of these
12. A jointed stem with hollow internode in known as
(a) Cladode (b) Phylloclade
(c) Culm (d) None of these
13. The tendrils occur in
(a) Passiflora (b) *Arachis*
(c) *Helianthus* (d) None of these
14. The function of offset is
(a) Vegetative propagation (b) Micropropogation
(c) Sexual reproduction (d) None of these
15. Presence phylloclade or cladode is the characteristic feature of
(a) Halophyte (b) Mesophyte
(c) Hydrophyte (d) Xerophytic plant

16. The decussate phyllotaxy occur in
    (a) *Calotropis* (b) *Annona*
    (c) *Azadiracta* (d) *Citrus*
17. The stipule occur at the base of
    (a) Stem (b) Inflorescence
    (c) Leaf (d) None of these
18. The rachis is the part of
    (a) Compound leaf (b) Inflorescence
    (c) Simple leaf c. (d) None of these
19. A secondary leaf let in a pinnately compound leaf is termed as
    (a) Pinnule (b) Rachilla
    (c) Petiole (d) None of these
20. The carpel is the part of
    (a) Fruit (b) Stem
    (c) Flower (d) None of these
21. The flower without perianth occur in
    (a) *Magnolia* (b) *Solanum*
    (c) *Ipomoea* (d) None of these
22. The maturation of gynoecium before androecium in termed as
    (a) Protogyny (b) Protoandrae
    (c) Eugyny (d) None of these
23. The thalamus occur in
    (a) *Annona squimosa* (b) *Coriandrum sativum*
    (c) *Apium poppy* (d) None of these
24. The example of dense umbel type of inflorescence is
    (a) *Arachis hypogea* (b) *Polyalthia longifolia*
    (c) *Citrus sinensis* (d) None of these
25. Which of the following in medicinal plant
    (a) *Argemone mexicana* (b) *Saccharum officinarum*
    (c) *Sorghum vulgare* (d) *None of these*
26. The leaf margin of *Capparis spinosa* is
    (a) Dentate (b) Entire
    (c) Dissected (d) None of these
27. All the pulse crops are angiosperms and are
    (a) Dicotyledons (b) Both a and b
    (c) Monocots (d) None of these

28. The habitat of aquatic plants is described as
(a) Hydrophytic (b) Halophytic
(c) Xerophytic (d) None of these
29. The plants growing in scanty of water are considered as
(a) Mesophytes (b) Halophytic
(c) Xerophytes (d) None of these
30. Plants growing on branches of large trees are termed as
(a) Epiphytes (b) Hydrophytic
(c) Xerophytes (d) Halophytic
31. Which of the following is an epiphyte?
(a) Orchids (b) Both a and b
(c) Cuscuta (d) None of these
32. Which of the angiospermic plant is a plant parasite?
(a) Sunflower (b) *Mentha*
(c) *Catharanthus* (d) *Loranthus*
33. The angiosperms grow an land are termed as
(a) Submerged (b) Terrestrial
(c) Aquatic (d) None of these
34. The wing petals and standard petals occur in flowers of family
(a) Rutaceae (b) Mimosaceae
(c) Caesalpinaceae (d) Papilionaceae
35. A boat shaped petal of Papilionaceous form of corolla is termed as
(a) Keel petal (b) Standard petals
(c) Wings (d) None of these
36. The cruciform type of corolla occur in
(a) Pea (b) Banana
(c) Brinjal (d) Radish
37. Which of the following in dicot plant
(a) Gram (b) Grasses
(c) Cereals (d) None of these
38. The tetradynamous condition occur in
(a) *Brassica nigra* (b) *Datura stramonium*
(c) *Hibiscus rosa sinensis* (d) None of these
39. The unilocular ovary looks like bilocular because of false septum in
(a) *Mangifera indica* (b) *Raphanus sativus*
(c) *Helianthus annuus* (d) None of these

40. The false septum that occur in ovary is known as
    (a) Replum (b) Labellum
    (c) Rostellum (d) None of these
41. Family of *Hibiscus rosa sinensis* is
    (a) Malvaceae (b) Magnoliaceae
    (c) Meliaceae (d) Apiaceae
42. The schizocarp fruit consists of many indehiscent mericarps in
    (a) *Acacia nilotica* (b) *Abutilon indicum*
    (c) *Cajanua cajan* (d) None of these
43. The reticulate venation and taproot system in the characteristic feature of
    (a) Dicot plants (b) Both a and b
    (c) Monocot plants (d) None of these
44. The angiospermic plants are
    (a) Heterotrophs (b) Parasitic
    (c) Autotrophs (d) None of these
45. The cotton is the member of family
    (a) Caesalpinaceae (b) Solanaceae
    (c) Malvaceae (d) Mimoceae
46. The phenomenon of separation of leaf from plant is termed as
    (a) Leaf fall (b) Abscission
    (c) Leaf destruction (d) None of these
47. One seeded indehiscent fruit with leathery pericarp is termed as
    (a) Pome (b) Pod
    (c) Achene (d) None of these
48. The roots which grow from the trunk above the ground instead of starting underground are termed as
    (a) Epiphytic (b) Hanging root
    (c) Adventitious (d) Tap root
49. The epiphytes are also known as
    (a) Air plants (b) Land plants
    (c) Terrestrial plants (d) None of these
50. The best example of succulent plant is
    (a) Rose (b) Neem
    (c) Aloe (d) Coriander
51. Which term is used for enlarged woody base of the stem or trunk located below the ground?
    (a) Root (b) Tuber
    (c) Caudex (d) None of these

52. Which term is used for embryonic leaf which in situated within a seed?
(a) Cotyledon (b) Seedling
(c) Embryo (d) None of these
53. Which term is used for plants that lose their leaves seasonally?
(a) Defoliation (b) Terrestrial
(c) Deciduous (d) None of these
54. Which term is used for smooth edges of leaf margin?
(a) Toothed (b) Serrate
(c) Entire (d) Dentate
55. Which term is used for part of the stem that is above the first leaf?
(a) Cotyledon (b) Epicotyls
(c) Pair of leaf (d) Hypocotyls
56. Which term is used for part of the flower that holds the anther?
(a) Style (b) Androecium
(c) Filament (d) Anther lobe
57. Which is the family of barley?
(a) Meliaceae (b) Graminae
(c) Malvaceae (d) Papilionaceae
58. Who introduced the concept of Binomial nomenclature?
(a) Bentham (b) Engler
(c) Linnaeus (d) Hutchinson
59. Which term is used to a reduced leaf like structure which is associated with a flower?
(a) Bract (b) Pedicel
(c) Stipule (d) None of above
60. Which term is used for group sepals of the flower?
(a) Petal (b) Corolla
(c) Calyx (d) None of above
61. Which is the female reproductive organ of flower?
(a) Filament (b) Carpel
(c) Stigma (d) None of above
62. The parallel venation in the characteristic feature of
(a) Dicot (b) Hydrophytes
(c) Monocots (d) None of these
63. Which term is used for leaf lamina that divides twice into leaflets?
(a) Pinnate compound leaf (b) Tripinnate compound leaf
(c) Bipinnate compound leaf (d) None of these

64. When two leaflets are articulated to the petiole, the leaf is termed as
(a) Unifoliate (b) Bifoliate
(c) Bipinnate (d) None of these

65. Which term is used for leaf having small leafy structure at the base of the petiole?
(a) Bracteate (b) Ligulate
(c) Stipulate (d) None of these

66. Which term is used when the leaf arises from main stem only?
(a) Sessile (c) Radical
(b) Cauline (d) Petiolate

67. The leaf without stalk is termed as
(a) Petiolate (b) Stalked
(c) Sessile (d) None of these

68. The root nodules of family Fabaceae contain
(a) Fungus (b) Bacteria
(c) Algae (d) Bryophyte

69. Potato is a modified
(a) Root (b) Branch
(c) Stem (d) None of these

70. What is the function of adventitious roots
(a) Support (b) Food storage
(c) Absorption of water (d) Respiration

71. The Royal Botanic Garden was started as private garden of
(a) C.E. Bessey (b) Hans Hallier
(c) Sir Henery Capel (d) John Hutchinson

72. Where is the National Botanic Garden?
(a) Madras (b) Bangalore
(c) Mumbai (d) Lucknow

73. The National Botanic Garden is situated near
(a) Ganga river (b) Yamuna river
(c) Gomti river (d) Narmada

74. If a flower consists of a large standard petal, two wing petals and two inner boat shaped keel petals, such a corolla is termed as
(a) Cruciform (b) Papilionacious
(c) Campanulate (d) None of these

75. Which type of inflorescence occurs in family Lamiaceae?
(a) Recemose (b) Cymose
(c) Verticillaster (d) Solitary

76. Which is true in case of flower of family Lamiaceae?
    (a) Bisexual actinomorphic
    (b) Unisexual actinomorphic
    (c) Unisexual
    (d) Hermaphrodite zygomorphic
77. Which is the member of family Lamiaceae?
    (a) *Mentha arvensis* (c) *Vinca rosea*
    (b) *Coriandrum sativum* (d) *Adhatoda vasica*
78. Ocimum is the member of family
    (a) Solanaceae (b) Acanthaceae
    (c) Lamiaceae (d) Papilionaceae
79. The non symmetrical flower is termed as
    (a) Zygomorphic (b) Actinomorphic
    (c) Bisexual (d) None of above
80. The propagation of many plant of the family Lamiaceae takes place by
    (a) Sexual method (b) Vegetative method
    (c) By conjugation method (d) None of these
81. How is the leaf margin of genus *Ocimum*?
    (a) Entire (b) Serrate
    (c) Incised (d) Toothed
82. Which term is used for style in the flower that arises from the base of the ovary in between the four locule?
    (a) Androbasic style (b) Lowermost style
    (c) Gynobasic style (d) None of these
83. When all the flower parts originated from the base of ovary, the position of ovary in termed as
    (a) Interior (b) Superior
    (c) Half interior (d) None of these
84. Stem of *Ocimum sanctum* is
    (a) Round (b) Triangular
    (c) Waved (d) Quadrangular
85. Which is the member of Lamiaceae?
    (a) *Salvia officinalis* (b) *Andrographis paniculata*
    (c) *Allium sativum* (d) *Avena sativa*
86. How many carpels occur in most of the plants of family lamiaceae?
    (a) 3 (b) 2
    (c) 5 (d) 4

87. Which term is used for a form of Corolla with two lobed petals, fused, zygomorphic?
    (a) Papilionaceous (b) Bilabiate
    (c) Infundibuliform (d) None of these
88. Which the member is of is the member of family labiatae?
    (a) *Solanum nigrum* (b) *Annona squimosa*
    (c) *Mentha piperata* (d) None of these
89. The family Nyctaginaceae is the family of group of
    (a) Aromatic plants (b) Monocot plants
    (c) None of these (d) Dicot plants
90. Which is the member of family nyctaginaceae?
    (a) Bougainvillea (b) Sapota
    (c) Asparagus (d) Oryza
91. Which is the family of four – o - clock plants?
    (a) Solanaceae (b) Labiatae
    (c) Nyctaginaceae (d) Graminae
92. Which term is used for arrangement of sepals & petals in a flower?
    (a) Aestivation (b) Placentation
    (c) Actinomorphic (d) None of these

Answer key: TAXONOMY - II

1. (a) 2. (b) 3. (a) 4. (c) 5. (b) 6. (a) 7. (c) 8. (a) 9. (b) 10. (a) 11. (a) 12. (c) 13. (a) 14. (a) 15. (d) 16. (a) 17. (c) 18. (a) 19. (a) 20. (c) 21. (a) 22. (a) 23. (a) 24. (b) 25. (a) 26. (b) 27. (a) 28. (a) 29. (c) 30. (a) 31. (a) 32. (d) 33. (b) 34. (d) 35. (a) 36. (d) 37. (a) 38. (a) 39. (b) 40. (a) 41. (a) 42. (b) 43. (a) 44. (c) 45. (c) 46. (b) 47. (c) 48. (c) 49. (a) 50. (c) 51. (c) 52. (a) 53. (c) 54. (c) 55. (b) 56. (c) 57. (b) 58. (c) 59. (a) 60. (c) 61. (b) 62. (c) 63. (c) 64. (b) 65. (c) 66. (b) 67. (c) 68. (b) (69. (c) 70. (a) 71. (c) 72. (d) 73. (c) 74. (b) 75. (c) 76. (d) 77. (a) 78. (c) 79. (a) 80. (b) (81. (b) 82. (c) 83. (b) 84. (d) 85. (a) 86. (b) 87. (b) 88. (c) 89. (d) 90. (a) 91. (c) 92. (a)

TAXONOMY - III

1. Which term is used for non-differentiated sepals & petals of flower?
    (a) Calyx (b) Perianth
    (c) Corolla (d) None of these.
2. In four 'o' clock plant the stamens are alternate to
    (a) Calyx (b) Tepals
    (c) Corolla (d) None of these

3. Which type of filaments occurs in flower of *Mirabilis jalapa*?
   (a) Unequal filament (b) Equal filaments
   (c) Two long two short (d) None of them.
4. Which is the family of *Boerhavia diffusa*?
   (a) Nyctaginaceae (b) Acanthaceae
   (c) Solanaceae (d) Poaceae
5. The Sadabahar (*Vinca rosea*) is a
   (a) Perennial shrub (b) Biannual shrub
   (c) Perennial herb (d) None of these
6. Which of the following is a member of family apocynaceace?
   (a) *Plumeria acutifolia* (b) *Crinum defixum*
   (c) *Annona squimosa* (d) *Fumaria indica*
7. The leaves of *Nerium odorum* are
   (a) Stipulate (b) Exstipulate
   (c) Bracteate (d) None of these
8. When the main axis ends in a flower and similarly the lateral axis also ends in a flower, Such type of inflorescence is termed as
   (a) Recemose (b) Catkin
   (c) Cymose (d) Spadix
9. In which of the following branched tap root occurs?
   (a) *Bamboo* (b) *Triticum vulgarae*
   (c) *Vinca rosea* (d) None of these
10. Which term is used for attachment of stamen to petals of flower?
   (a) Polypetalous (b) Free
   (c) Epipetalous (d) None of these
11. Which term is used for smooth surface of stem?
   (a) Spiney (b) Glabrous
   (c) Fistular (d) None of these
12. Which type of inflorescence occurs in genus *Plumeria*?
   (a) Axillary cyme (b) Terminal cyme
   (c) Recemose (d) None of these
13. Which is the member of family apocynaceace?
   (a) *Rauwolfia serpentina* (b) *Lycopersicon esculentum*
   (c) *Crotalaria sericea* (d) None of these
14. Which one is the common name of *Carrisa carandas*?
   (a) Tree (b) Prostrate Herb
   (c) Spiny shrub (d) None of these

15. Which plant contains alkaloids in its roots?
    (a) *Rauwolfia serpentina* (b) *Triticum vulgarae*
    (c) *Vinca rosea* (d) None of these
16. Which is the largest family of fabaceae?
    (a) Mimosaceae (b) Caesalpinaceae
    (c) Papilionaceae (d) None of these
17. Root nodules occur in the plants of family
    (a) Papilionaceae (b) Annonaceae
    (c) Cruciferae (d) Solanaceae
18. Bean is the member of family
    (a) Papilionaceae (b) Cruciferae
    (c) Solanaceae (d) None of these
19. Which type of aestivation occurs in corolla of family Papilionaceae?
    (a) Valvate (b) Imbricate
    (c) Ascending imbricate (d) Descending imbricate
20. Which type of fruit occurs in of plants of family Papilionaceae?
    (a) Pome (b) Legume
    (c) Drupe (d) None of these
21. The form of corolla of *Pisum sativum* is described as
    (a) Cruciform (b) Infundibuliform
    (c) Papilionacious (d) Bell shaped
22. The *Pisum sativum* is a climber, which climb with the help of
    (a) Stem tendril (b) Leaf tendril
    (c) Scaly tendril (d) None of these
23. Which type of stipule occurs in *Pisum sativum*?
    (a) Foliaceous (b) Scaly
    (c) Narrow (d) None of these
24. When the filaments unit in two bundles, the condition is termed as
    (a) Monodelphous (b) Polydelphous
    (c) Didelphous (d) None of these
25. When calyx, corolla & stamens arise from the base of ovary, the position of ovary is termed as
    (a) Semi-inferior (b) Superior
    (c) Interior (d) None of these
26. The anthers of *Lythrus sativus* are
    (a) Basifixed (b) Dorsifixed
    (c) Versatile (d) None of these

27. The *Dalbergia sisso* is a yield
    (a) Resin (b) Gum
    (c) Wood (d) None of these
28. The *Crotalaria sericea* is grown for its
    (a) Flowers (b) Green manure
    (c) Roots (d) None of these
29. The large sized petal of papilionacious type of corolla is termed as
    (a) Normal petal (b) Keel petal
    (c) Wing (d) Standard petal
30. The genus *Solanum nigrum* is a
    (a) Small annual herb (b) Large shrub
    (c) Small tree (d) None of these
31. Which one is the shape of corolla of *Daters stramonium*?
    (a) Oval (b) Funnel shaped
    (c) rectangular (d) None of these
32. Which is the family of Potato & Brinjal?
    (a) Poaceae (b) Mimoceae
    (c) Papilionaceae (d) Solanaceae
33. How is the aestivation of *Withania somnifera*?
    (a) Imbricate (b) Twisted
    (c) Valvate (d) None of these
34. The botanical name of red pepper is
    (a) *Solanum nigrum* (b) *Capsicum frutescens*
    (c) *Cyphomandra betacea* (d) None of these
35. Which of the following Is famous for its medicinal value?
    (a) *Solanum tuberosum* (b) *Solanum melengena*
    (c) *Withania somnifera* (d) *Ricinus communis*
36. Kateli is the vernacular name of
    (a) *Solanum xanthocarpum* (b) *Solanum indicum*
    (c) *Solanum ferox* (d) *Solanum nigrum*
37. Which is the family of Tobacco?
    (a) Caesalpinaceae (b) Annonaceae
    (c) Solanaceae (d) None of these
38. Which is the botanical name of Jasmine?
    (a) *Vinca rosea* (b) *Rosa sinensis*
    (c) *Cestrum nocturnum* (d)*Triticum vulgarae*

39. The *Datura suaveolens* is a native of
    (a) Mexico (b) India
    (c) Australia (d) Canada
40. Which of the plant consists of narcotic and soporific properties?
    (a) Azadiracta indica (b) *Dalbergia sisso*
    (c) *Withania somnifera* (d) None of these
41. The flowers of *Withania somnifera* are
    (a) Sub-sessile (b) Petiolate
    (c) Sessile (d) None of these.
42. The flowers having gynoecium & androecium are termed as
    (a) Pistillate (b) Bisexual
    (c) Staminate (d) Unisexual
43. Which one is true in case of family Solanaceae is
    (a) Syngenesious (b) Synandrous
    (c) Polyandrous (d) None of the above
44. In floral formula calyx is represented by symbol
    (a) C (b) A
    (c) + (d) K
45. Which symbol is used to represent zygomorphic nature of flower?
    (a) % (b) +
    (c) K (d) C
46. Flower of Tulip is a
    (a) Modified shoot (b) Modified root
    (c) Modified flower (d) Modified petiole
47. Which of the following plant consists of zygomorphic flower?
    (a) *Caesalpinia pulcherima* (b) *Annona squimosa*
    (c) *Coriandrum sativum* (d) None of these
48. The example of actinomorphic flower is
    (a) *Caesalpinia* (b) Rose
    (c) Hibiscus (d) None of these
49. Which is the example of marginal placentation?
    (a) Pea (b) Cucumber
    (c) Onion (d) Mango
50. Wind pollination occurs in
    (a) Mentha (b) Mosses
    (c) Bryophytes (d) Grasses

51. Insect pollination occurs in
   (a) *Caesalpinia* (b) Bamboo
   (c) Both a and b (d) None of these
52. In which plant half inferior ovary occurs in flower
   (a) Peach (b) *Mentha*
   (c) Fenugreek (d) *Coriander*
53. From which plant pillows are prepared
   (a) Aloe (b) Hemp
   (c) Agave (d) Silk cotton tree
54. Nagpur is popular for
   (a) Oranges (b) Mango
   (c) Papaya (d) Banana
55. A large sized flower occurs in
   (a) Lantana (b) Citrus
   (c) Gram (d) Rafflesia
56. The wood of which tree is used to make railway sleepers
   (a) Pine (b) Sandle wood
   (c) Annona (d) Mulberry
57. In corm, buds are present at
   (a) Lateral side of corm (b) Lower side of corm
   (c) Top of corm (d) None of these
58. When male & female flowers are borne on different plants, the plant is described as
   (a) Bisexual (b) Unisexual
   (c) Dioecious (d) None of these
59. Which term is used for flower having only pistil
   (a) Unisexual flowers (b) Staminate flower
   (c) Bisexual flowers (d) None of these
60. Which one is a thin long structure grow from ovary
   (a) Style (b) Filament
   (c) Stigma (d) Anther
61. The grain like structure occurs in ovary called as
   (a) Ovules (b) Androecium
   (c) Stigma (d) Stamen
62. Which one is not a part of shoot of plant?
   (a) Root (b) Branch
   (c) Stem (d) Peduncle

63. Which type of tissue used for storage of food in plants?
    (a) Pith (b) Endodermis
    (c) Cortex (d) Parenchyma
64. Which are is responsible to increase length of stem
    (a) Apical meristems (b) Lateral branches
    (c) Basal node (d) Floral axis
65. Where is the first Indian Botanical Garden?
    (a) Shibpur – Kolkata (b) Kufri – Simla
    (c) Lal Bagh- Bangalore (d)None of these
66. Which type of pollination occurs in *Vallisnaria* ?
    (a) Zoophily (b) Anemophily
    (c) Hydrophily (d) None of these
67. Which type of ovule occur in *Pisum sativum*
    (a) Anatropus (b) Orthotropus
    (c) Amphitropus (d) None of these
68. Which one is the function of Tapetum?
    (a) Nutrition (b) Photosynthesis
    (c) Respiration (d) Both b & c
69. Self pollination occurs in
    (a) Apple (b) Pear
    (c) Wheat (d) Pumkins
70. Which term is used for fertilized egg?
    (a) Zygote (b) Seedling
    (c) Ovary (d) Stigma
71. Function of suspensor is
    (a) Provide nutrition (b) Photosynthesis
    (c) Exchange of gases (d) None of these
72. Brinjal is the member of family
    (a) Asclepidiaceace (b) Rutaceae
    (c) Myrtaceae (d) Solanaceae
73. Carrot is the member of family
    (a) Cruciferae (b) Annonaceae
    (c) Caesalpiniaceae (d) Solanaceae
74. In which plant Anatropus ovule occurs
    (a) *Helianthus* (b) Lemna
    (c) Poppy (d) None of these

75. From which of the following parthenocarpic fruit develops
    (a) Pollen grain (b) Ovary
    (c) Style (d) Stigma
76. In which, a tri-merous flower occurs
    (a)Radish (b) *Catharanthus*
    (c) Asphodelus (d) Rose
77. Stylopodium occurs in family
    (a) Cruciferae (b) Mimosaceae
    (c) Caesalpinaceae (d) Apiaceae
78. Bilabiate corolla occurs in
    (a) *Ocimum* (b) *Ricinus*
    (c) *Aloe* (d) *Withania*
79. Which one is the family of cereals?
    (a) Poaceae (b) Papilionaceae
    (c) Mimosaceae (d) Asclepiadaceace
80. Botanical name of lentil is
    (a) *Pisum sativum* (b) *Sorghum vulgarae*
    (c) *Lens culinaris* (d) *Glycine max*
81. Family Papilionaceae concerned with
    (a) Monodelphous (c) Didelphous
    (b) Both a and c (d) Didelphous
82. Which is the example of family papilionaceae?
    (a) *Cajanus cajan* (b) *Annona squemosa*
    (c) *Tamarindus indica* (d) *Coriandrum sativum*
83. In which family stipellate gynoecium occurs
    (a) Papilionaceae (b) Annonaceae
    (c) Graminae (d) Acanthaceae
84. In which family raceme type of inflorescence occurs
    (a) Verbenaceae (b) Caryophyllaceae
    (c) Rubiaceae (d) Fabaceae
85. Which one are xerophytic angiosperms?
    (a) *Aloe vera* (b) *Triticum vulgarae*
    (c) *Pisum satiuvm* (d) *Linum usitatissimum*
86. Which of the following is a climber?
    (a) *Benincasa hispida* (b) *Duranta repens*
    (c) *Mimosa pudica* (d) *Acacia catechu*

87. Which type of inflorescence occur in asteraceae
    (a) Head (b) Catkin
    (c) Spadix (d) Verticelaster
88. Which one is a beautiful hedge plant?
    (a) *Callicarpa longifolia* (b) *Malus domestica*
    (c) *Sterculia guttata* (d) *Cucumis melo*
89. Which is the largest family of flowering plants?
    (a)Asclepidiaceace (b) Asteraceae
    (c) Malvaceae (d) Amaranthaceae
90. As per recent record how many species are included under a family asteraceae
    (a) 28000 (b) 24000
    (c) 40000 (d) 25000
91. Which type of habit occurs in *Aloe vera*?
    (a)Mesophyte (b) Xerophyte
    (c) Both a and b (d) Halophyte
92. Which term is used for organizing taxonomical information of plants?
    (a) Systematics (b) Identification
    (c) Phylogenetic (d) Arrangement of plants
93. Who is pioneer to classify organisms?
    (a) H.H. Thomas (b) Camerarium
    (c) Linnaeus (d) None of these
94. Which organization provides rules for naming plants?
    (a) ICBN (b) CSIR
    (c) DST (d) ICRISAT
95. Father of taxonomy is
    (a) Aristotle (b) Linnaeus
    (c) Earnst Haeckel (d) None of these
96. A concept of Tautonym is
    (a) These are the repeated sequence
    (b) It is name of fish
    (c) It is name of genus & species
    (d) It is the name of genus
97. The term used for a duplicate specimen of original type
    (a) Lectotype (b) Holotype
    (c) Isotype (d) Neotype

98. Which one is the part of androecium?
   (a) Anther (b) Ovule
   (c) Style (d) Stigma
99. In which family carnivorous plants are included
   (a) Lentibulariaceae (b) Solanaceae
   (c) Nepenthaceae (d) Droseraceae
100. How many petals occur in flower of Tamarind?
   (a) 6 (b) 5
   (c) 10 (d) 2

Answer key: TAXONOMY - III

1. (b) 2. (b) 3. (a) 4. (a) 5. (c) 6. (a) 7. (b) 8. (c) 9. (c) 10. (c) 11. (b), 12. (b) 13. (a) 14. (c) 15. (c) 16. (c) 17. (a) 18. (a) 19. (c) 20. (b) 21. (c) 22. (b) 23. (a) 24. (c) 25. (b) 26. (b) 27. (c) 28. (c) 29. (d) 30. (a) 31. (b) 32. (d) 33. (c) 34. (b) 35. (c) 36. (a) 37. (c) 38. (c) 39. (a) 40. (c) 41. (a) 42. (b) 43. (c) 44. (d) 45. (a) 46. (a) 47. (a) 48. (c) 49. (a) 50. (d) 51. (a) 52. (a) 53. (d) 54. (a) 55. (d) 56. (a) 57. (c) 58. (c) 59. (a) 60. (a) 61. (c) 62. (a) 63. (d) 64. (a) 65. (a) 66. (c) 67. (b) 68. (a) 69. (c) 70. (a) 71. (a) 72. (d) 73. (a) 74. (a) 75. (b) 76. (c) 77. (d) 78. (a) 79. (a) 80. (c) 81. (c) 82. (a) 83. (a) 84. (d) 85. (a) 86. (a) 87. (a) 88. (a) 89. (b) 90. (b) 91. (b) 92. (a) 93. (c) 94. (a) 95. (b) 96. (c) 97. (c) 98. (a) 99. (a) 100. (b)

TAXONOMY - IV

1. Who is the Father of Botany?
   (a) Theophrastus (b) Darwin
   (c) Lamarck (d) None of these
2. The pioneer to distinguish non-flowering and seed plants is
   (a) Andrea Cesalpino (b) Linnaeus
   (c) John Ray (d) None of these
3. Anthophyta is the division of
   (a) All angiosperms (b) Pteridophytes
   (c) Gymnosperms (d) Bryophyta
4. Oswald Tippo classified angiosperm under the phylum
   (a) Tracheophyta (b) Gametophyte
   (c) Spermophyta (d) None of these
5. The artificial system of plants classification is firstly given by
   (a) Gaspard Bauhin (b) Theophrastus
   (c) Luca Ghini (d) None of these

6. The another taxonomist proposed artificial system of plants classification was
   (a) Armen Takhtajan (b) John Hutchinson
   (c) Carl Linnaeus (d) Dahlgreen
7. Who has firstly considered features of vascular tissue for classification of plants?
   (a) A.P. de Candolle (b) Hutchinson
   (c) Bentham and Hooker (d) None of these
8. Bentham and Hooker has given the classification of plants which is called as
   (a) Phylogenetic (b) Natural
   (c) Artificial (d) None of these
9. The book Plantarum was authorized by
   (a) Bentham and Hooker (b) Linnaeus
   (c) A.P. de Candolle (d) Hutchinson
10. Who has placed angiosperms between dicot and monocot?
   (a) Theophrastus (b) A.P. de Candolle
   (c) Bentham and Hooker (d) None of these
11. The Bentham and Hookers system of classification is a
   (a) Natural (b) Phylogenetic
   (c) Artificial (d) None of these
12. Which is the non-Phyllogenetic system of classification?
   (a) Pre-Darwinian system (b) Both a and b
   (c) Post Darwinian (d) None of these
13. Who is the first to coin the term taxonomy?
   (a) Carolus Linnaeus (b) Hooker
   (c) Bentham (d) de Candolle (1813)
14. The nomenclature of plants is regulated by
   (a) ICBN (b) NBRI
   (c) IUCN (d) None of these
15. The phylogenetic classification of plants given by
   (a) Carolus Linnaeus (b) de Candolle
   (c) Adolf Engler (d) None of these
16. Cladistic and Patristic are the terms used to express affinities in
   (a) Phylogenetic contest (b) Artificial
   (c) Natural (d) None of these

17. Which of the classification is based on gross morphological characters of plants and extensive herbarium?
    (a) Omega taxonomy (b) Lambda taxonomy
    (c) Beta taxonomy (d) Alpha taxonomy
18. The term alpha taxonomy is coined by
    (a) Turrill (1942) (b) Dahlgreen
    (c) Heywood (d) None of these
19. Which of the term designated to be related to modern taxonomy?
    (a) Alpha taxonomy (b) Beta taxonomy
    (c) Omega taxonomy (d) Lambda taxonomy
20. The branch of taxonomy where classification of plant kingdom is made on the basis of phylogenetic relationships using numerical data.
    (a) Numerical taxonomy (b) Chemotaxonomy
    (c) Cytotexonomy (d) None of these
21. Which is the basic unit of taxonomic works?
    (a) Taxa (b) Family
    (c) Genus (d) Species
22. A group of plants with common evolutionary origin but without genetic mixing termed as
    (a) Intra-species (b) Cenospecies
    (c) Sub. Species (d) None of these
23. A basic bio-systematic unit is known as
    (a) Prototype (b) Ecotype
    (c) Holotype (d) None of these
24. The study deals with every natural group of plants in classification has an invariant, generalized patterns is term as
    (a) Ecotype (b) Holotype
    (c) Archetype (d) None of these
25. Which one is the analytical device used for the determination of the names of the plants included in it termed as
    (a) Bracketed key (b) Yoked key
    (c) Indented key (d) Ione of these
26. Which device is used to identify an unknown plants
    (a) Indented key or Yoked key (b) Both of these
    (c) Bracketed key (d) None of these
27. How many plants were described by Theophrastus (370-285 BC) in his book Historia Plantarum?
    (a) 480 (b) 3000
    (c) 2000 (d) 358

28. Who is the first to find differences between monocot and dicot
    (a) Tippo (b) Cisalpino
    (c) Albert Magnus (1193-1280) (d) None of these
29. Who is first to note concept of superior of inferior condition of ovary
    (a) Andrea Cisalpino (1519-1603) (b) Ray John
    (c) Hutchinson (d) None of these
30. John Roy (1625-1705 AD) wrote a book in three volume is
    (a) Species plantarum (b) Hostoria Plantarum
    (c) Genera plantarum (d) None of these
31. The genera Plantarum and classes Plantarum of Linnaeus appears in
    (a) 1737 & 1738 respectively (b) 1780
    (c) 1853 and 1838 (d) None of these
32. The book "Species Plantarum" of Linnaeus was published in
    (a) 1758 (b) 1853
    (c) 1653 (d) 1753
33. The Linnaeus proposed a system of classification called
    (a) Sexual system (b) Natural system
    (c) Asexual system (d) None of these
34. Who gave an artificial key for identifying plants?
    (a) J.B. Lamarck (1744-1829) (b) de Candolle
    (c) Albert Magnus (1193-1280) (d) Hutchinson
35. Who is the first author of genera Plantarum?
    (a) Cisalpino
    (b) Tippo
    (c) Lamarck (1744-1829)
    (d) Antoine de Jassieu (1686-1758)
36. Who has used the same title genera Plantarum for his book?
    (a) Stephan Endlicher (1805-1849) (b) Englar
    (c) Linnaeus (d) None of these
37. Bentham and hooker published the book of same title Genera Plantarum in Latin in
    (a) 1823-1837 (b) 1867-1893
    (c)1862-1883 (d) None of these
38. Bentham and hooker divided dicot into
    (a) Gamopetalae and Monochlamydeae
    (b) Polypetalae and Gamopetalae
    (c) Polypetalae and Monochlamydeae
    (d) Polypetalae, Gamopetalae and Monochlamydeae

39. Who kept gymnosperms between Dicotyledons and monocotyledons?
(a) Bentham and Hooker (b) A.P. Candolle
(c) Hutchinson (d) Takhtajan
40. Darwin in 1859 published a book
(a) Origin of plants (b) Origin of genus
(c) Origin of species (d) None of these
41. The classification of plants proposed by Darwin in 1859 is a
(a) Artificial (b) Natural
(c) Phylogenetic system (d) None of these
42. A German Botanist August Wilhem Eichler (1839-1887) he divided whole plant kingdom into
(a) Cryptogam and Phanerograms
(b) Mono and dicotyledonous
(c) Saprophytic and gametophytic
(d) None of these
43. Who published a 20 volume work entitled 'Die Naturlichen Pflanzen Families (1887-1899)
(a) Adolph Engler & A.E Prantle (b) Hutchinson
(c) Bentham and hooker (d) V.N. Naik
44. Adolph Engler (1944-1930) considered
(a) Monocots as more advanced
(b) Dicotyledons as more primitive than Monocotyledons
(c) Monocots as more primitive than Dicotyledons
(d) None of these
45. Charles E. Bessey (1844-1915) proposed system of classification which is
(a) Phyllogenetic (b) Natural
(c) Artificial (d) None of these
46. Charles E Bessey regarded that the origin of angiosperm from
(a) Gymnosperms like Bennettitales (b) Bryophyta
(c) Pteridophytes (d) Algae
47. Bessey considered the flowering plants to have originated from
(a) Gnetalian group (b) Pentoxylales
(c) Strobiliferous cycads (d) None of these
48. John Hutchinson (1884-1972) British botanist, proposed a system of classification of plants which was based on
(a) Bentham & Hooker (b) Linnaeus
(c) A.P. Candolle (d) None of these

49. John Hutchinson in 1926 published first volume entitled the families of flowering plants consists of
(a) Pteridophytes (b) Gymnosperms
(c) Monocotyledon (d) Dicotyledons
50. John Hutchinson British taxonomist published second volume entitled the families of flowering plant consists of
(a) Monocotyledon plants (b) Pteridophytes
(c) Dicotyledons (d) None of these
51. The third edition of john Hutchinson British taxonomist entitled the families of flowering plants appeared in
(a) 1963 (b) 1968
(c) 1973 (d) 1977
52. Who considered that the dicot are primitive and monocots are advanced
(a) Hutchinson in 1959 (b) Engler and Prantle
(c) Bentham and Hooker (d) None of these
53. Which of the order was primitive according to Bentham and Hooker?
(a) Malvales (b) Rosales
(c) Ranales (d) None of these
54. Which classification of flowering plant contains principles of floral evolution?
(a) Bentham & Hookers system (b) Hutchinson in 1959
(c) Engler and Prantle (d) Takhtajan
55. According to Bentham and hooker, floral anatomy, wood anatomy as well as palynology confirms that the most primitive order is
(a) Rosales (b) Ranales
(c) Malvales (d) None of these
56. The dicotyledons are divided into 3 large groups i.e Polypetalae, Gamopetalae and
(a) Tripetalae (b) Monochlamydeae
(c) Hexapetalae (d) None of these
57. In classification by Engler & Prantl (1887-1899) which group of plants placed before angiosperms
(a) Gymnosperms (b) Bryophytes
(c) Pteridophytes (d) None of these
58. Carolus Linnaeus named plants in
(a) English (b) Latin language
(c) Greek language (d) None of these

59. The name of the plant which is different in different states is termed as
    (a) Vernacular name (b) Both a and b
    (c) Scientific name (d) None of these
60. The rules of nomenclature of plants laid down in
    (a) 1763 (b) 1753
    (c) 1783 (d) None of these
61. The international rules of botanical nomenclature made in 1930 at
    (a) Cambridge (b) USA
    (c) Moscow (d) None of these
62. Which is the basic unit of taxonomy?
    (a) Family (b) Genus
    (c) Species (d) Order
63. Many species forms a group of individual which is called as
    (a) Population (b) Both a and b
    (c) Community (d) None of these
64. The experimental taxonomy is related with study of species such as morphological, cytological, genetical and ecological is termed as
    (a) Phytogeography (b) Biosystematics
    (c) Phytochemistry (d) None of these
65. Which of the following in the basic unit in biosystematics
    (a) Ecotype (b) Both a and b
    (c) Ecospecies (d) None of these
66. Linnaeus (1753) published his basic work in taxonomy in
    (a) Genera Plantarum (b) Both a and b
    (c) The Species Plantarum (d) None of these
67. Study related with the chemical description of plant taxon
    (a) Chemotaxonomy (b) Cladistics
    (c) Numerical taxonomy (d) None of these
68. A numerical evaluation of the similarity between groups of organisms and ordering of these groups into higher ranking taxon on the basis of similarities known as
    (a) Numerical taxonomy (b) Cladistics
    (c) Chemotaxonomy (d) None of these
69. The phenomenon of confinement of species, genera or other group to a small area beyond which their existence is not found in termed as
    (a) Local (b) Exotic
    (c) Endemism (d) None of these

70. The central national herbarium (herbarium of Indian botanic garden) consists of 5 million plants which is present at
    (a) Kolkata, Hawrah (b) NBRI Lucknow
    (c) Lal Bagh Bangluru (d) None of these
71. Herbarium of Forest Research Institute Dehradun consists of
    (a) 100,000plants (b) 200000 plants
    (c) 300,000 plants (d) None of these
72. Blatter Herbarium, St. Xaviers College, Fort, consists of 100,000 plants which is situated at
    (a) Madras (b) Chennai
    (c) Bangalore (d) Mumbai
73. World's No. 1 herbarium center which consists of 6,000,000 plants is
    (a) Royal Botanic Garden, Kew London
    (b) University Botanical garden Moscow
    (c) NBRI Lucknow
    (d) IBG Hawrah

Answer key: TAXONOMY - IV

1. (a) 2. (c) 3. (a) 4. (a) 5. (b) 6. (c) 7. (a) 8. (b) 9. (a) 10. (c) 11. (a) 12. (a) 13. (d) 14. (b) 15. (c) 16. (a) 17. (d) 18. (a) 19. (c) 20. (a) 21. (d) 22. (b) 23. (b) 24. (c) 25. (a) 26. (a) 27. (a) 28. (c) 29. (a) 30. (b) 31. (a) 32. (d) 33. (a) 34. (a) 35. (d) 36. (a) 37. (c) 38. (d) 39. (a) 40. (c) 41. (c) 42. (a) 43. (a) 44. (c) 45. (a) 46. (a) 47. (c) 48. (a) 49. (d) 50. (a) 51.(c) 52. (a) 53. (c) 54. (a) 55. (b) 56. (b) 57. (a) 58. (b) 59. (a) 60. (b) 61. (a) 62. (c) 63. (a) 64. (b) 65. (a) 66. (c) 67. (a) 68. (b) 69. (c) 70. (a) 71. (c) 72. (d) 73. (a)

TAXONOMY - V

1. A author name of particular species in always written in
   (a) Roman (b) Greek
   (c) Spanish (d) None of these
2. As a rule the valid name of an organism is the Botanical name after
   (a) 1753 (b) 1773
   (c) 1758 (d) None of these
3. The highly reduced male and female gametophytes occur in
   (a) Pteridophytes (b) Bryophyte
   (c) Angiosperm (d) None of these
4. Which division of plant kingdom consists of dominant terrestrial flora?
   (a) Spermatophyte (b) Mosses
   (c) Ferns (d) None of these

5. Which of the following do not contain chlorophyll?
   (a) Bryophytes (b) Gymnosperms
   (c) Angiosperms (d) Fungi
6. Which organism contain usually non vacuolated cells
   (a) Prokaryotic (b) Both a and b
   (c) Eukaryotic (d) None of these
7. The science of naming of plant is known as
   (a) Classification (b) Nomenclature
   (c) Identification (d) None of these
8. The term Systematics was coined by
   (a) Huxley (b) Brown
   (c) Englar (d) Darwin
9. The algae differ from bryophyte in
   (a) Bicellular sex organ (b) Both a and b
   (c) Unicellular sex organ (d) None of these
10. The gymnouspermic plants are distinguished from angiosperms by
    (a) Naked ovules (b) Absence of ovule
    (c) Small ovule (d) None of these
11. The artificial system of plant classification is made on the basis of
    (a) Few, one or two or variable character
    (b) Anatomical character
    (c) Hidden character
    (d) None of these
12. The natural system of classification is made on the basis of
    (a) Dissimilar character (b) Both a and b
    (c) All the similarities between plants (d) None of these
13. The interrelationship of plants and phylogeny between taxa based on how the chromosomes are arranged
    (a) Chemotaxonomy (b) Karyotaxonomy
    (c) Cytotexonomy (d) None of these
14. The study of phenomenon of cytotexonomy is based on
    (a) Cytochromes- "c" (b) Phytochromes
    (c) Chromosomes (d) None of these
15. The study of origin of evolutionary variation and classification of plant is termed as
    (a) Anatomy (b) Classical taxonomy
    (c) Natural (d) None of these

16. Which one is the first step in the study of taxonomy of plants?
    (a) Nomenclature (b) Classification
    (c) Description (d) Identification
17. How can we confirm that two plants are taxonomically closely related?
    (a) It those plant store carbohydrates in the same type of molecule
    (b) Presence of same number of stamens
    (c) Presence of same number of petals
    (d) None of these
18. The study of botany concerned with classification identification an naming of plant in term as
    (a) Numerical taxonomy (b) Cytotexonomy
    (c) Plant taxonomy (d) Phytology
19. The plant which does not bear flowers and seeds are group as
    (a) Cryptogams (b) Angiosperms
    (c) Gymnosperms (d) None of these
20. Which of the following group is of Thallophyta?
    (a) Bryophyte (b) Gymnosperms
    (c) Pteridophytes (d) Algae and fungi
21. In which plant grow embryo vascular system in absent
    (a) Bryophyte (b) Gymnosperms
    (c) Pteridophytes (d) None of these
22. The mosses and liverworts are kept under
    (a) Algae (b) Pteridophytes
    (c) Bryophyte (d) None of these
23. For which characteristics of bryophytes , they are considered advanced than Thallophytes
    (a) Multicellular jackted gametangia and sporangia
    (b) Presence of root
    (c) Presence of fruits
    (d) None of these
24. Which of the following lack true to roots?
    (a) Gymnosperms (b) Angiosperms
    (c) Bryophytes (d) None of these
25. In which group of plant the gametophytes are leafy
    (a) Bryophytes (b) Algae
    (c) Fungi (d) None of these

26. Which of the following is heterosporous archegoniate?
    (a) Lichens (b) Algae
    (c) Fungi (d) Pteridophytes
27. The independent alternation of generation occur in
    (a) Pteridophytes (b) Algae
    (c) Fungi (d) None of these
28. How the bryophytes are differ than Pteridophytes
    (a) Formation of fruits (b) Seed formation
    (c) Absence of vascular tissue (d) None of these
29. The ovules are naked in gymnosperms because
    (a) Ovary wall is absent (b) Ovules are absent
    (c) Ovules are not visible (d) None of these
30. One of the important evolutionary features of alternation generation from algae to flowering plant is
    (a) Gradual elaboration of sporophyte
    (b) Both of these
    (c) Gametophyte
    (d) None of these
31. The angiosperms consist of
    (a) Absence of companion cells (b) Vessels
    (c) Absence of vessels (d) None of these
32. The angiospermic plant are differs from a gymnosperm in the absence of
    (a) Vessels (b) Companion cells
    (c) Naked ovule (d) None of these
33. The magnification of electron microscope is up to
    (a) 100,000 times (b) 1.500000 times
    (c) 200,000 times (d) 50,000 times
34. The exobiology is the study of
    (a) Life in forest (b) Life in other city
    (c) Life on other country (d) Life on other planets
35. The study of biological problems by statically is termed as
    (a) Genetic engineering (b) Biometry
    (c) Biotechnology (d) None of these
36. The gymnosperm differ from angiosperm in
    (a) Presence of naked seeds
    (b) Presence of companion cells
    (c) Vessel present
    (d) None of these

37. The gymnosperm are the plant which
    (a) Produces seeds in cones but no flowers
    (b) Produces fruits
    (c) Produces flowers
    (d) None of these
38. The plant division into angiosperms and gymnosperms ends with suffix 'sperms' it means that both produce
    (a) Flowers (b) Inflorescence
    (c) Ovules and seeds (d) None of these
39. Who is the 1st written maximum on plant?
    (a) de Candole (b) Hutchinson
    (c) Takhtajan (d)Theophrastus
40. First time the term species was coined by
    (a) John Ray (b) Gregor Mendel
    (c) John Hutchinson (d) None of these
41. Who is first to coin the term taxonomy
    (a) A.P de Condole (b) Robert brown
    (c) Theophrastus (d) None of these
42. Who is the father of taxonomy?
    (a) Theophrastus (b) Darwin
    (c) Linnaeus (d) None of these
43. The word ending area indicates
    (a) Division (b) Family
    (c) Order (d) None of these
44. Adolf Mayer coined the term
    (a) Order (b) Genus
    (c) Family (d) Taxon
45. The International code of Binomial nomenclature was made uniform throughout the world in
    (a) 1975 (b) 1978
    (c) 1953 (d) 1982
46. The name of plant are given in Latin because
    (a) Universal language (b) Both a and b
    (c) Latin language in an ancient (d) None of these
47. The female nucleus (eggs) do not occur in archegonia in
    (a) Angiosperms (b) Pteridophytes
    (c) Bryophyte (d) None of these

48. Which group of plant has maximum power of adoptability?
    (a) Pteridophytes (b) Angiosperm
    (c) Gymnosperm (d) None of these
49. Which organism are generally classified as protists.
    (a) Protozoa, few algae and fungi (b) Bryophyte
    (c) Lichen (d) None of these
50. The division of plant kingdom into prokariota and eukaryote is based on the characters of
    (a) Ribosome (b) Both a and b
    (c) Nucleus only (d) None of these

Answer key: TAXONOMY - V

1. (a) 2. (a) 3. (c) 4. (a) 5. (d) 6. (a) 7. (b) 8. (c) 9. (c) 10. (a) 11. (a) 12. (c) 13. (b) 14. (a) 15. (b) 16. (d) 17. (a) 18. (c) 19. (a) 20. (d) 21. (a) 22. (c) 23. (a) 24. (c) 25. (a) 26. (d) 27. (a) 28. (c) 29. (a) 30. (a) 31. (b) 32. (c) 33. (c) 34. (d) 35. (b) 36. (a) 37. (a) 38. (c) 39. (d) 40. (a) 41. (a) 42. (c) 43. (b) 44. (d) 45. (a) 46. (c) 47. (a) 48. (b) 49. (a) 50. (c)

TAXONOMY - VI

1. What is the correct descending sequence of taxonomic categories?
    (a) Division class, order, family, genus, species
    (b) Division class, order, family, genus,
    (c) Division order, family, genus, species
    (d) Division class, family, genus, species
2. Who is firstly coined the term Phylum?
    (a) Ghini (b) Pinto
    (c) Cuvier (d) None of these
3. The word with suffix is the character of rank of an order is
    (a) ales (b) les
    (c) eles (d) elas
4. Who proposed the use of term taxon for plant?
    (a) Herman Johannes Lam in 1948
    (b) Gregor Mendel
    (c) Charls Darwin
    (d) None of these
5. Which system of nomenclature for an organism in given by Linnaeus
    (a) Binomial system (b) Polynomial system
    (c) Traditional system (d) None of these

6. The binomial nomenclature of an organisms composed of
   (a) Species and Genus (b) Both a and b
   (c) Genus and second (d) None of these
7. The concept of binomial nomenclature explained in detail by Linnaeus in
   (a) Species Plantarum (b) Floral plantarum
   (c) Genera Plantarum (d) None of these
8. The book Systema Naturae was written by
   (a) Hutchinson (b) Takhtajan
   (c) Carolus Linnaeus (d) None of these
9. The international code of binomial nomenclature rule is applicable for
   (a) Naming of plant (b) Identification of plants
   (c) Classification of plants (d) None of these
10. Which of the following are included in Tracheophyta?
    (a) Pteridophytes, gymnosperms and Angiosperm
    (b) Algae and bryophyte
    (c) Algae and fungi
    (d) Bacteria and fungi
11. The binomial nomenclature means
    (a) Two generic names (b) Two species names
    (c) Generic name and species name (d) None of these
12. The branch of cultivation of grasses is termed as
    (a) Agrostology (b) Floriculture
    (c) Apiculture (d) Horticulture
13. The *Coriandrum sativum* is member of family
    (a) Apiaceae (b) Solanaceae
    (c) Solanaceae (d) Euphorbiaceae
14. Which of the following is a cultivated plant?
    (a) *Cassia tora* (b) *Tephrosia purpurea*
    (c) *Cucumis sativus* (d) None of these
15. A cremocarp type of fruit occur in
    (a) *Coriandrum sativum* (b) *Cassia tora*
    (c) *Cucumis sativus* (d) *Terminalia chebula*
16. Which type of inflorescence occur in *Foeniculum vulgare*
    (a) Recemose (b) Cymose
    (c) Compound umbel (d) None of these
17. A disc like stylopodium occur at the base of the style in
    (a) *Foeniculum vulgare* (b) *Allium*
    (c) *Cassia tora* (d) *Aegle*

18. Which of the following is a ornamental plant
    (a) *Cassia angustifolia* (b) *Coriandrum sativum*
    (c) *Ixora parviflora* (d) None of these
19. The family of *Eclipta alba* is
    (a) Asclepidiaceace (b) Malvaceae
    (c) Malvaceae (d) Compositae
20. Botanical name of sunflower is
    (a) *Helianthus annuus* (b) *Withania somnifera*
    (c) *Catharanthus roseus* (d) *Annona squimosa*
21. Presence of ray and disc florets is a characteristic feature of family
    (a) Compositae (b) Mimosaceae
    (c) Meliaceae (d) Apiaceae
22. Ray floret are the
    (a) Female flower (b) Both a and b
    (c) Male flowers (d) None of these
23. The involucres of bract is a characteristic feature of family
    (a) Compositae (b) Caesalpinaceae
    (c) Malvaceae (d) Papaveraceae
24. Which plant consists of decumbent type of stem?
    (a) *Rosa indica* (b) *Tridax procumbence*
    (c) *Helianthus annuus* (d) None of these
25. The family of *Achras sapota* is
    (a) Sapotaceae (b) Magnoliaceae
    (c) Anacardiaceae (d) None of these
26. The fruit of *Achras sapota* is a
    (a) Drupe (b) Capsule
    (c) Nut (d) Fleshy berry
27. The *Madhuca india* is a mesophyte occur in
    (a) Deciduous forest (b) Alpine forest
    (c) Evergreen forest (d) None of these
28. The Botanical name of Sadabahar is
    (a) *Tamarindus indica* (b) *Vinca rosea*
    (c) *Nerium indicum* (d) None of these
29. Which of the following require dry soil for growth?
    (a) Calotropis gigantea (b) *Saccharum officinarum*
    (c) *Zingiber officinale* (d) None of these

30. The presence of a pair of caudicle (pollinium) is a characteristics feature of
    (a) *Acacia nilotica* (b) *Mimosa pudica*
    (c) *Cassia angustifolia* (d) *Calotropis gigantea*
31. Which of the following is an ornamental climbing shrub?
    (a) *Cryptostegia grandiflora* (b) *Curcuma longa*
    (c) *Catharanthus roseus* (d) None of these
32. The family of *Ipomoea palmata* is
    (a) Asclepiadaceace (b) Cucurbitaceae
    (c) Convolvulaceae (d) None of these
33. The leaves are absent in
    (a) *Cuscuta reflexa* (b) *Vinca rosea*
    (c) *Alstonia scholaria* (d) None of these
34. The roots are absent but haustoria are present in plant like
    (a) *Cuscuta* (b) *Curcuma*
    (c) *Ipomoea* (d) *Asparagus*
35. Which of the following in wild plant growing on waste land?
    (a) *Curcuma longa* (b) *Helianthus annuus*
    (c) *Solanum nigrum* (d) None of these
36. The thorns on the leaf occur in
    (a) *Solanum nigrum* (b) *Raphanus sativus*
    (c) *Solanum tuberosum* (d) *Daccus carrota*
37. Family of *Withania somnifera* is
    (a) Piperaceae (b) Solanaceae'
    (c) Convolvulaceae (d) None of these
38. Which is the plant used as medicine
    (a) *Withania somnifera* (b) *Solanum tuberosum*
    (c) *Solanum melongiana* (d) None of these
39. Which plant grow in wet or marshy places
    (a) *Annona squimosa* (b) *Mangifera indica*
    (c) *Bacopa monnieri* (d) *Alstonia scolaris*
40. The persistent style occurs in
    (a) *Bacopa monnieri* (b) *Musa paradiscicca*
    (c) *Cassia tora* (d) None of these
41. Family of *Bacopa monnieri* is
    (a) Anacardiaceae (b) Myrtaceae
    (c) Annonaceae (d) Scrophulariaceae

42. The *Adhatoda vasica* is a member of family
    (a) Acanthaceae (b) Solanaceae
    (c) Papilionaceae (d) Mimosaceae
43. The *Adhatoda vasica* is a
    (a) Annual herb (b) Climber
    (c) Perennial shrub (d) Annual Shrub
44. The best wood yielding plant is
    (a) *Tectona grandis* (b) *Annona squimosa*
    (c) *Cassia angustifolia* (d) None of these
45. The *Vitex nigundo* is a member of family
    (a) Verbenaceae (b) Myrtaceae
    (c) Apocynaceae (d) None of these
46. The cymose panicle type of inflorescence occur in
    (a) *Delonix regia* (b) *Mentha piperata*
    (c) *Daccus carota* (d) *Vitex nigundo*
47. A carcerulus type of fruit occur in
    (a) *Ocimum sanctum* (b) *Coriander sativum*
    (c) *Mimosa pudica* (d) None of these
48. The gland dotted aromatic leaves occur in
    (a) *Zea maize* (b) Sugarcane
    (c) *Ocimum sanctum* (d) All of these
49. A Verticelaster type of inflorescence is a characteristic feature of family
    (a) Acanthaceae (b) Apiaceae
    (c) Malvaceae (d) Labiatae
50. Which of the following represents most of the characteristic features of a particular plant
    (a) Floral formula and floral diagram
    (b) Androecium and gynoecium
    (c) Calyx and corolla
    (d) None of these
51. Which of the following is the member of family amaranthaceae?
    (a) *Achyranthes aspera* (b) *Melia azadiracta*
    (c) *Adatoda vasica* (d) *Azadiracta indica*
52. The persistent perianth and spiny bracteoles occur in
    (a) *Cassia tora* (b) *Mimosa pudica*
    (c) *Achyranthes aspera* (d) None of these

53. Which of the following angiosperm used as vegetable
    (a) *Amaranthus spinosus* (b) *Curcuma longa*
    (c) *Citrus aurantifolia* (d) None of these
54. The tapels are present in
    (a) *Mirabilis jalapa* (b) China rose
    (c) *Chenopodium album* (d) None of these
55. The plant *Euphorbia hirta* is a
    (a) Monoecious (b) Both a and b
    (c) Dioecious (d) None of these
56. Which term is used for collection of dried and pressed plants?
    (a) Museum specimen (b) Herbarium
    (c) Preservation (d) None of these
57. Herbaria are generally associated with
    (a) DST
    (b) ICRISAT
    (c) CSIR
    (d) Educational Research Organization
58. Conservatory material & data of plants is also termed as
    (a) Museum specimen (b) Transparency
    (c) Herbarium (d) None of these
59. A three coccoid schizocarpic capsule occur in
    (a) *Ricinus communis* (b) *Hibiscus rosa-sinensis*
    (c) *Cucumis sativus* (d) None of these
60. Presence of milk latex in the characteristic feature of family
    (a) Euphorbiaceae (b) Annonaceae
    (c) Malvaceae (d) Nyctaginaceae
61. The family of *Ficus glomarata* is
    (a) Anacardiaceae (b) Papilionaceae
    (c) Caesalpinaceae (d) Moraceae
62. The fruit of which plant are edible
    (a) *Ficus glomarata* (b) *Ricinus communis*
    (c) *Gossipium herbacium* (d) None of these
63. The *Phoenix* is a member of family
    (a) Orchidaceae (b) Palmae
    (c) Scitaminae (d) None of these
64. Which of the following angiosperm possesses prominent leaf bases on stem?
    (a) *Cocos nucifera* (b) *Ricinus communis*
    (c) *Jatropha curcus* (d) None of these

65. A fibrous drup occur in
(a) *Cocos nucifera* (b) *Ricinus communis*
(c) *Annona squimosa* (d) None of these
66. A aromatic herb perennating trough underground rhizome is
(a) *Daccus carrota* (b) *Raphanus sativus*
(c) *Zingiber officiale* (d) None of these
67. Which of the following plant grow in canal banks?
(a) *Zeuxine sulcata* (b) *Alocasia indica*
(c) *Vanda roxburghii* (d) None of these
68. Which of the following in a orchid?
(a) *Vanda roxburghii* (b) *Pistia stratiotes*
(c) *Allium cepa* (d) *None of these*
69. Which is the member of family Liliaceae
(a) *Tamarindus indica* (b) *Terminalia chebula*
(c) *Cajanus cajan* (d) *Asparagus officinalis*
70. The rhizome of which plant are edible
(a) *Alocasia indica* (b) *Pistia shatiotes*
(c) *Vanda roxburghii* (d) *None of these*
71. The family of *Alocasia indica* is
(a) Araceae (b) Graminae
(c) Palmae (d) Apocynaceae
72. Which of the following is floating stolon bearing herb?
(a) *Alocasia indica* (b) *Pistia stratiotes*
(c) *Vanda roxburghii* (d) None of these
73. The wheat (*Triticum aestivum*) is the member of family
(a) Poaceae (b) Araceae
(c) Palmae (d) Orchidaceae
74. The inflorescence of wheat plant is
(a) Recemose (b) Cymose
(c) Spike (d) None of these
75. The *Zea mays* is a
(a) Cereal (b) Pulse
(c) Spice (d) Aromatic plant
76. Jowar and bamboo are examples of
(a) Monocot plants (b) Both a and b
(c) Dicot plants (d) None of these

77. Which family of angiosperm consists of large number of plants?
(a) Malvaceae (b) Caesalpinaceae
(c) Fabaeceae (d) Compositae
78. Which angiosperm in an aromatic plant
(a) *Ocimum* (b) *Ricinus*
(c) *Solanum* (d) *Triticum*
79. The reproductive organ of angiosperms is
(a) Stipule (b) Calyx
(c) Petal (d) Flower
80. The sterile stamens in the flower are termed as
(a) Staminode (b) Carpel
(c) Stamens (d) None of these
81. A following is the example of one seeded drupe
(a) *Triticum vulgarae* (b) *Ricinus communis*
(c) *Calotropis gigantea* (d) *Melia azadirachta*
82. Which of the following plant have prickles?
(a) *Rosa indica* (b) *Solanum tuberosum*
(c) *Melia azadirachta* (d) None of these
83. Quincuncial type of aestivation occur in
(a) Sorghum (b) Daccus
(c) Rose (d) Sunflower
84. Which one is the plant of family Papilionaceae?
(a) Trigonella (b) Sugarcane
(c) Potato (d) Tamarind
85. The *Crotalaria juncea* (Papilionaceae) is a
(a) Climber (b) Creeper
(c) Tree (d) Herb
86. The terminal leaflet of compound leaf modified to a tendril in
(a) *Pisum sativum* (b) *Cassia tora*
(c) *Delonix regia* (d) None of these
87. The plant bears aerial flowers and fruits mature in soil in
(a) *Arachis hypogea* (b) *Cassia tora*
(c) *Raphanus sativus* (d) None of these
88. Diadelphous condition occur in
(a) *Raphanus sativus* (b) *Pisum sativum*
(c) *Tamarindus indicus* (d) None of these

89. Descending imbricate aestivation occur in
    (a) *Lythrus odoratus* (b) *Cassia tora*
    (c) *Justicia adhatoda* (d) None of these
90. Which plant consists of zygomorphic flower?
    (a) Dalbergia sisso (b) *Cassia tora*
    (c) *Delonix regia* (d) None of these
91. The marginal placentation occur in
    (a) *Allium* (b) *Sorghum*
    (c) *Mangifera* (d) Pea
92. The sheathing leaf base occurs in plants of family
    (a) Graminae (b) Meliaceae
    (c) Orchidaceae (d) None of these
93. The paripinnate compound leaf occur in
    (a) *Cassia tora* (b) *Ricinus communis*
    (c) *Sorghum vulgarae* (d) None of these
94. Tamarindus indica is a
    (a) Climber (b) Herb
    (c) Shrub (d) Large tree
95. The leaf of *Caesalpinia pulcherima* is
    (a) Bipinnate compound (b) Tripinnate
    (c) Unipinnate (d) None of these
96. A globose head type of inflorescence occur in
    (a) *Mimosa pudica* (b) *Abutilon indica*
    (c) Cassia tora (d) None of these
97. The *Mimosa pudica* stipules are modified to
    (a) Tendril (b) Involucres
    (c) Stipule (d) Spine
98. Which one is called as touch me not plants?
    (a) *Mimosa pudica* (b) *Delonix regia*
    (c) *Daccus carota* (d) None of these
99. Which plant yield gum of commercial value?
    (a) *Caesalpinia pulcherima* (b) *Terminalia indica*
    (c) *Mentha piperata* (d) *Acacia nilotica*
100. The fruit type of *Acacia nilotica* is
    (a) Lomentum (b) Legume
    (c) Drupe (d) Pod

Answer key: TAXONOMY - VI

1. (a) 2. (c) 3. (b) 4. (a) 5. (a) 6. (c) 7. (a) 8. (c) 9. (a) 10. (a) 11. (c) 12. (a) 13. (a) 14. (c) 15. (a) 16. (c) 17. (a) 18. (c) 19. (d) 20. (a) 21. (a) 22. (c) 23. (a) 24. (b) 25. (a) 26. (d) 27. (a) 28. (b) 29. (a) 30. (d) 31. (a) 32. (c) 33. (a) 34. (a) 35. (c) 36. (a) 37. (c) 38. (d) 39. (c) 40. (a) 41. (d) 42. (a) 43. (c) 44. (a) 45. (a) 46. (d) 47. (a) 48. (c) 49. (d) 50. (a) 51. (a) 52. (c) 53. (a) 54. (c) 55. (a) 56. (c) 57. (d) 58. (c) 59. (a) 60. (a) 61. (d) 62. (a) 63. (b) 64. (a) 65. (a) 66. (c) 67. (a) 68. (a) 69. (d) 70. (a) 71. (a) 72. (b) 73. (c) 74. (c) 75. (a) 76. (a) 77. (d) 78. (a) 79. (d) 80. (a) 81. (d) 82. (a) 83. (c) 84. (a) 85. (d) 86. (a) 87. (a) 88. (b) 89. (a) 90. (a) 91. (d) 92. (a) 93. (a) 94. (d) 95. (a) 96. (a) 97. (d) 98. (a) 99. (d) 100. (a)

TAXONOMY - VII

1. Which of the following in a deciduous tree growing in dry places?
   (a) *Albizzia lebbek* (b) *Murraya paniculata*
   (c) *Alstonia scolaris* (d) None of these
2. Monodelphous condition of stamen occur in
   (a) *Raphanus sativus* (b) *Acacia nilotica*
   (c) *Cassia tora* (d) *Hibiscus rosa sinensis*
3. Which one is a tall tree with non endospermic seeds?
   (a) *Eucalyptus lanceolatus* (b) Both a and b
   (c) *Polyanthia longifolia* (d) None of these
4. The family of *Psidum guajava* is
   (a) Myrtaceae (b) Magnoliaceae
   (c) Meliaceae (d) None of these
5. Fruit of guava is a
   (a) Many seeded berry (b) Drupe
   (c) Capsule (d) None of these
6. The fruit of *Ficus carica* is a
   (a) Follicle (b) Hypanthodium
   (c) Hesperidium (d) None of these
7. The leaf of Perithecium grass in an example of
   (a) Decompound leaf (b) Simple
   (c) compound (d) None of these
8. The sorosis of pineapple is a type of
   (a) Multiple fruit (b) Etaerio of berries
   (c) Simple fruit (d) None of these

9. A single seeded dehiscent fruit with thin wall in described as
   (a) Drupe (b) Capsule
   (c) Legume (d) Utricle
10. The one seeded dry indehiscent fruit with bony shell derived from. Compound syconium is termed as
   (a) Nut (b) Berry
   (c) Capsule (d) Achene
11. The petals are absent in flower of
   (a) *Terminalia bellerica* (b) *Cassia tora*
   (c) *Hibiscus rosa-sinensis* (d) *Cucumis sativus*
12. A five angled achene type of fruit occur in
   (a) *Mangifera indica* (b) *Aegle marmelos*
   (c) *Cucumis sativus* (d) *Quiqualis indica*
13. Which one is the climbing herb?
   (a) *Cucurbita maxima* (b) *Ficus religiosa*
   (c) *Annona squimosa* (d) *Tamarindus indica*
14. The *Cucurbita maxima* is a
   (a) Monoecious and dicot plant
   (b) Monoecious and monocot plant
   (c) Dioecious and dicot plant
   (d) None of these
15. The type of fruit occur in *Luffa cylindrica* is a
   (a) Drupe (b) Capsule
   (c) Legume (d) Pepo
16. The flowers without petiole termed as
   (a) Sessile (b) Stalked
   (c) Petiolate (d) Androgynous
17. The ovules are attached to ovary wall with the help of
   (a) Placenta (b) Gynophore
   (c) Receptacle (d) None of these
18. The roots of *Momordica charantia* appear like a chain of beads which is described as
   (a) Moniliform (b) Scalariform
   (c) Polyads (d) None of these
19. The *Coriandrum sativum* is member of family
   (a) Euphorbiaceae (b) Solanaceae
   (c) Solanaceae (d) Apiaceae

20. Which of the following is a cultivated plant?
(a) *Cucumis sativus* (b) *Tephrosia purpurea*
(c) *Cassia tora* (d) None of these
21. A cremocarp type of fruit occur in
(a) *Coriandrum sativum* (b) *Cassia tora*
(c) *Cucumis sativus* (d) *Terminalia chebula*
22. Which type of inflorescence occur in *Foeniculum vulgare*
(a) Recemose (b) Cymose
(c) Compound umbel (d) None of these
23. A disc like stylopodium occur at the base of the style in
(a) *Foeniculum vulgare* (b) *Allium*
(c) *Cassia tora* (d) *Aegle*
24. Which of the following is a ornamental plant
(a) *Coriandrum sativum* (b) *Ixora paviflora*
(c) *Cassia angustifolia* (d) None of these
25. The family of *Eclipta alba* is
(a) Compositae (b) Malvaceae
(c) Malvaceae (d) Asclepidiaceace
26. Botanical name of sunflower is
(a) *Helianthus annuus* (b) *Withania somnifera*
(c) *Catharanthus roseus* (d) *Annona squimosa*
27. Presence of ray and disc florets is a characteristic feature of family
(a) Solanaceae (b) Mimosaceae
(c) Meliaceae (d) Compositae
28. Ray floret are the
(a) Male flowers (b) Both a and b
(c) Female flower (d) None of these
29. The involucres of bract is a characteristic feature of family
(a) Caesalpinaceae (b) Compositae
(c) Malvaceae (d) Papaveraceae
30. Which plant consists of decumbent type of stem?
(a) *Tridax procumbence* (b) *Rosa indica*
(c) *Helianthus annuus* (d) None of these
31. The family of *Manikara zapota* is
(a) Anacardiaceae (b) Magnoliaceae
(c) Sapotaceae (d) None of these

32. The fruit of *Manikara zapota* is a
    (a) Fleshy berry (b) Capsule
    (c) Nut (d) Drupe
33. The *Madhuca india* is a mesophyte occur in
    (a) Deciduous forest (b) Alpine forest
    (c) Evergreen forest (d) None of these
34. The botanical name of Sadabahar is
    (a) *Nerium indicum* (b) *Caesalpinia pulcherima*
    (c) *Vinca rosea* (d) None of these
35. Which of the following require dry soil for growth?
    (a) Calotropis gigantea (b) *Saccharum officinarum*
    (c) *Zingiber officinale* (d) None of these
36. The presence of a pair of caudicle (pollinium) is a characteristics feature of
    (a) *Calotropis gigantea* (b) *Mimosa pudica*
    (c) *Cassia angustifolia* (d) *Acacia nilotica*
37. Which of the following is an ornamental climbing shrub?
    (a) *Catharanthus roseus* (b) *Curcuma longa*
    (c) *Cryptostegia grandiflora* (d) None of these
38. The family of *Ipomoea palmata* is
    (a) Convolvulaceae (b) Cucurbitaceae
    (c) Asclepiadaceace (d) None of these
39. The leaves are absent in
    (a) *Cuscuta reflexa* (b) *Vinca rosea*
    (c) *Alstonia scholaria* (d) None of these
40. The roots are absent but haustoria are present in plant like
    (a) Asparagus (b) Curcuma
    (c) *Ipomoea* (d) *Cuscuta*
41. Which of the following in wild plant growing on waste land?
    (a) *Solanum nigrum* (b) *Helianthus annuus*
    (c) Curcuma longa (d) None of these
42. The thorns on the leaf occur in
    (a) *Solanum tuberosum* (b) *Raphanus sativus*
    (c) *Solanum nigrum* (d) *Daucus carota*
43. Family of *Withania somnifera* is
    (a) Solanaceae (b) Malvaceae
    (c) Convolvulaceae (d) None of these

44. Which is the plant used as medicine
    (a) *Withania somnifera* (b) *Solanum tuberosum*
    (c) *Solanum melongiana* (d) None of these
45. Which plant grow in wet or marshy places
    (a) *Alstonia scolaris* (b) *Mangifera indica*
    (c) *Annona squimosa* (d) *Bacopa monnieri*
46. The persistent style occurs in
    (a) *Bacopa monnieri* (b) *Annona squimosa*
    (c) *Cassia tora* (d) None of these
47. Family of *Bacopa monnieri* is
    (a) Annonaceae (b) Myrtaceae
    (c) Scrophulariaceae (d) Anacardiaceae
48. The *Justicia adhatoda* is a member of family
    (a) Acanthaceae (b) Solanaceae
    (c) Papilionaceae (d) Mimosaceae
49. The *Justicia adhatoda* is a
    (a) Perennial shrub (b) Climber
    (c) Annual herb (d) Annual Shrub
50. The best wood yielding plant is
    (a) *Cassia angustifolia* (b) *Annona squimosa*
    (c) *Tectona grandis* (d) None of these
51. The *Vitex nigundo* is a member of family
    (a) Verbenaceae (b) Myrtaceae
    (c) Apocynaceae (d) None of these
52. The cymose panicle type of inflorescence occur in
    (a) *Vitex nigundo* (b) *Mentha piperata*
    (c) *Daccus carota* (d) *Delonix regia*
53. A carcerulus type of fruit occur in
    (a) *Mimosa pudica* (b) *Coriander sativum*
    (c) *Ocimum sanctum* (d) None of these
54. The gland dotted aromatic leaves occur in
    (a) *Ocimum sanctum* (b) Sugarcane
    (c) Jowar (d) All of these
55. Verticelaster type of inflorescence in characteristic features of family
    (a) Acanthaceae (b) Apiaceae
    (c) Solanaceae (d) Labiatae

56. Which of the following represents most of the characteristic features of a particular plant?
(a) Floral formula and floral diagram
(b) Androecium and gynoecium
(c) Calyx and corolla
(d) None of these

57. Which of the following is the member of family Amaranthaceae?
(a) *Achyranthes aspera* (b) *Melia azadiracta*
(c) *Ipomoea palmata* (d) *Azadiracta indica*

58. The persistent perianth and spiny bracteoles occur in
(a) *Mimosa pudica* (b) *Achyranthes aspera*
(c) *Melia azadiracta* (d) None of these

59. Which of the following angiosperm used as vegetable
(a) *Amaranthus spinosus* (b) *Curcuma longa*
(c) *Annona squemosa* (d) None of these

60. The tapels are present in
(a) *Chenopodium album* (b) China rose
(c) *Mirabilis jalapa* (d) None of these

61. The plant *Euphorbia hirta* is a
(a) Dioecious (b) Both a and b
(c) Monoecious (d) None of these

62. Which term is used for collection of dried and pressed plants?
(a) Museum specimen (b) Herbarium
(c) Preservation (d) None of these

63. Herbaria are generally associated with
(a) DST
(b) ICRISAT
(c) CSIR
(d) Educational Research Organization

64. Conservatory material & data of plants is also termed as
(a) Museum specimen (b) Transparency
(c) Herbarium (d) None of these

65. A three coccoid schizocarpic capsule occur in
(a) *Ricinus communis* (b) *Hibiscus rosa-sinensis*
(c) *Cucumis sativus* (d) None of these

66. Presence of milk latex in the characteristic feature of family
(a) Nyctaginaceae (b) Annonaceae
(c) Caesalpinaceae (d) Euphorbiaceae

67. The family of *Ficus glomarata* is
    (a) Moraceae (b) Papilionaceae
    (c) Caesalpinaceae (d) Anacardiaceae
68. The fruit of which plant are edible
    (a) *Ficus glomarata* (b) *Ricinus communis*
    (c) *Gossipium herbacium* (d) None of these
69. The *Phoenix* is a member of family
    (a) Orchidaceae (b) Palmae
    (c) Scitaminae (d) None of these
70. Which of the following angiosperm possesses prominent leaf bases on stem
    (a) *Cocos nucifera* (b) *Ricinus communis*
    (c) *Jatropha curcus* (d) *None of these*
71. A fibrous drup occur in
    (a) *Tectona grandis* (b) *Ricinus communis*
    (c) *Cocos nucifera* (d) None of these
72. A aromatic herb perennating trough underground rhizome is
    (a) *Zingiber officinale* (b) *Raphanus sativus*
    (c) *Daccus carrota* (d) None of these
73. Which of the following plant grow in canal banks?
    (a) *Zeuxine sulcata* (b) *Alocasia indica*
    (c) *Vanda roxburghii* (d) None of these
74. Which of the following in an orchid?
    (a) *Pistia stratiotes* (b) *Vanda roxburghii*
    (c) *Allium cepa* (d) *None of these*
75. Which is the member of family Liliaceae?
    (a) *Asparagus officinalis* (b) *Terminalia chebula*
    (c) *Cajanus cajan* (d) *Tamarindus indica*
76. The rhizome of which plant are edible
    (a) *Alocasia indica* (b) *Pistia stratiotes*
    (c) *Vanda roxburghii* (d) *None of these*
77. The family of *Alocasia indica* is
    (a) Apocynaceae (b) Graminae
    (c) Palmae (d) Araceae
78. Which of the following is floating stolon bearing herb?
    (a) *Pistia stratiotes* (b) *Alocasia indica*
    (c) *Vanda roxburghii* (d) None of these

79. The wheat (*Triticum aestivum*) is the member of family
    (a) Malvaceae (b) Araceae
    (c) Asclepidiaceace (d) Poaceae
80. The inflorescence of wheat plant is
    (a) Spike (b) Cymose
    (c) Recemose (d) None of these
81. The *Zea mays* is a
    (a) Spice (b) Pulse
    (c) Cereal (d) Aromatic plant
82. Who is the Father of Botany?
    (a) Theophrastus (b) Darwin
    (c) Lamarck (d) None of these
83. The pioneer to distinguish non-flowering and seed plants is
    (a) Caesalpino (b) Linnaeus
    (c) John Ray (d) None of these
84. Anthophyta is the division of
    (a) All angiosperms (b) Pteridophyta
    (c) Gymnosperms (d) Bryophyta
85. Oswald Tippo classified angiosperm under the phylum
    (a) Tracheophyta (b) Gametophyte
    (c) Spermophyta (d) None of these
86. The artificial system of plants classification is firstly given by
    (a) Linnaeus (b) Gaspard Bauhin
    (c) Theophrastus (d) None of these
87. The another taxonomist proposed artificial system of plants classification was
    (a) Linnaeus (b) Hutchinson
    (c) Takhtajan (d) None if these
88. Who has firstly considered features of vascular tissue for classification of plants?
    (a) Bentham and Hooker (b) Hutchinson
    (c) A.P. de Candolle (d) None of these
89. Bentham and Hooker has given the classification of plants which is called as
    (a) Natural (b) Phylogenetic
    (c) Artificial (d) None of these
90. The book Plantarum was authorized by
    (a) Bentham and Hooker (b) Linnaeus
    (c) A.P. de Candolle (d) Hutchinson

91. Who has placed angiosperms between dicot and monocot?
    (a) John Ray (b) Bentham and Hooker
    (c) Theophrastus (d) None of these
92. The Bentham and Hookers system of classification is a
    (a) Natural (b) Phylogenetic
    (c) Artificial (d) None of these
93. Which is the non-Phyllogenetic system of classification?
    (a) Pre-Darwinian system (b) Both a and b
    (c) Post Darwinian (d) None of these
94. Who is the first to coin the term taxonomy
    (a) de Candolle (1813) (b) Takhtajan
    (c) Bentham & Hooker (d) Linnaeus
95. The nomenclature of plants is regulated by
    (a) NBRI (b) ICBN
    (c) IUCN (d) None of these
96. The phylogenetic classification of plants given by
    (a) Adolf Engler (b) de Candolle
    (c) Linnaeus (d) None of these
97. Cladistic and Patristic are the terms used to express affinities in
    (a) Phylogenetic contest (b) Artificial
    (c) Natural (d) None of these
98. Which of the classification is based on gross morphological characters of plants and extensive herbarium?
    (a) Omega taxonomy (b) Lambda taxonomy
    (c) Beta taxonomy (d) Alpha taxonomy
99. The term alpha taxonomy is coined by
    (a) William Bertram Turrill (1942) (b) Hutchinson
    (c) John Heywood (d) None of these
100. Which of the term designated to be related to modern taxonomy?
    (a) Omega taxonomy (b) Beta taxonomy
    (c) Alpha taxonomy (d) Lambda taxonomy

Answer key: TAXONOMY - VII

1. (a) 2. (d) 3. (a) 4. (a) 5. (a) 6. (b) 7. (a) 8. (a) 9. (d) 10. (a) 11. (a) 12. (d) 13. (a) 14. (a) 15. (d) 16. (a) 17. (a) 18. (a) 19. (d) 20. (a) 21. (a) 22. (c) 23. (a) 24. (b) 25. (a) 26. (a) 27. (d) 28. (a) 29. (b) 30. (a) 31. (c) 32. (a) 33. (a) 34. (c) 35. (a) 36. (a) 37. (c) 38. (a) 39. (a) 40. (d) 41. (a) 42. (c) 43. (a) 44. (a) 45. (d) 46. (a) 47. (c) 48. (a) 49. (a) 50. (c) 51. (a) 52. (a)

53. (c) 54. (a) 55. (d) 56. (a) 57. (a) 58. (c) 59. (a) 60. (a) 61. (c) 62. (c) 63. (d) 64. (c) 65. (a) 66. (d) 67. (a) 68. (a) 69. (b) 70. (a) 71. (c) 72. (a) 73. (a) 74. (b) 75. (a) 76. (a) 77. (d) 78. (b) 79. (d) 80. (a) 81. (c) 82. (a) 83. (c) 84. (a) 85. (a) 86. (c) 87. (a) 88. (c) 89. (a) 90 (a) 91. (b) 92. (a) 93. (a) 94. (a) 95. (b) 96. (a) 97. (a) 98. (d) 99. (a) 100. (a)

TAXONOMY - VIII

1. The branch of taxonomy where classification of plant kingdom is made on the basis of phylogenetic relationships using numerical data.
   (a) Cytotexonomy (b) Chemotaxonomy
   (c) Numerical taxonomy (d) None of these
2. Which is the basic unit of taxonomic works?
   (a) Taxa (b) Family
   (c) Genus (d) Species
3. A group of plants with common evolutionary origin but without genetic mixing termed as
   (a) Cenospecies (b) Both a and b
   (c) Sub. Species (d) None of these
4. A basic bio-systematic unit is known as
   (a) Prototype (b) Ecotype
   (c) Holotype (d) None of these
5. The study deals with every natural group of plants in classification has an invariant, generalized patterns is term as
   (a) Archetype (b) Holotype
   (c) Ecotype (d) None of these
6. Which one is the analytical device used for the determination of the names of the plants included in it termed as
   (a) Yoked key (b) Bracketed key
   (c) Indented key (d) None of these
7. Which device is used to identify unknown plants?
   (a) Indented key or Yoked key (b) Both of these
   (c) Bracketed key (d) None of these
8. How many plants were described by Theophrastus (370-285 BC) in his book Historia Plantarum?
   (a) 480 (b) 3000
   (c) 2000 (d) 358
9. Who is the first to find differences between monocot and dicot?
   (a) Albert Magnus (1193-1280) (b) Cisalpino
   (c) Tippo (d) None of these

10. Who is first to note concept of superior of inferior condition of ovary
    (a) Oswald Tippo (1942) (b) Both a and b
    (c) Andrea Cisalpino (1519-1603) (d) None of these
11. John Roy (1625-1705 AD) wrote a book in three volumes is
    (a) Historia Plantarum (b) Species plantarum
    (c) Genera plantarum (d) None of these
12. The genera Plantarum and classes Plantarum of Linnaeus appears in
    (a) 1737 & 1738 respectively (b) 1780
    (c) 1853 and 1838 (d) None of these
13. The book Species Plantarum of Linnaeus was published in
    (a) 1755 (b) 1853
    (c) 1653 (d) 1753
14. Who gave an artificial key for identifying plants?
    (a) J.B. Lamarck (1744-1829) (b) Albert Magnus (1193-1280)
    (c) Tippo (d) Cisalpino
15. Who is the first author of genera Plantarum?
    (a) Antoine de Jassieu (1686-1758) J.B.
    (b) Lamarck (1744-1829)
    (c) Cisalpino
    (d) None of these
16. Who has used the same title "Genera Plantarum" for his book?
    (a) Stephan Endlicher (1805-1849)
    (b) Gaspard Bauhin (1560-16-24)
    (c) Carl Linnaeus
    (d) None of these
17. Bentham and hooker published the book of same title Genera Plantarum in Latin
    (a) 1867-1893 (b) 1862-1883
    (c) 1823-1837 (d) None of these
18. Bentham and hooker divided dicot into
    (a) Polypetalae, Gamopetalae and Monochlamydeae
    (b) Polypetalae and Gamopetalae
    (c) Polypetalae and Monochlamydeae
    (d) Gamopetalae and Monochlamydeae
19. Who kept gymnosperms between Dicotyledons and monocotyledons?
    (a) Bentham and Hooker (b) A.P. Candolle
    (c) Hutchinson (d) Takhtajan

20. Darwin in 1859 published a book
    (a) Origin of plants (b) Origin of genus
    (c) Origin of species (d) None of these
21. The classification of plants proposed by Darwin in 1859 is a
    (a) Natural (b) Phylogenetic system
    (c) Artificial (d) None of these
22. A German botanist August Wilhem Eichler (1839-1887) he divided whole plant kingdom into
    (a) Cryptogamae and Phanerogamae
    (b) Sporophyte and gametophytic
    (c) Mono and dicotyledonous
    (d) None of these
23. Who published a 20 volume work entitled 'Die Naturlichen Pflanzenfamilien (1887-1915)
    (a) Adolph Engler & A.E Prantle (b) John Hutchinson
    (c) Bentham and hooker (d) V.N. Naik
24. Adolph Engler (1944-1930) considered
    (a) Monocots as more advanced
    (b) Dicotyledons as more primitive than Monocotyledons
    (c) Monocots as more primitive than Dicotyledons
    (d) None of these
25. Charles E. Bessey (1844-1915) proposed system of classification which is
    (a) Phyllogenetic (b) Natural
    (c) Artificial (d) None of these
26. Charles Edwin Bessey regarded that the origin of angiosperm from
    (a) Gymnosperms like Bennettitales (b) Bryophyta
    (c) Pteridophytes (d) Algae
27. Bessey considered the flowering plants to have originated from
    (a) Gnetalian group (b) Pentoxylales
    (c) Strobiliferous cycads (d) None of these
28. John Hutchinson (1884-1972) British botanist, proposed a system of classification of plants which was based on
    (a) Bentham & Hooker (b) Carl Linnaeus
    (c) Augustin Pyramus de Candolle (d) None of these
29. John Hutchinson in 1926 published first volume entitled the families of flowering plants consists of
    (a) Bryophyte (b) Gymnosperms
    (c) Monocotyledon (d) Dicotyledons

30. John Hutchinson British taxonomist published second volume entitled the families of flowering plant consists of
    (a) Monocotyledon plants (b) Pteridophytes
    (c) Dicotyledons (d) None of these
31. The third edition of john Hutchinson British taxonomist entitled the families of flowering plants appeared in
    (a) 1977 (b) 1968
    (c) 1963 (d) 1973
32. Who considered that the dicot are primitive and monocots are advanced
    (a) Hutchinson in 1959 (b) Engler and Prantle
    (c) Bentham and Hooker (d) None of these
33. Which of the order was primitive according to Bentham and Hooker?
    (a) Rosales (b) Ranales
    (c) Malvales (d) None of these
34. Which classification of flowering plant contains principles of floral evolution?
    (a) Bentham & Hookers system (b) Hutchinson in 1959
    (c) Engler and Prantle (d) Takhtajan
35. According to Bentham and hooker, floral anatomy, wood anatomy as well as palynology confirms that the most primitive order is
    (a) Malvales (b) Rosales
    (c) Ranales (d) None of these
36. The dicotyledons are divided into 3 large groups i.e. Polypetalae, Gamopetalae and
    (a) Monochlamydeae (b) Tripetalae
    (c) Hexapetalae (d) None of these
37. In classification by Engler & Prantle (1887-1899) which group of plants placed before angiosperms
    (a) Gymnosperms (b) Bryophytes
    (c) Pteridophytes (d) None of these
38. Carolus Linnaeus named plants in
    (a) Greek language (b) English
    (c) Latin language (d) None of these
39. The name of the plant which is different in different states is termed as
    (a) Vernacular name (b) Both a and b
    (c) Scientific name (d) None of these
40. The rules of nomenclature of plants laid down by
    (a) 1853 (b) 1763
    (c) 1753 (d) None of these

41. The international rules of botanical nomenclature made in 1930 at
    (a) Cambridge (b) USA
    (c) Moscow (d) None of these
42. Which is the basic unit of taxonomy?
    (a) Order (b) Genus
    (c) Family (d) Species
43. Many species forms a group of individual which is called as
    (a) Population (b) Both a and b
    (c) Community (d) None of these
44. The experimental taxonomy is related with study of species such as morphological, cytological, genetical and ecological is termed as
    (a) Phytogeography (b) Biosystematics
    (c) Phytochemistry (d) None of these
45. Which of the following in the basic unit in biosystematics
    (a) Ecotype (b) Both a and b
    (c) Ecospecies (d) None of these
46. Linnaeus (1753) published his basic work in taxonomy in
    (a) The Species Plantarum (b) Both a and b
    (c) Genera Plantarum (d) None of these
47. Study related with the chemical description of plant taxon
    (a) Numerical taxonomy (b) Cladistics
    (c) Chemotaxonomy (d) None of these
48. A numerical evaluation of the similarity between groups of organisms and ordering of these groups into higher ranking taxon on the basis of similarities known as
    (a) Chemotaxonomy (b) Cladistics
    (c) Numerical taxonomy (d) None of these
49. The phenomenon of confinement of species, genera or other group to a small area beyond which their existence is not found in termed as
    (a) Endemism (b) Exotic
    (c) Local (d) None of these
50. The central national herbarium (herbarium of Indian botanic garden consists of 5 million plants which is present at
    (a) NBRI Lucknow (b) Kolkata, Hawrah
    (c) Lal Bagh Bangalore (d) None of these
51. Herbarium of Forest Research Institute Dehradun consists of
    (a) 100,000 plants (b) 200000 plants
    (c) 300,000 plants (d) None of these

52. Blatter Herbarium, St. Xaviers College, Fort, consists of 100,000 plants which is situated at
(a) Mumbai (b) Chennai
(c) Kolkata (d) Madras

53. World's No.1 herbarium center which consists of 6,000,000 plants is
(a) Royal Botanic Garden, Kew London
(b) University Botanical garden Moscow
(c) NBRI Lucknow
(d) IBG Hawrah

54. Which of the following is a polycarpic plant?
(a) Sorghum (b) Bamboo
(c) Pear (d) None of these

55. When a plant produce fruits only once in its life time is termed as
(a) Multicarpic (b) Monocarpic
(c) Polycarpic (d) None of these

56. Presence of tap root is characteristics feature of
(a) Gymnosperm (b) Bryophyte
(c) Pteridophytes (d) None of these

57. Maize produces fibrous roots which initiate from
(a) Middle node (b) Lower node
(c) Upper node (d) None of these

58. The roots develop from any part of plant except radical termed as
(a) Adventitious (b) Parasitic root
(c) Tap root (d) None of these

59. The prop roots are the
(a) Buttress root (b) Conical root
(c) Adventitious roots (d) None of these

60. The hanging roots of banyan tree are termed as
(a) food storage root (b) Parasitic root
(c) Adventitious roots (d) Prop roots

61. The roots originated from branches of Ficus bengalensis are
(a) Positively geotropic (b) Positively phototrophic
(c) Negatively geotropic (d) None of these

62. The food sucking roots found in
(a) Tectona (b) Mangroves
(c) Cuscuta (d) None of these

63. The roots which occur in Cuscuta are termed as
    (a) Parasitic root (b) Adventitious roots
    (c) Prop roots (d) Hanging root
64. The respiratory roots are occurs in
    (a) Adventitious root (b) Pnematophores
    (c) Prop roots (d) None of these
65. Which of the following produces Pnematophores?
    (a) Avicennia (b) Ficus
    (c) Cuscuta (d) None of these
66. The *Ipomoea batatas* is a
    (a) Underground stem (b) Rhizome
    (c) Underground root (d) Corm
67. Which part of sweet potato is edible?
    (a) Adventitious tuberous roots (b) Prop roots
    (c) Pnematophores (d) Adventitious roots
68. Which of the following is plant have climbing roots
    (a) Maize (b) *Amaranthus*
    (c) Betel (d) Fenugreek
69. In which plants epiphytic roots are found
    (a) Orchids (b) Ficus
    (c) Cuscuta (d) Rose
70. Which type of roots form velamen tissue?
    (a) Hanging root (b) Adventitious roots
    (c) Prop roots (d) Hanging root
71. The photosynthetic roots are found in
    (a) Taeniophyllum (b) Avicennia
    (c) Cuscuta (d) None of these
72. The stem of banana is a
    (a) True stem (b) Both a and b
    (c) False stem (d) None of these
73. The bud which gives rise to leafy shoot is termed as
    (a) Vegetative bud (b) both a and b
    (c) Axillary bud (d) None of these
74. The accessory buds develop at the side of
    (a) Radial bud (b) Axillary bud
    (c) Apical bud (d) None of these
75. The origin of branches of stem is
    (a) Exogenous (b) Mesogenous
    (c) Endogenous (d) None of these

76. The main reason of underground modification of stem is
    (a) Creeping (b) Procumbence
    (c) Perennation (d) None of these
77. Which of the following is characteristic feature of underground modified stem?
    (a) Nodes and internodes (b) Both a and b
    (c) Stolon (d) None of these
78. The underground swollen edible portion of onion is called as
    (a) Corm (b) Bulb
    (c) Underground rhizome (d) None of these
79. In which plant the stem performs the functions of food storage and perennation
    (a) Ginger (b) Radish
    (c) Carrot (d) None of these
80. The function of eyes of potato is
    (a) Avegetative propagation (b) Both a and b
    (c) Vegetative propagation (d) None of these
81. Which of the following in sub aerial modified stem?
    (a) Rhizome (b) Stolon
    (c) Corm (d) None of these
82. The corn is
    (a) An underground vertical stem (b) Rhizome
    (c) Bulb (d) None of these
83. Which plant propagates by offset is?
    (a) Coconut (b) Agave
    (c) Cuscuta (d) None of these
84. Why the ginger is called stem not a root because
    (a) It consists of nodes and internodes
    (b) It consists of chlorophyll
    (c) It consists of leaves
    (d) None of these
85. Why the thorn is called as modified branch
    (a) Because it originate from the axil of leaf
    (b) Woody
    (c) Hard like stem
    (d) None of these

86. The pickles which occur in rose are
(a) Endogenous in origin (b) Both a and b
(c) Exogenous in origin (d) None of these
87. In Opuntia the photosynthesis takes place in
(a) Phylloclade (b) Phyllosphere
(c) Phylloplane (d) None of these
88. Phylloclade is a
(a) Modified scale (b) Modified bract b.
(c) Modified root (d) Modified stem
89. The disc like stem occur in
(a) Onion (b) Maize
(c) Sunflower (d) None of these
90. Which of the following produces stolon?
(a) Onion (b) Ginger
(c) Ocimum (d) Mint
91. Which one is the example of phylloclade?
(a) Opuntia (b) Asparagus
(c) Cuscuta (d) Bamboo
92. The main function of leaf is
(a) Reproduction (b) Both a and b
(c) Photosynthesis (d) None of these
93. The petiole less leaf is termed as
(a) Sessile (b) Scaly leaf
(c) Petiolate (d) Succulent
94. The term vernation is used for
(a) Arrangement of leaves in bud (b) Arrangement of petals
(c) Arrangement of sepals (d) None of these
95. The leaf has parallel vernation in
(a) Santalum (b) Gram
(c) Caesalpinia (d) Grass
96. In which plant leaf lamina is highly reduced
(a) Halophyte (b) Mesophyte
(c) Hygrophyte (d) Xerophytes
97. Which plant store food in leaves?
(a) Ginger (b) Onion
(c) Carrot (d) None of these

98. The phyllotaxy is the
    (a) Arrangement of leaves in stem (b) Arrangement of petals
    (c) Arrangement of sepals (d) Arrangement of ovules
99. The mode of arrangement of leaves in bud is termed as
    (a) Pollination (b) Germination
    (c) Vernation (d) None of these
100. The margin of which plant is spiney
    (a) Withania (b) Citrus
    (c) Ficus (d) Aloe vera

Answer key: TAXONOMY - VIII

1. (c) 2. (d) 3. (a) 4. (b) 5. (a) 6. (b) 7. (a) 8. (a) 9. (a) 10. (c) 11. (a) 12. (a) 13. (d) 14. (a) 15. (a) 16. (a) 17. (b) 18. (a) 19. (a) 20. (c) 21. (b) 22. (a) 23. (a) 24. (c) 25. (a) 26. (a) 27. (c) 28. (a) 29. (d) 30. (a) 31. (d) 32. (a) 33. (b) 34. (a) 35. (c) 36. (a) 37. (a) 38. (c) 39. (a) 40. (c) 41. (a) 42. (d) 43. (a) 44. (b) 45. (a) 46. (a) 47. (c) 48. (c) 49. (a) 50. (b) 51. c), 52. a), 53. a), 54. c), 55. (b) 56. (a) 57. (b) 58. (a) 59. (c) 60. (d) 61. (a) 62. (c) 63. (a) 64. (b) 65. (a) 66. (c) 67. (a) 68. (c) 69. (a) 70. (a) 71. (a) 72. (c) 73. (a) 74. (b) 75. (a) 76. (c) 77. (a) 78. (b) 79. (a) 80. (c) 81. (b) 82. (a) 83. (b) 84. (a) 85. (a) 86. (c) 87. (a) 88. (d) 89. (a) 90. (d) 91. (a) 92. (c) 93. (a) 94. (a) 95. (d) 96. (d) 97. (b) 98. (a) 99. (c) 100. (d)

TAXONOMY-IX

1. In case of Nepenthes, the pitchers are developed from
    (a) Lamina (b) Veins
    (c) Midrib (d) None of these
2. Bipinnate leaf is characteristic feature of family
    (a) Mimosaceae (b) Meliaceae
    (c) Malvaceae (d) Acanthaceae
3. The simple leaf occur in
    (a) *Tamarind* (b) *Acacia*
    (c) *Annona* (d) *Caesalpinia*
4. The imparipinnate leaves occur in
    (a) Rose (b) Santalum
    (c) Tamarind (d) None of these
5. The adnate type of stipule occur in
    (a) Withania (b) Mentha
    (c) Neem (d) Rose

6. Which plant consists of interpetiolar stipule?
(a) Ixora (b) Nelumbo
(c) Rose (d) None of these
7. The onion bulb is a modified
(a) Stipule (b) Bract
(c) Leaf (d) Rhizome
8. The tendril of sweet pea is a modified
(a) Leaflet (c) Stem
(c) Petiole (d) None of these
9. The spine, thorns, pickles in plant function as
(a) Defensive organs (b) Both a and b
(c) Ornamental organ (d) None of these
10. The vegetative reproduction by bulbils takes place in
(a) Butea (b) Tectona
(c) Mimosa (d) Agave
11. The hooks present in Artabotrys is a modified
(a) Inflorescence axis (b) Root
(c) Leaf (d) Bract
12. The black pepper plant is a
(a) Creeper (b) Climber
(c) Runner (d) None of these
13. The function of leaf veins is
(a) Transport of water, minerals (b) Transpiration
(c) Photosynthesis (d) None of these
14. In Ficus, the bud scales represent
(a) Trichomes (b) Both a and b
(c) Stipules (d) None of these
15. The tendrillar petiole occur in
(a) Clematis (b) Mangifera
(c) Gossipium (d) None of these
16. Folding of young leaves itself in the bud is called
(a) Ptyxis (b) Epicalyx
(c) Scaly leaf (d) Calyx
17. The stalk of leaflet is known as
(a) Androphore (b) Receptacle
(c) Petiole (d) Petiolule

18. The tubular hollow long petioles occur in
    (a) *Carica papaya* (b) *Ficus religiosa*
    (c) *Delonix regia* (d) None of these
19. The winged petiole occurs in
    (a) Asparagus (b) Papaya
    (c) Banana (d) Citrus
20. The time taken for the development of two adjacent leaves is called
    (a) Plastochron Index (b) Phytochron
    (c) Cystochrone (d) None of these
21. Which of the following helps in counting age of plants?
    (a) Phytochron (b) Plastochron Index
    (c) Cystochrone (d) None of these
22. Which one produces a compound leaf but looks like simple leaf?
    (a) Citrus (b) Solanum
    (c) Ficus (d) None of these
23. The root develops from
    (a) Radical (b) Node
    (c) Stem (d) None of these
24. The stem develops from
    (a) Radical (b) Node
    (c) Plumule (d) None of these
25. The rhizome differs from root because it consists of
    (a) Scale leaves and buds (b) Both a and b
    (c) Absence of root leaves (d) None of these
26. Which of the following is a root?
    (a) Brinjal (b) Potato
    (c) Ginger (d) Carrot
27. The function of adventitious roots of Pistia is
    (a) Balancing the plant (b) Both a and b
    (c) Photosynthesis (d) None of these
28. The garlic and onion bulbs consists of
    (a) Greatly reduced stem (b) Elongated stem
    (c) Well developed stem (d) None of these
29. The potatoes are borne as
    (a) Twinners (b) Runner
    (c) Creeper (d) Stolons

30. When the petiole is modified to a green leafy structure it is known as
    (a) Phyllode (b) Both a and b
    (c) Cladode (d) None of these
31. The spines of citrus are morphologically
    (a) Terminal leaf of a terminal branch (b) Stipule of lower branch
    (c) Axillary (d) None of these
32. The leaf lamina of Calotropis is
    (a) Oblique (b) Obtuse
    (c) Auricular (d) None of these
33. Which of the following in the non-carnivorous pitcher plant
    (a) *Dischida* (b) *Drocera*
    (c) *Nepenthes* (d) *Dionaea*
34. The petiole modified into tendrils are found in
    (a) *Solanum* (c) *Ipomea*
    (b) Clematis (d) None of these
35. The name of taxon is permanently attached with
    (a) Holotype (b) Phylum
    (c) Order (d) Heterotype
36. In which year Paris code was formulated
    (a) 1944 (b) 1960
    (c) 1958 (d) 1956
37. In which year Vienna code is formulated
    (a) 2006 (b) 1920
    (c) 2005 (d) 2010
38. As per which ICN rule number the specific name should always follows the generic name
    (a) Rule no. 285 (b) Rule no. 286
    (c) Rule no. 287 (d) Rule any 288
39. As per which ICN rule number the specific name must distinguish a plant from all its relatives
    (a) Rule no. 254 (b) Rule no. 255
    (c) Rule no. 258 (d) Rule no. 257
40. Which of the following in a group in which every member shares a common ancestor
    (a) Clade (b) Phyllod
    (c) Phylloclade (d) None of these
41. Which of the following occurs in family Rannunculaceace?
    (a) Umbelliferae (b) Verticelaster
    (c) Cymose (d) None of these

42. How many sepals occur in family Rannunculaceace?
(a) 3 (b) 6
(c) 4 (d) 5
43. Which type of fruit occur in family rannunculaceace
(a) Etaerio (b) Drupe
(c) Capsule (d) None of these
44. How many sepals occur in family brassicaceace?
(a) 7 (b) 5
(c) 6 (d) 4
45. Which type of corolla occur in family brassicaceace
(a) Cruciferous (b) Tubular
(c) Papilionacious (d) None of these
46. Which type of fruit occur in family brassicaceace
(a) Serosis (b) Legume
(c) Siliqua (d) Drupe
47. How many carpels occur in family fabaeceae?
(a) 5 (b) 3
(c) 4 (d) 2
48. How many sepals occurs in flower of family fabaeceae
(a) 5 (b) 3
(c) 4 (d) 2
49. Which type of food occur in family Papilionaceae (fabaeceae)
(a) Legume (b) Drup
(c) Aggregate (d) Berry
50. How many perianth occur in the flower of family euphorbiaceae
(a) 4 (b) 5
(c) 8 (d) 7
51. Taxonomically fruit of family euphorbiaceae is described as
(a) Hesperidium (b) Berry
(c) Pome (d) Regma
52. Which is the alternative term used for family commelinaceae?
(a) Spiderwort (b) Moss family
(c) Small family (d) Aquatic family
53. Which is the family of *Foeniculum vulgarae?*
(a) Solanaceae (b) Papilionaceae
(c) Euphorbiaceae (d) Apiaceae

54. Which epithet is used to indicate two authors of any new publication of new species?
    (a) in (b) ex
    (c) et (d) emend
55. The Binomials with identical genus name and specific epithet are called
    (a) Tautonym (b) Variety
    (c) Local name (d) Varietal name
56. The comprehensive information of the specific genus or family is termed as
    (a) Life cycle (b) Monograph
    (c) Life history (d) None of these
57. Which one is the demerit of Englar and Prantle classification of plant?
    (a) Dicotyledons are placed after monocotyledon
    (b) Monocotyledons are placed after dicotyledons
    (c) Both a and b
    (d) None of these
58. The numerical taxonomy is developed by
    (a) Darwin (b) Englar
    (c) Hutchinson (d) Sneath and Sokal
59. Who discovered the concept of double fertilization and triple fusion?
    (a) Nawaschin and Guignard (b) Linnaeus
    (c) Robert Morison (d) John Roy
60. Which is the male gametophyte of angiosperms?
    (a) Tapetum (b) Macrospores
    (c) Venter (d) Microspore
61. Penetration of pollen grains tube trough micropile is termed as
    (a) Apogamy (b) Progray
    (c) Syngamy (d) None of these
62. Who discovered concept of cellular totipotency
    (a) F.C. Steward (b) Carolus Linnaeus
    (c) Camerarius (d) de Candolle
63. The pollen grains occurs only in
    (a) Gymnosperms & angiosperms
    (b) Bryophytes & Pteridophytes
    (c) Virus & bacteria
    (d) Fungi & algae

64. Concept of pollination in absent in
    (a) Angiosperms (b) Gymnosperms
    (c) Bryophytes (d) None of these
65. In which plant pollination does not occurs
    (a) Psilotum (b) Pinus
    (c) Gnetum (d) Melia
66. The embryo sac occurs in
    (a) Ovule (b) Mesoderm
    (c) Endoderm (d) None of these
67. Which is concern with family Fabaeceae (Papilionaceae?)
    (a) Tetradynamous (b) Didelphous
    (c) Epistemanous (d) None of these
68. In which of the following, a group of plants can breed freely themselves
    (a) Taxa (b) Family
    (c) Order (d) Species
69. Who is pioneer to propose five kingdom arrangements to organism?
    (a) Whittaker (b) Robert Brown
    (c) Hooker (d) Henri Baillon
70. Which one consists of large number of organisms?
    (a) Family (b) Genus
    (c) Order (d) Class
71. Which is the basic unit of plant taxonomy?
    (a) Kingdom (b) Phylum
    (c) Species (d) Family
72. Which is the first step of study of taxonomy?
    (a) Preservation (b) Systmatics
    (c) Identification (d) Classification
73. The Botanical nomenclature designate
    (a) Order & genus (b) Order & family
    (c) Species (d) Genus & Species
74. Which of the following is correct taxonomic study?
    (a) Division –class-order-family-genus-species
    (b) Class-order-div-family-species
    (c) Genus –class-division-family-order
    (d) Family-order-genus- division-class
75. Who is pioneer to propose term Systematics?
    (a) Bailey (b) Heywood
    (c) Arthur Cronguist (d) John Ray

76. On which of the following modern classification is based on
(a) Anatomy (b) General characters
(c) Vegetative structure (d) None of these
77. What is taxon?
(a) An order
(b) A family
(c) A variety
(d) A taxonomic category of any rank
78. The writer of system of nature is
(a) Carl Linnaeus (b) Hutchinson
(c) Darwin (d) Theophrastus
79. Which term is used for classification which is based on morphological characters of plants?
(a) Simple (b) Natural
(c) Bio chemical (d) Both a & d
80. Which one possesses suckers?
(a) Tulip (b) Onion
(c) Carrot (d) Mint
81. Which consists of embryo
(a) Fruit (b) Immature plant
(c) Seeds (d) None of these
82. Which part of the plant attract agents of pollination
(a) Sepals (b) Anther
(c) Petals (d) stigma
83. From which of the following shoot of plants develops
(a) Radical (b) Epicotyls
(c) Hypocotyl (d) Plumule
84. Which is the second whorl of flower?
(a) Gynoecium (b) Androecium
(c) Calyx (d) Corolla
85. Which is the inner most whorl of flower
(a) Gynoecium (b) Androecium
(c) Calyx (d) Corolla
86. The fiber yielding cotton ball is a
(a) Plumed seed (b) Plumed fruit
(c) Soft seed (d) Pome fruit

87. The parachute like structure developed from plumed fruits is
    (a) Scale (b) Tendril
    (c) Glumes (d) Pappus
88. Which one is the winged seed?
    (a) Tacoma (b) Cactus
    (c) Daccus (d) Coriander
89. The winged fruits occurred in
    (a) Groundnut (b) Bamboo
    (c) Tectona (d) Samara
90. The light weighted, small seeds dispersed by
    (a) Wind (b) Human
    (c) Animals (d) None of these
91. In which of the following vegetative reproduction occurs through leaf
    (a) *Bryophyllum* (b) *Pisum*
    (c) *Sugarcane* (d) *Senna*
92. In which plant vegetative reproduction takes through root
    (a) Tomato (b) Tapioca
    (c) Sweet potato (d) None of these
93. Which term is used for food storing roots?
    (a) Tuberous root (b) Hanging root
    (c) Fibrous root (d) Stilt root
94. In which vegetative reproduction takes place by stems
    (a) Potato (b) Coriander
    (c) Citrus (d) All of these
95. Which tissue responsible for transportation of water in plants
    (a) Chlorenchyma (b) Collenchymas
    (c) Arenchyma (d) Vascular tissue
96. Which term is used for plant which has true roots, stems and leaves?
    (a) Thallophytes (b) Vascular plants
    (c) Bryophytes (d) None of these
97. Which one attracts insects for pollination?
    (a) Petals (b) Sepals
    (c) Epicalyx (d) Stipel
98. Which one is the example of non vascular plants?
    (a) *Daccus* (b) *Dalbergia*
    (c) Marchantia (d) *Cajanus*

99. Which term in used for waxy covering of leaf of land plant
    (a) Cuticle (b) Epidermis
    (c) Hypodermis (d) Endodermis
100. What is the function of xylem?
    (a) Transport food from leaves
    (b) Transport water & minerals
    (c) Exchange carbon dioxide with the atmosphere
    (d) All of these
101. Which code is formulated during 18th International Botanical Congress, Australia in July 2011
    (a) Melbourn code 2011 (b) Hutchinson 1959
    (c) S. L. Tandon (1970) (d) J. Cullen 1968

Answer key: TAXONOMY - IX

1. (a) 2. (a) 3. (c) 4. (a) 5. (d) 6. (a) 7. (c) 8. (a) 9. (a) 10. (d) 11. (a) 12. (b) 13. (a) 14. (c) 15. (a) 16. (a) 17. (d) 18. (a) 19. (d) 20. (a) 21. (b) 22. (a) 23. (a) 24. (c) 25. (a) 26. (d) 27. (a) 28. (a) 29. (d) 30. (a) 31. (a) 32. (c) 33. (a) 34. (b) 35. (a) 36. (d) 37. (b) 38. (a) 39. (d) 40. (a) 41. (c) 42. (d) 43. (a) 44. (d) 45. (a) 46. (c) 47. (d) 48. (a) 49. (a) 50. (b) 51. (d) 52. (a) 53. (d) 54. (c) 55. (a) 56. (b) 57. (a) 58. (d) 59. (a) 60. (d) 61. (b) 62. (a) 63. (a) 64. (c) 65. (a) 66. (a) 67. (b) 68. (d) 69. (a) 70. (d) 71. (c) 72. (c) 73. (d) 74. (a) 75. (d) 76. (a) 77. (d) 78. (a) 79. (b) 80. (d) 81. (c) 82. (c) 83. (d) 84. (d) 85. (a) 86. (b) 87. (d) 88. (a) 89. (d) 90. (a) 91. (a) 92. (b) 93. (a) 94. (a) 95. (d) 96. (b) 97. (a) 98. (c) 99. (a) 100. (b) 101. (a)

TAXONOMY - X

1. The scientific name of any plant consists of
    (a) Genus & species (b) Genus & variety
    (c) Species and variety (d) None of these
2. Members of which kingdom live in a unusual condition that is deep ocean trenches
    (a) Eubacteria (b) Thallophytes
    (c) Fungi (d) Archeobacteria
3. The two name naming system is described as
    (a) Binomial nomenclature (b) Plant systmatics
    (c) Taxonomy (d) None of these
4. Which one is the largest group of living things?
    (a) Domain (b) Kingdom
    (c) Phylum (d) Order

5. The term used for swollen part of pedicel is
(a) Stigma (b) Thalamus
(c) Pedicel (d) None of these
6. In phanerograms ovules bear on a cushion of tissue structure called
(a) Placenta (b) Receptacle
(c) Anther (d) Stigma
7. Monodelphous condition occurs in
(a) China rose (b) *Cajanus cajan*
(c) *Daccus carota* (d) None of these
8. When stamens attached to petals the phenomenon is termed as
(a) Imbricate (b) Epiphyllous
(c) Epipetalous (d) None of these
9. Epipetalous condition occur in
(a) Datura (b) Gram
(c) Carrot (d) None of these
10. Stigma is located at
(a) Below ovary (b) Tip of filament
(c) Base of ovary (d) Tip of style
11. Which of the following is characteristic feature of flowering plant?
(a) Fruits (b) Root hairs
(c) Seeds (d) Buds
12. Which term is used for the fruit developed without fertilization?
(a) Drupe (b) Pome fruit
(c) Schizocarp fruit (d) Parthenocarpic fruit
13. The outer most whorl of China rose is
(a) Epicalyx (b) Calyx
(c) Bracts (d) Sepals
14. A group of sepals of flower is termed as
(a) Calyx (b) Pedicel
(c) Androphore (d) Corolla
15. Which is the whorl situated inner to the calyx
(a) Corolla (b) Calyx
(c) Epicalyx (d) Perianth
16. Fern plants belongs to
(a) Pteridophytes (b) Bryophyte
(c) Gymnosperms (d) Angiosperms

17. Which of the following is a dye yielding plant?
    (a) Amla (b) Dalbergia
    (c) Carrot (d) Indigofera
18. Which of the following is a fodder yielding plant?
    (a) Sesbania (b) Azadiracta
    (c) Coriander (d) Mentha
19. Which family is called as potato family?
    (a) Nyctaginaceae (b) Solanaceae
    (c) Papilionaceae (d) Rutaceae
20. Term is used to describe flower with essentials & non essentials whorls is
    (a) Complete (b) Incomplete
    (c) Imperfect (d) None of these
21. A bisexual flower which never opens in its life span is termed as
    (a) Celistogamous (b) Unisexual
    (c) Gynandrous (d) None of these
22. In which of the following head inflorescence occurs
    (a) Rice (b) Maize
    (c) Sunflower (d) Jowar
23. Which term is used for flower which opens once in its life time?
    (a) Monocarpic (b) Polycarpic
    (c) Cliestorcarpic (d) Pericarpic
24. Which is the third whorl of a flower?
    (a) Petals (b) Sepals
    (c) Stamens (d) Style
25. Which one occurs in complete flower?
    (a) Calyx, corolla, androecium & gynoecium
    (b) Epicalyx, calyx, androecium & gynoecium
    (c) Calyx, bracts, androecium & gynoecium
    (d) Calyx, petiole, androecium & gynoecium
26. When calyx & corolla are similar it is called as
    (a) Corolla (b) Calyx
    (c) Perianth (d) Stamens
27. The scented nector secreting flower are mostly pollinated by
    (a) Insects (b) Wind
    (c) Animals (d) None of these
28. In which plant male & female flowers occur in the same plant
    (a) Hibiscus (b) Euphorbia
    (c) Pea (d) Pumpkin

29. When ovary is situated above all the whorls of the flower it is described as
    (a) Superior (b) Inferior
    (c) Semi inferior (d) Semi superior
30. Which is long form of sp.nov in plant taxonomy?
    (a) Specific nomenclature (b) Species novum
    (c) Species name (d) None of these
31. Which is the long form of ICNCP in plant systematic?
    (a) Internal code for nomenclature of cultivated plants
    (b) Intergeneric code for nomenclature of cultivated plants
    (c) International code for nomenclature of cultivated plants
    (d) None of these
32. Which are three parts of ICBN?
    (a) Principles, rules & recommendations
    (b) Principles, rare & recommendations
    (c) Practice, rules introductions and principles
    (d) Introduction, Principles & rules
33. What is the long form of ICBN
    (a) International Code of Botanical Nomenclature
    (b) International compulsory Botany nomenclature
    (c) International code of biological
    (d) None of these
34. Which is the following valid publication initial date?
    (a) 2nd may 1754 (b) 2nd may 1954
    (c) 1st may 1853 (d) 1st may 1753
35. Which is the basic unit of classification?
    (a) Species (b) Genus
    (c) Family (d) Phylum
36. Which suffix is used for denoting order of plant family?
    (a) als (b) ales
    (c) ceae (d) All are correct
37. Which suffix is used for denoting family?
    (a) aceae (b) caea
    (c) acaea (d) ales
38. Which of the epithets used in the Binomial nomenclature
    (a) Order name
    (b) Generic name & traditional name
    (c) Generic & specific name
    (d) None of these

39. The taxonomy of description & designation of species is termed as
(a) Alfa taxonomy (b) Plane taxonomy
(c) Simple taxonomy (d) Plant systematic
40. Which term is used for the name of plant accepted to the world and used internationally?
(a) Epithet (b) Generic name
(c) Vernacular name (d) Scientific name
41. A name with two epithets (one generic & another specific) is termed as
(a) Bionomial name (b) Biological name
(c) Plant name (d) Perfect name
42. Which is the alternative name for family compositae?
(a) Acanthaceae (b) Asclepidiaceace
(c) Solanaceae (d) Asteraceae
43. Alternative term for family umbelliferae
(a) Apiacece (b) Papilionaceae
(c) Caesalpinaceae (d) myrtaceae
44. The alternative term for family Papilionaceae
(a) Fabaceae (b) Annonaceae
(c) Solanaceae (d) Acanthaceae
45. The forest research institute Dehradun is established in the year
(a) 1817 (b) 1816
(c) 1812 (d) 1810
46. Total herbariums occurs at National Botanic Garden, Kolkata is
(a) 1,00,200 (b) 1,00,00
(c) 1,00,020 (d) 1,00,000
47. Which one is the world's important herbarium?
(a) New York botanical garden 7200000 USA
(b) Botanical garden 720000 UK
(c) National Botanic Garden, Darjeeling, India
(d) None of these
48. Who is the founder of largest & oldest plant museum in India?
(a) Psychopathological Society of India
(b) Asiatic Society of Bengal in Kolkata 1841
(c) Society of life Science
(d) None of these
49. Who is the founder of Asiatic Society of Bengal, Kolkata 1884?
(a) D.B.N. Chakraborthy (b) Dr. Deugeon
(c) Dr. Nathaniel Wallich (d) None of these

50. What is the long form of CNH
    (a) Central National Herbarium
    (b) Central Numbered Herbarium
    (c) Collection of new Herbarium
    (d) None of these
51. An institute for the preservation of those objects which best illustrate the phenomena of nature is termed as
    (a) Store house (b) Herbarium
    (c) Museum (d) Science lab
52. Which is the long form of FRI?
    (a) Forest Research Institute
    (b) Forest Reconstruction Institute
    (c) First Research Institute
    (d) None of these
53. The device used for plant press is made up of
    (a) Aluminum (b) Copper
    (c) Wood or iron (d) Plastic
54. Which term is used for collection of plant material after being dried?
    (a) Herbarium (b) Museum
    (c) Taxonomy (d) All of these
55. Who started Herbarium making
    (a) de Candole (b) Luca Ghini
    (c) Linnaeus (d) Theophrastus
56. Natural History Museum is situated as
    (a) London (b) USA
    (c) Canada (d) Germany
57. Which one is the standard size of herbarium?
    (a) 25.43 cm (b) 28.43 cm
    (c) 27.43 cm (d) 29.43cm
58. Which is the full form of DDT?
    (a) Dichloro Dipropyl Tricholoroethane
    (b) Dichloro Dimetnyl Tricholoroethane
    (c) Dichloro Diphenyl Tricholoroethane
    (d) Dichloro Diethyl Tricholoroethane
59. Secondary growth in plants occur by
    (a) Lateral meristems (b) Apical meristems
    (c) Epidermal cells (d) Hypodermis region

60. Total biogeographic zones in India are
   (a) 11 (b) 10
   (c) 12 (d) 14
61. How many types of forests occur in India?
   (a) 17 (b) 17
   (c) 16 (d) 20
62. Where is the location of great Indian Thar desert ?
   (a) Rajasthan (b) Maharashtra
   (c) Haryana (d) Uttar Pradesh
63. In India how much percentage of angiosperms flora is endemic
   (a) 27 (b) 28
   (c) 33 (d) 25
64. Which is the most common example of the in situ conversation?
   (a) Deciduous forests (b) Local gardens
   (c) Home gardens (d) National park
65. The location of sundarban is at
   (a) West Bengal (b)Tamilnadu
   (c) Kulu Manali (d) Masoori
66. Which is the smallest biosphere reserve?
   (a) Bangalore, Karnataka (b) Nanda devi, Utarakhand
   (c) Dibru-Saikhowa, Assam (d) Manas, Assam
67. Where is the head office of NBPGR
   (a) New Delhi (b) Calcutta
   (c) Mumbai (d) Bangalore
68. Core & buffer zones are important constituents of
   (a) Nilgiri forests (b) Grasslands
   (c) Deciduous forests (d) Biosphere reserve
69. Where is the location of Nanda Devi biosphere reverse?
   (a) Utarakhand (b) Rajasthan
   (c) Punjab (d) Bihar
70. Which is the long form of BSI?
   (a) Botanical screening of India
   (b) Biological Survey of India
   (c) Botanical Survey of India
   (d) Biological Survey of Indus River

71. Which is the long form of CBD
    (a) Convention on Biological Diversity
    (b) Convention on Botanical Diversity
    (c) Conservation of Biosphere Diversity
    (d) None of these
72. A variety of plant means
    (a) Lowest rank in taxon (b) Highest rank in taxon
    (c) Lowest rank of order (d) Lowest rank of family
73. Which is the following is a cup of tissue
    (a) Pericycle (b) Petiole
    (c) Hypodermis (d) Hypanthium
74. When floral parts connect to the main axis of the flower above the ovary it in termed as
    (a) Hypogynous ovary (b) Semi-inferior ovary
    (c) Superior ovary (d) Inferior ovary
75. When the flower part of ovary attached below the ovary it is termed as
    (a) Superior ovary (b) Epigynous ovary
    (c) Semi superior ovary (d) None of these
76. Which one is the dry fruit?
    (a) Peas (b) Hazelnuts
    (c) Mango (d) Guava
77. Which of the following g is a berry?
    (a) Squash (b) Mango
    (c) Pear (d) Pea pad
78. Fleshy simple fruit is
    (a) Annona (b) Ground nut
    (c) Avocado (d) None of these
79. Which one is characteristics feature of family mustard ?
    (a) Presence of pome type of fruit
    (b) Presence of Hesperidium type of fruit
    (c) Presence of berry type of fruit
    (d) Presence of silicle type of fruit
80. Which fruit are commonly called as stone fruits?
    (a) Drupe (b) Berry
    (c) Siliqua (d) Hypanthopodium
81. Which type of inflorescence consists of sessile flowers?
    (a) Spike (b) Cymose
    (c) Raceme (d) Verticelaster

82. Which is the family of *Albizzia lebbek*
(a) Rutaceae (b) Solanaceae
(c) Myrtaceae (d) Mimosaceae

83. Which one is planted as a air breaker?
(a) *Prosopis glandulosa* (b) *Catharanthus roseus*
(c) *Annona squimosa* (d) *Rosa sinensis*

84. Which is the family of pulses?
(a) Poaceae (b) Papilionaceae
(c) Asclepidiaceace (d) Caesalpinaceae

85. Which family is commonly called as the milk weed family?
(a) Asclepidiaceace (b) Asteraceae
(c) Annonaceae (d) Rutaceae

86. Translator mechanism is found in
(a) Solanaceae (b) Poaceae
(c) Asclepidiaceace (d) Myrtaceae

87. Descending imbricate form of corolla occurs in family
(a) Papilionaceae (b) Myrtaceae
(c) Asclepiadaceace (d) Nyctaginaceae

88. Botanical name of shisham is
(a) *Mentha piperata* (b) *Vitex nigundo*
(c) *Coriander sativum* (d) *Dalbergia sisso*

89. In which of the following gynostegium occurs
(a) Asclepidiaceace (b) Malvaceae
(c) Rutaceae (d) Moraceae

90. A two celled anther is termed as
(a) Dithecous (b) Monothecous
(c) Stamen (d) Filamentous

91. Structural modification of funiculus develops into a hook on which seeds rest in termed as
(a) Funicle (b) Junctor
(c) Jaculator (d) None of these

92. A zygomorphic, gamopetalous corolla with two lips is termed as
(a) Personate (b) Apocarpus
(c) Adnate (d) Cruciform

93. Jaculator occurs in family
(a) Chaenopodiaceae (b) Convolvulaceae
(c) Droseraceae (d) Acanthaceae

94. Which family is also termed as grass family?
    (a) Poaceae (b) Apocynaceace
    (c) Nymphaceae (d) Anacardiaceae
95. In poaceae perianth represented by 2/3 minute scales which is termed as
    (a) Scales (b) Lodicules
    (c) Jaculator (d) Culm
96. Which term is used for seed like fruit?
    (a) Caryopsis (b) Pepo
    (c) Samara (d) Pome
97. The tissue that store food outside the embryo is termed as
    (a) Endosperms (b) Tapetum
    (c) Periderm (d) Pith
98. Plants adopted for wind pollination are termed as
    (a) Cross pollination (b) Self pollination
    (c) Anemophilous pollination (d) None of these
99. Which is the fruit of family poaceae?
    (a) Caryopsis (b) Drupe
    (c) Sorosis (d) Compound berry
100. Botanical name of tomato is
    (a) *Artocarpus heterophyllus* (b) Lycopersicon esculentum
    (c) *Ficus bengalensis* (d) None of these

Answer key: TAXONOMY - X

1. (a) 2. (d) 3. (a) 4. (a) 5. (b) 6. (a) 7. (a) 8. (c) 9. (a) 10. (d) 11. (a) 12. (d) 13. (a) 14. (d) 15. (a) 16. (a) 17. (d) 18. (a) 19. (b) 20. (a) 21. (a) 22. (c) 23. (a) 24. (c) 25. (a) 26. (c) 27. (a) 28. (d) 29. (a) 30. (b) 31. (c) 32. (a) 33. (a) 34. (d) 35. (a) 36. (b) 37. (a) 38. (c) 39. (a) 40. (d) 41. (a) 42. (d) 43. (a) 44. (a) 45. (b) 46. (d) 47. (a) 48. (b) 49. (c) 50. (a) 51. (c) 52. (a) 53. (c) 54. (a) 55. (b) 56. (a) 57. (d) 58. (c) 59. (a) 60. (b) 61. (c) 62. (a) 63. (c) 64. (d) 65. (a) 66. (c) 67. (a) 68. (d) 69. (a) 70. (c) 71. (a) 72. (a) 73. (d) 74. (d) 75. (a) 76. (b) 77. (a) 78. (c) 79. (d) 80. (a) 81. (a) 82. (d) 83. (a) 84. (b) 85. (a) 86. (c) 87. (a) 88. (d) 89. (a) 90. (a) 91. (c) 92. (a) 93. (d) 94. (a) 95. (b) 96. (a) 97. (a) 98. (c) 99. (a) 100. (b)

TAXONOMY - XI

1. Which is the inflorescence of paddy?
   (a) Spike (b) Spadix
   (c) Catkin (d) Panicle
2. In poaceae the lodicules are
   (a) Perianth leaves (b) Bracts
   (c) Stipel (d) Foliage leaves
3. Which is the family of onion?
   (a) Rutaceae (b) Liliaceae
   (c) Myrtaceae (d) Cucurbitaceae
4. Which term is used for highly modified sepal of orchidaceous flower?
   (a) Lip or labellum (b) Peduncle
   (c) Modified bracts (d) Keel petals
5. Plants of which family consists of wings petals
   (a) Meliaceae (b) Solanaceae
   (c) Myrtaceae (d) Papilionaceae
6. Gynandrium in orchid flower occur by
   (a) Adnation of stamen, style and stigma
   (b) Absence of style & petiole
   (c) Adnation of style & stigma
   (d) None of these
7. The members of which family stands first as a source of food & folder
   (a) Cucurbitaceae (b) Capparidaceae
   (c) Solanaceae (d) Poaceae
8. Who is first to describe plant by using scientific taxonomical terminology
   (a) Theophrastus (370 -c a. 285 B C) (b) Linnaeus
   (c) Englar (d) Darwin
9. Who proposed firstly the term of bio-diversity
   (a) Jean Bauhin (b) John ray
   (c) Love joy (d) M.de Lobelins
10. How many percent flora constitute by India in comparison to the world
    (a) 2.1 (b) 2.2
    (c) 4.2 (d) 2.4
11. In which family trimerous hypogynous flowers occurs
    (a) Bignoniaceae (b) Malvaceae
    (c) Liliaceae (d) Caesalpinaceae

12. Perianth occurs in family
    (a) Liliaceae (b) Asteraceae
    (c) Solanaceae (d) Asclepidiaceace
13. All pulses belongs to family
    (a) Fabaceae (b) Myrtaceae
    (c) Rubiaceae (d) Rutaceae
14. Who proposed the phylogenetic classification of plants?
    (a) Edgar Anderson (b) Hutchinson
    (c) Turrill (d) Devis Heywood
15. Who is the author of Die Naturlichen Pflanzenfamilian
    (a) Engler and Prantl (b) J.R. Wettstein, 1935
    (c) Thomas, 1925 (d) Hallier
16. How many families are recognized by Hutchinson?
    (a) 412 (b) 410
    (c) 408 d) 411
17. The term taxonomy is gained by
    (a) De Candolle (b) Guppy
    (c) John Ray (d) Theophrastus
18. In which of the following Hutchinson published classification
    (a) The Families of Flowering Plants (b) Material Medica
    (c) Historia Naturalis (d) Historia Plantarum
19. What is the aim of taxonomy?
    (a) Identification, nomenclature and classification of plants
    (b) Identification and classification of plants
    (c) Identification and presentation
    (d) None of these
20. The study of taxonomy with intraspecific population and with phylogenetic trends is termed as
    (a) Omega taxonomy (b) Plant taxonomy
    (c) Beta taxonomy (d) Gamma taxonomy
21. Which character can differentiate from angiosperm to gymnosperm?
    (a) Xylem vessels (b) Closed seed
    (c) Enclosed seed (d) Presence of flower
22. Which scientist proposed phylogenetic system of plant classification?
    (a) Adolf Engler and Karl Prantl (b) Prantle & Eichler
    (c) Adolf Engler (d) Wetlslein

23. Which is largest family of dicotyledons?
    (a) Apiaceae (b) Papilionaceae
    (c) Asteraceae (d) Lamiaceae
24. Gamopetalous epigynous family is
    (a) Cucurbitaceae (b) Rosaceae
    (c) Meliaceae (d) Annonaceae
25. Which family consists of tetramerous flower?
    (a) Rubiaceae (b) Cruciferae
    (c)Tiliaceae (d) Malvaceae
26. In which family opdiplostemanous condition of androecium is common
    (a) Rutaceae (b) Caesalpinaceae
    (c) Compositae (d) Poaceae
27. Which plant does not show marginal placentation?
    (a) Tomato (b) Mimosa
    (c) Pea (d) Cassia
28. Which type of fruit occur in family Annonaceae
    (a) Samara (b) Multiple berry
    (c) Legume (d) None of these
29. In which of the following polypetalous irregular corolla occur
    (a) Caesalpinaceae (b) Papilionacious
    (c) Malvaceae (d) None of these
30. Which type of fruit occur in rose
    (a) Berry (b) Drup
    (c) Hip (d) Achene
31. In which of the following Hesperidium type of fruit occurs
    (a) Grapes (b) Citrus
    (c) Pea (d) Pepo
32. In which family gynobasic style arise from the base of ovary
    (a) Lamiaceae (b) Caesalpinaceae
    (c) Papilionaceae (d) None of these
33. Which type of inflorescence occur in *Tectona grandis*
    (a) Dichasial cyme (b) Panicle
    (c) Verticelaster (d) None of these
34. Who prepared classification in which gymnosperm placed between dicot and monocot
    (a) Bentham and hooker (b) Englar
    (c) Hutchinson (d) None of these

35. In which of the following cleistogamous flower occur
    (a) Tiliaceae (b) Cucurbitaceae
    (c) Rutaceae (d) Annonaceae
36. How is the habit Wolfia
    (a) Aquatic (b) Sub-terrestrial
    (c) Symbiotic (d) Halophytes
37. In China rose placentation is
    (a) Axile (b) Marginal
    (c) Basal (d) None of these
38. In which of the following numerous stamens occur
    (a) Malvaceae (b) Cruciferae
    (c) Papilionaceae (d) None of these
39. Phyllotaxy in *Calotropis procera* is
    (a) Alternate (b) Decussate
    (c) Whorled (d) opposite
40. In which family tetradynamous conditions occur
    (a) Crucifer (b) Caesalpinaceae
    (c) Papilionaceae (d) None of these
41. Which family shows didynamous conditions of flowers?
    (a) Caesalpinaceae (b) Papilionaceae
    (c) Rosaceae (d) Papavaraceae
42. Which is the example of family solanaceae
    (a) *Annona squemosa* (b) *Daccus carota*
    (c) *Cajanus cajan* (d) *Datura metal*
43. A form of corolla having four petals is termed as
    (a) Papilionaceae (b) Cruciferous
    (c) Solanaceae (d) None of these
44. Polydelphous condition of stamens occurs in
    (a) Sugarcane (b) Rose
    (c) Coriander (d) Citrus
45. Drupe type off fruit occurs in
    (a) *Mangifera indica* (b) *Dalbergia sisso*
    (c) *Lantana camera* (d) None of these
46. Which family is an example of monocarpellary conditions?
    (a) Fabaeceae (b) Annonaceae
    (c) Asclepidiaceace (d) None of these

47. Cereals are the group of plant which belongs to the family
    (a) Crucifer (b) Poaceae
    (c) Solanaceae (d) Lamiaceae
48. Which type of placentation occur in family Papilionaceae
    (a) Central (b) Marginal
    (c) Axile (d) Parietal
49. Tetradynamous conditions of androecium occurs in family
    (a) Cruciferous (b) Caesalpinaceae
    (c) Papilionaceae (d) Rubiaceae
50. Which type of stamen occur in cotton flower
    (a) Free (b) Diadelphous
    (c) Monodelphous (d) Polyandrous
51. The condition of stamens in the china rose is
    (a) Monodelphous (b) Diadelphous
    (c) Both a and b (d) None of these
52. Type of fruit of Coriandrum is
    (a) Dry schizocarp (b) Berry
    (c) Drupe (d) Capsule
53. Arrangement of stamens in family crucifer is
    (a) Outer 4 long and inner two short stamens
    (b) Outer 2 short and inner two short stamens
    (c) Outer 2 long and inner two long stamen
    (d) Outer 4 short and inner two long stamen
54. In which family monocarpellary condition occurs
    (a) Rubiaceae (b) Papilionaceae
    (c) Annonaceae (d) None of these
55. Which is the family of pulses?
    (a) Leguminoceae (Papilionaceae)
    (b) Leguminoceae (Mimoceae)
    (c) Leguminoceae (Caesalpinaceae)
    (d) None of these
56. Which is the family of cereals?
    (a) Asclepidiaceace (b) Caesalpinaceae
    (c) Annonaceae (d) Poaceae
57. Which type of placentation occur in family Papilionaceae
    (a) Axile (b) Marginal
    (c) Central (d) None of above

58. Which is the edible part of coconut?
(a) Embryo (b) Endosperm
(c) Synergids (d) Shell
59. Which is the edible part of *Daucus carota.*?
(a) Flowers (b) Leaves
(c) Tap root (d) Rhizome
60. Which is true in case of mustard flower?
(a) Perigynous (b) Ebractiate
(c) Pentamerous (d) Slightly zygomorphic
61. Which one occur in seed of sunflower
(a) Alkaloids (b) Aromatic oils
(c) Edible oil (d) None of these
62. Which term is used for modified stamens of family asclepidiaceace?
(a) Sinuous (b) Translator
(b) Both a and b (d) None of these
63. Which is the botanical name of sunflower?
(a) *Helianthus annuus* (b) *Hibiscus esculentus*
(c) *Hibiscus rose sinensis* (d) None of these
64. In china rose stamens are
(a) Polydelphous (b) Diadelphous
(b) Monodelphous (d) None of these
65. The botanical of Bajra is
(a) *Pennisetum glaucum* (b) *Catharanthus roseus*
(b) *Sorghum vulgare* (d) *Menthe piperita*
66. Which type of fruit occur in family labiatae
(a) Follicle (b) Capsule
(c) Nut let (d) None of these
67. Which of the following is a huge tree?
(a) *Ficus bengalensis* (b) *Ficus carica*
(c) *Lantana camera* (d) None of these
68. Which of the following is shrub?
(a) *Piper nigrum* (b) *Butea monosperma*
(c) *Annona squimosa* (d) None of these
69. Which of the following is English name of lantana camera?
(a) Prickly herb (b) Small tree
(c) Twines (d) Climber

70. Orchids are
(a) Epiphytes (b) Hydrophytes
(c) Mangrove (d) Mesophyte
71. Which is the example of explosive fruit?
(a) *Asparagus recemosus* (b) *Nicotiana tuberose*
(b) *Ruellia tuberose* (d) *Solanum nigrum*
72. Which family secrets sticky milky substances
(a) Asclepidiaceace (b) Composite
(c) Annonaceae (d) Papilionaceae
73. What is the botanical name of birds nest orchids
(a) Wolfia (b) Mint
(c) Dendrobium (d) Neottia
74. Which of the following inflorescence occur in wheat?
(a) Spike (b) Catkin
(c) Panicle (d) Verticillaster
75. Which type of inflorescence occurs in paddy?
(a) Catkin (b) Panicle
(c) Both a and b (d) None of these
76. From which tap root grows
(a) Radical (b) Funicle
(c) Germ tube (d) From Rhizome
77. Fibrous roots occur in
(a) Groundnut (b) Dicot
(c) Ricinus (d) Monocot
78. Which roots are called apogeotropic?
(a) Pnematophores (b) Fibrous root
(c) Tap root (d) Prop root
79. Prop roots occurs in
(a) *Gloriosa* (b) Banyan tree
(c) *Dalbergia* (d) *Triticum*
80. Which is the function of fasciculate roots?
(a) Storage of food (b) Protection
(c) Perennation (d) Support
81. Which type of root is modified as nodulated root?
(a) Adventitious root (b) Fibrous root
(c) Tap root (d) Prop roots

82. Rhizome of banana is a
    (a) Underground modification of stem
    (b) Underground modification of root
    (c) Modification of Inflorescence
    (d) None of these
83. Which one is involved in water absorption?
    (a) Adventitious roots (b) Root cap
    (c) Stilt root (d) Root hairs
84. Food storing regions of garlic are
    (a) Leaves (b) Fruits
    (c) Stem (d) Modified root
85. Aerial stem modification occurs in
    (a) Agave (b) Opuntia
    (c) Aloe (d) Ocimum
86. Which term is used for aerial stem?
    (a) Phyllode (b) Cladode
    (c) Phylloclade (d) None of these
87. Phylloclade is a
    (a) Aerial stem modification of Opuntia
    (b) Aerial stem modification of garlic
    (c) Aerial stem modification of Wolfia
    (d) Aerial stem modification of Bamboo
88. Free lateral stipule occur in
    (a) Sunflower (b) *Hibiscus*
    (c) *Sorghum* (d) *Tectona*
89. Which term is used for hollow stipules?
    (a) Ochreate (b) Bracteate
    (c) Tendrillar (d) Petaloid
90. In natural vegetation and wild life, the category of India is
    (a) One of the 12 mega-biodiversity countries of the world
    (b) One of the 8 mega-biodiversity of countries of the world
    (c) One of the 5 mega-biodiversity of the world
    (d) One of the 4 mega diversity of the world
91. How many Global Biodiversity hot spots are present in India?
    (a) 38 (b) 34
    (c) 37 (d) 35

92. How many flowering plants occur in India?
(a) 12000 (b) 13000
(c)1100 (d) 14000

93. The plants which grow at higher altitude where generally no tree specie are found are termed as
(a) Alpine species (b) Endangered species
(c) Xerophytic species (d) Epiphytic species

94. The forest trees losing foliage at the end of growing season are termed as
(a) Deciduous (b) Evergreen
(c) Aquatic (d) Hydrophytes

95. A variety & variability of life on the earth is described
(a) Biotechnology (b) Biodiversity
(c) Diversity (d) None of these

96. A species which is only found in a given location and nowhere else in the world is termed as
(a) Endemism (b) Symbolism
(c) Exotic Species (d) None of these

97. Which term is used for vegetation which is purely Indian in origin?
(a) Endemic species (b) Exotic Species
(c) Both a and b (d) None of these

98. Which of the following natural vegetation have originally come to India from abroad?
(a) Exotic Species (b) Endemic species
(c) Both a and b (d) None of these

99. Total Biographic regions occur in India are
(a) 15 (b) 12
(c) 14 (d) 10

100. Which is the family of *Rhododendron* of Himalayan region?
(a) Ericaceae (b) Annonaceae
(c) Meliaceae (d) None of these

Answer key: TAXONOMY - XI

1. (d) 2. (a) 3. (b) 4. (a) 5. (d) 6. (a) 7. (d) 8. (a) 9. (c) 10. (d) 11. (c) 12. (a) 13. (a) 14. (b) 15. (a) 16. (d) 17. (a) 18. (a) 19. (a) 20. (d) 21. (b) 22. (a) 23. (c) 24. (a) 25. (b) 26. (a) 27. (a) 28. (b) 29. (b) 30. (c) 31. (b) 32. (a) 33. (b) 34. (a) 35. (c) 36. (a) 37. (a) 38. (a) 39. (b) 40. (a) 41. (b) 42. (b) 43. (b) 44. (d) 45. (a) 46. (a) 47. (b) 48. (b) 49. (a) 50. (c) 51. (a) 52. (a) 53. (b) 54. (b) 55. (a) 56. (a) 57. (b) 58. (b) 59. (c) 60. (d) 61. (c) 62. (b)

63. (a) 64. (b) 65. (a) 66. (c) 67. (a) 68. (c) 69. (a) 70. (a) 71. (b) 72. (a) 73. (d) 74. (a) 75. (b) 76. (a) 77. (d) 78. (d) 79. (b) 80. (a) 81. (c) 82. (a) 83. (d) 84. (a) 85. (b) 86. (c) 87. (a) 88. (b) 89. (a) 90. (a) 91. (d) 92. (b) 93. (a) 94. (a) 95. (b) 96. (a) 97. (a) 98. (a) 99. (d) 100. (a)

TAXONOMY - XII

1. Which is the alternative term used for keel petals?
   (a) Epi-calyx (b) Carina
   (c) Corolla (d) Calyx
2. How is the arrangement of petals in flower of family Papilionaceae?
   (a) 1+2+(2) (b) 2+1+2
   (c) (1)+2+(2) (d) 1+(2)+(2)
3. Which term is used for flower having semi inferior ovary?
   (a) Epigynous (b) Hypogynous
   (c) Perigynous (d) None of these
4. When the floral parts are originated from base of ovary it is described as
   (a) Hypogynous (b) Epigynous
   (c) Inferior (d) None of these
5. In which type of inflorescence there types of sessile flowers occurs
   (a) Spike (b) Spadix
   (c) Hypanthodium inflorescence (d) Catkin
6. Which term is used for female flowers with short style from Hypanthodium Inflorescence?
   (a) Gall flowers (b) Small flowers
   (c) Group of flowers (d) Tetramerous flower
7. In which year modern system of Biological nomenclature initiated
   (a) 1865 (b) 1870
   (c) 1792 (d) 1758
8. In which of the following tepenoids have been used in the chemotaxonomy
   (a) Citrus plants (b) Papaya
   (c) Cherry (d) Guava
9. Which term is used for arrangement of petals & sepals in flower bud?
   (a) Aestivation (b) Placentation
   (c) Syngenesis (d) None of these
10. Perianth composed of
    (a) Filaments (b) Epicalyx
    (c) Calyx (d) Tepals

11. When arrangement of sepals & petals are parallel in flower it is termed as
    (a) Valvate (b) Imbricate
    (c) Twisted (d) Contorted
12. Which type of aestivation occurs in *Calotropis*?
    (a) Valvate (b) Vexillary
    (c) Imbricate (d) None of these
13. Twisted aestivation is characteristic
    (a) Malvaceae (b) Rutaceae
    (c) Asteraceae (d) Myrtaceae
14. In which plant ascending imbricate aestivation occurs
    (a) *Shorea robusta* (b) *Clerodendrum indicum*
    (c) *Lantana camera* (d) *Caesalpiniaceae pulcherima*
15. Which are parts of stamens?
    (a) Filament & Anther (b) Style & Anther
    (c) Style & Stigma (d) Anther & Stigma
16. Descending imbricate aestivation is characteristic feature of family
    (a) Papilionaceae (b) Caesalpinaceae
    (c) Utricaceae (d) Magnoliaceae
17. A dithecous anther occurs in family
    (a) Capparidaceae (b) Sterculiaceae
    (c) Papilionaceae (d) Malvaceae
18. The mododelphaous condition of stamens occurs in family
    (a) Malvaceae (b) Sapotaceae
    (c) Santalaceae d) Rutaceae
19. Didelphous condition in characteristic feature of family
    (a) Rutaceae (b) Annonacece
    (c) Rosaceae (d) Papilionaceae
20. Polydelphous condition of flowers occur in family
    (a) Rutaceae (b) Asteraceae
    (c) Amaranthaceae (d) Chaenopodiaceae
21. In which of the following polydelphous condition occur
    (a) *Mulberry* (b) *Trachyspermum*
    (c) *Eclipta* (d) *Citrus*
22. When the anthers are united & filaments are free in flower, the condition in described as
    (a) Syngenesious (b) Parthenogenesis
    (c) Both a and b (d) Spadix

23. Epipetalous condition occurs in family
    (a) Pedaliaceae (b) Solanaceae
    (c) Rubiaceae (d) Apocynaceace
24. Epiphyllous condition of stamens occur in family
    (a) Liliaceae (b) Rubiaceae
    (c) Anacardiaceae (d) Acanthaceae
25. In a flower, when two stamens are long & two are short, the phenomenon is termed as
    (a) Didynamous (b) Tetradynamous
    (c) Both a & b (d) None of these
26. The tetradynamous condition is
    (a) Two long stamens in inner whorl & two short in inner whorl
    (b) Four long stamens in inner whorl & two short in inner whorl.
    (c) Three long stamens in inner whorl & two short in inner whorl
    (d) None of these
27. Tetradynamous condition is characteristic feature of family
    (a) Cruciferae (b) Myrtaceae
    (c) Anacardiaceae (d) Papilionaceae
28. Aggregate fruits are derived from
    (a) Polycarpellary and apocarpus ovary
    (b) Monocarpellary and apocarpus ovary
    (c) Polycarpellary and syncarpus ovary
    (d) None of these
29. In which of the following whole leaf is changed to tendril
    (a) *Citrullus* (b) *Sterculia*
    (c) *Theobroma* (d) *Lythrus*
30. Mostly tendril occurs in
    (a) Aquatic plants
    (b) Weak Stemed plants
    (c) Xerophytic plants
    (d) None of these
31. The origin of root is initiated from
    (a) Pericycle (b) Cortex
    (c) Hypodermis (d) Endodermis
32. Leaf hooks occurs in
    (a) *Cryptostegia* (b) *Croton*
    (c) *Linum* (d) *Bignonia*

33. Which term is used for stipules occur on the leaflets
(a) Stiples (b) Stipule
(c) Bract (d) Pedicel
34. Stipels occur in
(a) Moringa (b) Green gram
(c) Bean (d) Tamarind
35. Spathe is a large sized
(a) Bract (b) Stipule
(c) Pedicel (d) Peduncle
36. Feathery stigma occurs in family
(a) Rannunculaceace (b) Graminae
(c) Cucurbitaceae (d) Rutaceae
37. In Capitulum type of inflorescence, a cluster of florets surrounded by whorl of bracts called as
(a) Involucres (b) Thalamus
(c) Corona (d) Pedicel
38. Dichasial cyme type of inflorescence occurs in
(a) Theobroma (b) Capparis
(c) Sterculia (d) Bougainvillea
39. In which of type of inflorescence a cup like inflorescence made up of bract that encloses naked flowers (without calyx & corolla)
(a) Cyathium (b) Verticillaster
(c) Spike (d) Catkin
40. In Cyathium type of inflorescence the ratio of male to female flower is
(a) Many female flowers: One male flower
(b) Many female flowers: two male flower
(c) Many female flowers: three male flower
(d) Many female flowers: five male flower
41. Which is the member of family compositae?
(a) *Asparagus* (b) Sunflower
(c) *Erythrina* (d) *Desmodium*
42. The florets of Capitulum type of inflorescence is a
(a) Individual flowers (b) Sterile flowers
(c) Both a and b (d) None of these
43. Which of the following do not store food?
(a) Stolon & offset (b) Radish
(c) Rhizome (d) Bulb

44. Mirabilis is dicot plants showing venation is
(a) Unicostate (b) Reticulate
(c) Multicostate (d) Parallel
45. The monocots such as Smilax & Trillium shows
(a) Parallel venation (b) Reticulate venation
(c) Both a and b (d) None of these
46. Which ore is an ornamental plant
(a) Petunia (b) Sorghum
(c) Cumin (d) Saccharum
47. Which type of placentation occurs in onion?
(a) Basal (b) Marginal
(c) Axile (d) None of these
48. Stilt root in maize develops from
(a) Lower node (b) Apical bud
(c) Lateral bud (d) None of these
49. Which term is used for development of different types of leaves in a same plant
(a) Heterophyllus (b) Homophyllous
(c) Both a and b (d) None of these
50. The term used for arrangement of leaves on branches of stem is termed as
(a) Aestivation (b) Phyllotaxy
(c) Placentation (d) Vernation
51. The phenomenon of ceiling of young leaf in described as
(a) Placentation (b) Vernation
(c) Venation (d) None of these
52. Which one of the example of Phyllode
(a) Parkinsonia (b) Tamarindus
(c) Pistia (d) Echornia
53. Assimilatory roots are found in
(a) Agave (b) Aloe
(c) Trapa (d) Cactus
54. In which of the following spongy roots are found
(a) Jussiaea (b) Sorghum
(c) Jasmine (d) None of these
55. Maturation of flowers in recemose type of inflorescence is in
(a) Intermediate succession (b) Basipetal succession
(c) Acropetal succession (d) None of these

56. Maturation of flowers in cymose type of inflorescence is
    (a) Basipetal succession (b) Acropetal succession
    (c) Both a & b (d) None of these
57. In which region maximum growth of root occurs
    (a) At the apex (b) Behind the apex
    (c) Base of root (d) None of these
58. In which plant roots are modified to thorns
    (a) Coriandrum (b) Mint
    (c) Bamboo (d) Acanthorhiza
59. Which one is the function of prop roots?
    (a) Absorption of water
    (b) Formation of new branches
    (c) Balancing support to tree
    (d) None of these
60. Which plant composed of epiphytic roots?
    (a) Orchids (b) Aloe
    (c) Hydrophytes (d) Xerophytes
61. In which velamen type of tissue occurs
    (a) Mesophyte (b) Aerial roots of orchids
    (c) Hydrophytes (d) None of these
62. In which group of plants roots are freely developed
    (a) Hydrophytes (b) Xerophytes
    (c) Mesophyte (d) both b & c
63. Which is the primary function of stem?
    (a) To bear cortex (b) To bear flowers
    (c) To bear & support leaves (d) None of these
64. In which of the following false aerial stem occurs
    (a) Banana (b) Tilia
    (c) *Sterculia* (d) Croton
65. What is the function of underground modification of stem?
    (a) Respiration (b) Reproduction
    (c) Transpiration (d) Perennation
66. On which potatoes are developed
    (a) Stolons (b) Rhizome
    (c) Rhizophore (d) Gynophore
67. In Opuntia, photosynthesis occurs in
    (a) Internodes (b) Phylloclade
    (c) Node (d) None of these

68. Which one is a modified stem?
(a) Corm (b) Carrot
(c) Radish (d) Chilly

69. Which one is not a modified stem?
(a) Loranthus (b) Cuscuta
(c) Striga (d) Pitcher of Nepenthes

70. In which plant a horizontal underground stem occurs
(a) *Curcuma longa* (b) *Ixora parviflora*
(c) *Adina cordifolia* (d) *Chinchona officinalis*

71. The suckers are produced by
(a) Mint (b) Cardamom
(c) Olea (d) Onion

72. The leaf extract of which one is used to prepare syrup against cough
(a) *Vinca rosea* (b) *Solanum nigrum*
(c) *Adhatoda vasaka* (d) None of these

73. The symmetry of flower of *Barleria prionitis* is
(a) Pleuromorphic (b) Zygomorphic
(c) Actinomorphic (d) None of these

74. The plant *Acanthus ilicifolicus* is a
(a) Mesophyte (b) Saprophyte
(c) Halophyte (d) Parasite.

75. The corolla of most of the plants of family acanthaceae is
(a) Polypetalous (b) Tripetalous
(c) Gamopetalous (d) None of these

76. The androecium with four stamens, two are larger and two are small, the phenomenon is termed as
(a) Tetradynamous (b) Dithecous
(c) Didynamous (d) None of these

77. Most of the plants of family Acanthaceae grow well in
(a) On branches of large trees (b) Damp & marshy places
(c) On dry land (d) None of above

78. Which is the genus of family acanthaceae
(a) *Justicia* (b) *Lagenaria*
(c) *Prunus* (d) None of these

79. A highly reduced nonfunctional stamen is termed as
(a) Androecium (b) Staminode
(c) Stamen (d) None of these

80. In pentamerous flower, when both the edges of one sepal or petal completely inside, one petal edges completely outside and the edges of 3 petal or sepal are alternate, such arrangement in termed as
    (a) Valvate (b) Imbricate
    (c) Twisted (d) None of these
81. The margin of leaf of *Adhatoda vasica* is
    (a) Serrate (b) Incised
    (c) Entire (d) Dentate
82. The anthers facing inward are termed as
    (a) Versatile (b) Extrorse
    (c) Introrse (d) Adnate
83. Shape of corolla of *Ruellia prostrata* of family Acanthaceae is
    (a) Campanulate (b) Funnel shaped
    (c) Ligulate (d) Urceolate.
84. When the placenta develops from the central axis, it is termed as
    (a) Parietal placentation (b) Basal placentation
    (c) Axile placentation (d) None of these
85. Which is the member of family Acanthaceae?
    (a) *Solanum nigrum* (b) *Cymbopogon nardus*
    (c) *Thunbergia grandiflora* (d) None of these
86. Dominant feature of family Liliaceae is
    (a) A corolla like perianth (b) A sepal like perianth
    (c) Petaloid calyx (d) None of these
87. Which is the member of family Liliaceae?
    (a) *Acacia nilotica* (b) *Adhatoda vasaka*
    (c) *Aloe vera* (d) None of these
88. *Gloriosa superba* is a
    (a) Tree (b) Herb
    (c) Shrub (d) None of these
89. A special aerial stem on which inflorescence may develop is known as
    (a) Rhizome (b) Scape
    (c) Runner (d) None of these.
90. The plant roots of family Liliaceae are
    (a) Adventitious & fibrous (b) Branched tap root
    (c) Tap root (d) None of these
91. A leaf with single lamina termed as
    (a) Simple leaf (b) Unipinnate leaf
    (c) Bipinnate leaf (d) Compound leaf

92. Anthers of *Gloriosa superba* described as
    (a) Extrorse (b) Versatile
    (c) Introrse (d) Adnate
93. In the plants of family Liliaceae, the anther is attached to the top of filament; the phenomenon is termed as
    (a) Dorsifixed (b) Dithecous
    (c) Basifixed (d) None of these
94. The fruit of *Asparagus* is berry
    (a) Berry (b) Pome
    (c) Drupe (d) Capsule
95. Acacia is a member of family Mimosaceae which is a
    (a) Halophytic (b) Hydrophytic
    (c) Xerophytic (d) None of these
96. The genus *Mimosa pudica* is a
    (a) Shrub (b) Herb
    (c) Small shrub (d) Climber
97. The leaf of *Mimosa pudica* is a
    (a) Simple leaf (b) Compound leaf
    (c) Tripinnate leaf (d) None of these
98. The fruit of *Acacia* is a
    (a) Legume (b) Drupe
    (c) Pome (d) None of these.
99. The phenomenon of united sepals is termed as
    (a) Polypetalous (b) Free petals
    (c) Gamopetalous (d) None of these
100. In Acacia the stipule is modified to
    (a) Tendril (b) Spine
    (c) Trichomes (d) None of these
101. Which term is used for stamens attached so Gynoecium
    (a) Gynandrous (b) Synandrous
    (c) Monodelphous (d) Polydelphous

Answer key: TAXONOMY - XII

1. (b) 2. (a) 3. (c) 4. (a) 5. (c) 6. (a) 7. (d) 8. (a) 9. (a) 10. (d) 11. (a) 12. (a) 13. (a) 14. (d) 15. (a) 16. (a) 17. (d) 18. (a) 19. (d) 20. (a) 21. (d) 22. (a) 23. (b) 24. (a) 25. (a) 26. (b) 27. (a) 28. (a) 29. (d) 30. (b) 31. (a) 32. (d) 33. (a) 34. (c) 35. (a) 36. (b) 37. (a) 38. (d) 39. (a) 40. (a) 41. (b) 42. (a) 43. (a) 44. (d) 45. (b) 46. (a) 47. (c) 48. (a) 49. (a) 50. (b) 51. (b) 52. (a)

53. (c) 54. (a) 55. (c) 56. (a) 57. (b) 58. (d) 59. (c) 60. (a) 61. (b) 62. (a) 63. (c) 64. (a) 65. (d) 66. (a) 67. (b) 68. (a) 69. (d) 70. (a) 71. (a) 72. (a) 73. (b) 74. (c) 75. (c) 76. (c) 77. (b) 78. (a) 79. (b) 80. (b) 81. (c) 82. (c) 83. (b) 84. (c) 85. (c) 86. (a) 87. (c) 88. (b) 89. (b) 90. (a) 91. (a) 92. (c) 93. (c) 94. (a) 95 (c) 96. (b) 97. (b) 98. (a) 99. (c) 100. (b) 101. (a)

TAXONOMY - XIII

1. The leaf of Acacia is a
   (a) Simple leaf (b) Unipinnate leaf
   (c) Bipinnate compound leaf (d) None of these
2. The stem surface of *Mimosa pudica* is clothed with
   (a) Deflexed bristles (b) Spines
   (c) Small dots (d) None of these
3. Bark of which plant used for tanning purpose
   (a) *Mimosa pudica* (b) *Coriandrum sativum*
   (c) *Acacia arabica* (d) None of these
4. When ovary is one chambered & the placenta develop along the junction of two margins of the carpel, the placentation is termed as
   (a) Axile (b) Basal
   (c) Marginal (d) Parietal
5. The member of Mimosaceae, *Albizzia procera* yield
   (a) Week wood (b) Porous wood
   (c) Stronger wood (d) Black wood
6. Most of the plants of family Annonaceae are
   (a) Small herbs (b) Large tree
   (c) Small trees (d) None of these
7. Which is the member of family Annonaceae?
   (a) *Polyanthia longifolia* (b) *Acacia Arabica*
   (c) *Abutilon indicum* (d) *Albizzia lebbek*
8. The petals of *Annona squamosa* are
   (a) Thin (b) Papery
   (c) Fleshy (d) Membranous
9. Arrangement of stamens in *Annona squimosa* are
   (a) Circular (b) Alternate
   (c) Spiral (d) None of these
10. The type of fruit of *Annona* is termed as
   (a) An etaerio of berries (b) Pome
   (c) Berry (d) None of these

11. The *Polyanthia longifolia* is grown as a
    (a) Fruit yielding plant (b) Grain yielding plant
    (c) Ornamental plant (d) None of these
12. The central conical structure of fruit of Annona is termed as
    (a) Stalk (b) Thalamus
    (c) Base (d) Endosperm
13. The leaves of which plant possesses insecticidal property.
    (a) *Polyanthia longifolia* (b) *Artabotrys uncinatus*
    (c) *Annona squimosa* (d) None of these
14. Which plant yield edible fruits
    (a) *Polyanthia longifolia* (b) *Cassia tora*
    (c) *Annona squimosa* (d) None of these
15. When petals or sepals are present in a circle & their margins simply remain in contact with each other but do not overlap, the aestivation is termed as
    (a) Imbricate (b) Twisted
    (c)Valvate (d) None of these
16. The genus Annona squimosa is a
    (a) Herb (b) Shrub
    (c)Tree (d) None of these
17. The stamens are free to variously united in the plants of family
    (a) Acanthaceae (b) Caesalpinaceae
    (c) Solanaceae (d) Apocynaceae
18. Genus Parkinsonia of the family Caesalpinaceae is a
    (a) Halophyte (b) Xerophyte
    (c) Mesophyte (d) Hydrophyte
19. The flower of *Caesalpinia pulcherima* is
    (a) Zygomorphic (b) Symmetrical
    (c) Actinomorphic (d) None of these
20. Which is the member of family Caesalpinaceae
    (a) *Arachis hypogeal* (b) *Vinca rosea*
    (c) *Cassia fistula* (d) None of these
21. In *Cassia fistula*, the sepals are free, it is termed as
    (a) Gamosepalous (b) Calyx
    (c) Polysepalous (d) None of these
22. The aestivation of corolla of *Cassia fistula* is
    (a) Imbricate (b) Ascending imbricate
    (c) Descending imbricate (d) Valvate

23. The member of Caesalpinaceae *Saraca indica* is a native of
    (a) Egypt (b) Brazil
    (c) Indonesia (d) India
24. Kachnar is the vernacular name of
    (a) *Bauhinia variegate* (b) *Bauhinia nalabarica*
    (c) *Bauhinia purpurea* (d) *Bauhinia tomentosa*
25. The pulp of which plant is used as a purgative
    (a) *Cassia alata* (b) *Cassia auriculata*
    (c) *Cassia fistula* (d) *Cassia siamea*
26. The *Parkinsonia aculeata,* is cultivated as
    (a) Food crop (b) Ornamental plant
    (c) Oil yielding crop (d) Fodder crop
27. The genus Haematoxylon of Caesalpinaceae yield
    (a) Tannin (b) Gum
    (c) Resin (d) Dye
28. Flowers of *Cassia tora* of Caesalpinaceae used as source of
    (a) Dye (b) Vegetable
    (c) Scent (d) None of these
29. The placentation in pods of *Caesalpinia pulcherima* is
    (a) Central (c) Marginal
    (b) Axile (d) Basal
30. How many whorls of stamens occur in *Caesalpinia pulcherima*
    (a) 3 (b) 1
    (c) 2 (d) 4
31. Flower of poaceae subtended by two bracts which are termed as
    (a) Lemma & bract (b) Lemma & scale
    (c) Lemma & palea (d) None of these
32. Edible grain yielding plants of family poaceae are termed as
    (a) Crop (b) Cereal crop
    (c) Pulses (d) None of these
33. Bamboos in a
    (a) Large shrub (b) Largest woody grass
    (c) Large herb (d) None of these
34. The plants of family poaceae possesses
    (a) Tap root
    (b) Adventitious fibrous roots
    (c) Branched tap root
    (d) None of these

35. At the junction of leaf sheath and leaf blade of poaceae a thin membranous out growth is present which is known as
(a) Stipule (b) Bract
(c) Ligule (d) None of these

36. In many species of plants of poaceae there are two lateral, pointed outgrowths above the ligules are known as
(a) Auricles (b) Tillers
(c) Bracts (d) None of these

37. The aerial stem of plants of family poaceae is commonly known as
(a) Herb (b) Trunk
(c) Stick (d) Culm

38. The type of venation in the plants of poaceae is
(a) Reticulate unicostate (b) Reticulate multicostate
(c) Reticulate (d) Parallel

39. Nodes of *Oryza sativa* are
(a) Pointed (b) Flat
(c) Swollen (d) None of these

40. The flowers of *Oryza sativa* are
(a) Pedicellate (b) Sub-sessile
(c) Sessile (d) None of these

41. The Botanical name of wheat is
(a) *Triticum aestivum* (b) *Hordeum vulgare*
(c) *Avena sativa* (d) *Pennisetum typhoides*

42. Which is the member of family poaceae (Graminaceae)
(a) *Nerium indicum* (c) *Avena sativa*
(b) *Ocimum basilicum* (d) *Allium cepa*

43. The flowers of family poaceae are
(a) Actinomorphic (b) Dimorphic
(c) Zygomorphic (d) None of these

44. The anthers of family poaceae are
(a) Monothecous (b) Dithecous
(c) Versatile (d) None of these

45. The type of inflorescence which occurs in grasses is a
(a) Spike (b) Raceme
(c) Solitary (d) Cymose

46. The central axis of spikelet type of inflorescence is termed as
(a) Pedicel (b) Stalk
(c) Rachilla (d) None of these

47. The fruit of *Oryza sativa* is known as
    (a) Berry (b) Caryopsis
    (c) Pome (d) None of these
48. The bamboo is a
    (a) Grass (b) Shrub
    (c) Tree (d) Herb
49. How is the shape of guard cells of stomata
    (a) Kidney shaped (b) Peltate
    (c) Oval (d) Rectangular
50. A maximum light may be absorbed by leaf due to
    (a) Strong Petiole
    (b) Strong turger pressure in xylem
    (c) Strong turger pressure in mesophyll cells
    (d) Closed stomata
51. Which one is the function of guard cells?
    (a) Regulate the rate of photosynthesis
    (b) Regulate the rate of transpiration
    (c) Regulate the rate of vegetative reproduction
    (d) Regulate the rate of respiration
52. What is the function of needle like leaves in plants?
    (a) Reduce water loss (b) Increase photosynthesis
    (c) Protect leaf (d) Support plant
53. What is the function of stomata?
    (a) Reduce (b) Transpiration
    (c) Reduce Respiration (d) Reduce Photosynthesis
54. Which is the following is a tunicate bulb
    (a) Onion (b) Ginger
    (c) Clove (d) Potato
55. Which is the central axis of the plant?
    (a) Root (b) Peduncle
    (c) Petiole (d) Stem
56. Which one is a part of tunicate bulb?
    (a) Fleshy scales & basal plate
    (b) Fleshy scales & elongated stem
    (c) Thin scales & basal nodes
    (d) None of these

57. Which term is used for a large thick rhizome of ginger?
(a) Pachymorph (b) Polyploidy
(c) Polymorphs (d) Cladode

58. Which is the example of stolen producing plant?
(a) Mulberry (b) Strawberry
(c) Mentha (d) Ocimum

59. A fleshy tap root occurs in
(a) Carrots & Beets (b) Ginger
(c) Garlic (d) Potato

60. Which is the example of tuberous root?
(a) Sweet potato (b) Pea
(c) Lentil (d) Colocasia

61. Which type of pollination occur in cleistogamous type of flower
(a) Water pollination (b) Self pollination
(c) Both a and b (d) None of these

62. Which one is concerned with mango?
(a) Pericarp is fleshy (b) Both a and c
(c) Placenta is fleshy (d) Funiculus is fleshy

63. The position of ovary of China rose is
(a) Inferior (b) Superior
(c) Semi-inferior (d) Semi-superior

64. Mostly which part of flower is brightly coloured
(a) Petals (b) Epicalyx
(c) Bracts (d) Stamen

65. Which one is the function of root hairs?
(a) Absorb water & oxygen
(b) Absorb water & support root
(c) Absorb water & salts only
(d) Transpiration

66. Which family consists of large number of plants?
(a) Asteraceae (b) Rutaceae
(c) Cruciferae (d) Meliaceae

67. In which the pockets of pollen grain occur?
(a) Mimosoidae (b) Solanaceae
(c) Myrtaceae (d) None of these

68. Which monocot plant consists of reticulate venation?
(a) Smilax (b) Bamboo
(c) Sorghum (d) Sugarcane

69. In which plant flower enters in soil after fertilization?
    (a) *Ricinus* (b) Groundnut
    (c) Safflower (d) *Cassia*
70. Which pulse contains more protein than meat?
    (a) Soyabean (b) Sunflower
    (c) Hemp (d) *Cardamun*

Answer key: TAXONOMY - XIII

1. (c) 2. (a) 3. (c) 4. (c) 5. (c) 6. (c) 7. (a) 8. (c) 9. (c) 10. (a) 11. (c) 12. (b) 13. (c) 14. (c) 15. (c) 16. (b) 17. (b) 18. (b) 19. (a) 20. (c) 21. (c) 22. (b) 23. (d) 24. (a) 25. (c) 26. (b) 27. (d) 28. (b) 29. (c) 30. (c) 31. (c) 32. (b) 33. (b) 34. (b) 35. (c) 36. (a) 37. (d) 38. (d) 39. (c) 40. (c) 41. (a) 42. (c) 43. (c) 44. (b) 45. (a) 46. (c) 47. (b) 48. (a) 49. (a) 50. (a) 51. (b) 52. (a) 53. (b) 54. (a) 55. (d) 56. (a) 57. (a) 58. (b) 59. (a) 60. (a) 61. (b) 62. (a) 63. (b) 64. (a) 65. (a) 66. (a) 67. (a) 68. (a) 69. (b) 70 (a)

CHAPTER – 4

Anatomy - I to IV

ANATOMY - I

1. Function of pericycle is
   (a) Formation of branching (b) Storage of food
   (c) Mechanical support (d) None of these
2. The dead tissue present at the central region of tree is termed as
   (a) Heart wood (b) Both a and b
   (c) Sap wood (d) None of these
3. Which one is living wood of tree
   (a) Heart wood (b) Hard wood
   (c) Sap wood (d) None of these
4. Tree grows each year and cells are deposited at peripheral region of stem is termed as
   (a) Annual ring (b) Phellogen
   (c) Periderm (d) None of these
5. Which part of tree produce annual rings
   (a) Cambium (b) Cortex
   (c) Hypodermis (d) None of these
6. Cork is a
   (a) Phellogen layer of bark (b) Cortex
   (c) Hypodermis (d) None of these
7. The bark is
   (a) Outermost layer of tree (b) Innermost layer of tree
   (c) Vascular tissue (d) None of these
8. Which one protects tree from extreme adverse temperature
   (a) Hypodermis (b) Water conducting tissue
   (c) Bark (d) Cortex
9. Chemical formula of cork is
   (a) $C_{123}H_{182}O_{58}N$ (b) $C_{124}H_{183}O_{58}N$
   (c) $C_{125}H_{184}O_{58}N$ (d) $C_{126}H_{185}O_{58}N$

10. In which of the following cambium is absent?
   (a) Closed collateral vascular bundle
   (b) Open collateral vascular bundle
   (c) Both a and b
   (d) None of these
11. In which type of vascular bundle consists of cambium between xylem and phloem?
   (a) Open collateral vascular bundle
   (b) Closed collateral vascular bundle
   (c) Both a and b
   (d) None of these
12. The example of closed collateral vascular bundle is
   (a) *Cajanus cajan* (b) *Dalbergia sisso*
   (c) *Moringa* (d) *Asparagus*
13. Open collateral vascular bundles occur in
   (a) Stems of dicot (b) Root of monocot
   (c) Stem of monocot (d) None of these
14. When one type of vascular tissue surrounded by other vascular tissue such type of vascular bundle is termed as
   (a) Open vascular bundle
   (b) Concentric vascular bundle
   (c) Closed vascular bundle
   (d) None of these
15. Tissue takes part in storage of food is
   (a) Sclerenchyma (b) Xylem
   (c) Parenchyma (d) None of these
16. Which tissue is essential for the process of photosynthesis?
   (a) Trachids (b) Chlorophyll
   (c) Parenchyma (d) Sclerenchyma
17. The term used for cytoplasmic strands of cell is
   (a) Cell wall (b) Sieve tubes
   (c) Plasmodesmata (d) None of these
18. Food conducting vascular tissue is termed as
   (a) Sieve tube (b) Trachids
   (c) Xylem (d) Phloem

19. The cell with lack of cell organelles is termed as
    (a) Elongated (b) Prokaryotic
    (c) Eukaryotic (d) None of these
20. The first young root of emerging seedling is termed as
    (a) Radical (b) Plumule
    (c) Tap root (d) Fibrous root
21. Cell concerned with longitudinal conduction of food is termed as
    (a) Xylem parenchyma (b) Sieve tubes
    (c) Transverse tissue (d) None of these
22. Tubular porous walled vascular elements are termed as
    (a) Vessels (b) Sieve tubes
    (c) Phloem parenchyma (d) None of these
23. Water conducting tissue of flowering plant if termed as
    (a) Plastids (b) Sieve tubes
    (c) Xylem (d) Phloem parenchyma
24. How many nuclei occur in antipodal cell?
    (a) Eight (b) Five
    (c) Fifteen (d) Twelve
25. Function of cortex is
    (a) Mechanical support (b) Transpiration
    (c) Storage of food (d) None of these
26. The plant tissue situated inside the endodermis is called as
    (a) Stele (b) Pericycle
    (c) Plasmodesmata (d) Pith
27. The ATPs are produced in
    (a) Nucleus (b) Chloroplast and cristae
    (c) Golgi complex (d) Endoplasmic reticulum
28. Long form of ATP is
    (a) Adenosine Tri Phosphate (b) Adenosine Tetra Phosphate
    (c) Adenosine Twelve Phosphate (d) Adenosine Two Phosphate
29. Which is the main energy storage and transfer molecule in the cell
    (a) NADP (b) ATP
    (c) ADP (d) None of these
30. The plant cell organelle that synthesizes and store starch is
    (a) Leucoplast (b) Chloroplast
    (c) Amyloplast (d) Chromoplast

31. The cell membrane is made up of
    (a) Fat and protein (b) Protein
    (c) Lipid (d) Carbohydrate
32. The term used for folded inner membrane of mitochondria is
    (a) Setae (b) Cristae
    (c) Sieve tube (d) None of these
33. Most of the cellular activities occur in
    (a) Cytoplasm (b) Nucleoplasm
    (c) Mitochondria (d) Golgi complex
34. Rough walled endoplasmic reticulum is because of
    (a) Ribosome (b) Nucleus
    (c) Plastids (d) None of these
35. Which organelle of cell converts glucose into ATP?
    (a) Endoplasmic reticulum (b) Chloroplast
    (c) Mitochondria (d) Plastids
36. Polyarch type of xylem occurs in
    (a) Monocot root (b) Dicot root
    (c) Both a & b (d) None of these
37. Triarch type of xylem occurs in
    (a) Monocot root (b) Dicot root
    (c) Both a & b (d) None of these
38. Pith is absent in
    (a) Monocot stem (b) Dicot stem
    (c) Both a & b (d) None of these
39. Xylem and phloem are components of
    (a) Cortex (b) Vascular tissue
    (c) Stele (d) None of these
40. Actively dividing tissue is termed as
    (a) Meristematic tissue (b) Parenchymatous tissue
    (c) Sclerenchymatous tissue (d) None of these
41. Secondary growth is absent in
    (a) Dalbergia (b) Maize
    (c) Both a & b (d) None of these
42. The outermost layer of stele in a dicot stem is
    (a) Cortex (b) Endodermis
    (c) Pericycle (d) Hypodermis

43. Commercial cork is nothing but a dead tissue with thickened walls by the deposition of
    (a) Cuticle (b) Cellulose
    (c) Lignin (d) Suberin
44. Bi-collateral, conjoint vascular bundles are common in
    (a) Wolfia (b) Sunflower
    (c) Ricinus (d) Cucurbit
45. The cells with excessive length are common in the tissues of:
    (a) Parenchyma (b) Sclerenchyma
    (c) Collenchymas (d) Guard cells
46. Roots show one of the following characters
    (a) Exogenous origin
    (b) Presence of leaves and buds
    (c) Endogenous origin
    (d) Divisible into nodes and internodes
47. A water proofing substance secreted by cork and endodermal cells is
    (a) Cutin (b) Gum
    (c) Suberin (d) Mucous
48. What are the parts of the periderm
    (a) Periblem, phellogen, phelloderm
    (b) Periblem, phellogen, phelloderm
    (c) Cork, Cellulose, phelloderm
    (d) Cork, cork cambium, phelloderm
49. The histogen theory was proposed by:
    (a) Darwin (b) John Ray
    (c) Bailey (d) Hanstein
50. The lateral roots take their origin from
    (a) Sieve tube (b) Pericycle
    (c) Cortex (d) None of these
51. The bark is made up of
    (a) Phloem parenchyma (b) Endidermis
    (v) Cork (d) Phelloderm
52. Which are the special openings seen on tree trunk through which respiration is made possible
    (a) Water stomata (b) Stomata
    (c) Lenticels (d) Cracks of the bark

53. A tumor like tissues of xylem parenchyma cells developing over the wounds is called as
    (a) Tyloses (b) Gall
    (c) Callus (d) None of these
54. The chief function of velamen tissues is to
    (a) Prevent water loss (b) Transpiration
    (c) Respiration (d) None of these
55. Periderm is composed of
    (a) Phellogen and phellem
    (b) Phelloderm , phellogen and phellem
    (c) Cork-cambium secondary cortex, cork
    (d) Cork, bark, secondary cortex
56. Epidermal tissues acts generally is
    (a) A protective tissues (b) Absorbing tissues
    (c) Photosynthesis tissues (d) Conducting tissues
57. Submerged leaf posses
    (a) Stomata on both surfaces
    (b) (b) Stomata on the upper surface
    (c) Stomata on the lower surface
    (d) No stomata on any surface
58. Which of the following can be seen in monocot root
    (a) A large hypodermis (b) No pith
    (c) Medullary ray (d) Endarch xylem
59. Parenchyma cells are characterized by
    (a) Presence of thickening at the corner
    (b) Presence of uniforms thickening
    (c) Presence of intercellular spaces
    (d) Presence of lignified
60. Function of sclerenchyma help in
    (a) Photosynthesis (b) Conduction
    (c) Support (d) Absorption
61. Root hairs arises from
    (a) Pericycle (b) Endodermis
    (c) Cortex (d) Epiblema
62. The example of multiple epidermis is found in
    (a) Banyan leaf (b) Sunflower leaf
    (c) Nerium (d) Hibiscus leaf

63. Cortex is the region found between
    (a) Epidermis and stele
    (b) Hypodermis and endodermis
    (c) Endodermis and pith
    (d) Endodermis and vascular bundle
64. The bark tissues is
    (a) Living (b) Non living
    (c) Respiratory tissue (d) None of these
65. Trapa is a
    (a) Xerophyte (b) Halophytes
    (c) Hydrophyte (d) Mesophytes
66. Tunica corpus theory was proposed by
    (a) Matthias (b) Casper
    (c) Marcello (d) Schmidt
67. In angiospermic plants the leaf gap is found in
    (a) Internode (b) Node
    (c) Root apex (d) Lateral branch
68. Knots are formed in wood because of
    (a) Injuries caused by animals
    (b) Branches fall of leaves scarp
    (c) Natural growth of trees
    (d) None of these
69. What are hydathodes?
    (a) Opening in the bark
    (b) Pores through which gas exchange takes plant
    (c) Openings in the leaf through which water is forced out
    (d) Stomata in water plant
70. The presence of casparian strips is a specific featured of
    (a) Parenchyma (b) Chlorenchyma
    (c) Endodermis (d) None of these
71. Which is the example of anomalous secondary growth?
    (a) Sorghum (b) Sunflower
    (c) Bougainvillea (d) None of these
72. Hypodermis originate from
    (a) Epidermis (b) Mesoderm
    (c) Stele (d) None of these

73. The branch of botany which deals with study of external features of different plant is termed as
(a) Cytology (b) Morphology
(c) Anatomy (d) Embryology
74. The sieve tubes are found in
(a) Trachids (b) Wood fibers
(c) Phloem (d) Xylem
75. The cork cell wall is made up of
(a) Fat (b) Suberin
(b) Cellulose (d) Protein
76. Which is the water secreting gland occurs in plants
(a) Tylosis (b) Tannin glands
(b) Hydathodes (d) Pericycle
77. A lateral meristems that produces secondary growth is termed as
(a) Cambium (b) medullary rays
(c) Phloem (d) Pitch
78. An unevenly thickened cell walls occur in
(a) Collenchymas (b) Sieve tubes
(c) Apical (d) Parenchyma
79. The cell walls of which tissue impregnated with suberin
(a) Hypodems (b) Epidemics
(c) Pericycle (d) Cork
80. An impermeable layer of cutin of outer walls of epidermis is termed as
(a) Cuticle (b) Cork
(c) Epidermis (d) Hypodermis
81. A type of stele which consists of a ring of vascular tissue surrounding pith is termed as
(a) Siphonostele (b) Actinostele
(c) Porotostele (d) Mixed porotostele
82. The central vascular cylinder of stem or root is termed as
(a) Stele (b) Cambium
(c) Pith (d) Pericycle
83. From which one cork is produced
(a) Phellogen (b) Pericycle
(c) Endodermis (d) Cortex

84. Which is concerned with monocot leaf?
(a) Mesophyll is not differentiated into palisade of spongy tissue
(b) Reticulate venation
(c) Petiolate leaves
(d) Cyme inflorescence

85. Which is not the member of the family rannunculaceace?
(a) Mentha (b) Coriander
(c) Sorghum (d) Horse tail

86. Which family is called as a pink family?
(a) Caryophyllaceae (b) Tiliaceae
(c) Malvaceae (d) Euphorbiaceae

87. Which plant is commonly grown in Europe for preparation of perfumes?
(a) *Dianthus* (b) *Sesbania sesban*
(c) *Tectona* (d) *Eucalyptus citriodora*

88. When stamen are arranged in two whorls of five each outer stamens situated opposite to petals termed as
(a) Opdiplostemanous (b) Epistemanous
(c) Gynandrous (d) Diandrous

89. A straight ovule with the micropile opposite to petals is termed as
(a) Anatrophous (b) Orthotropus
(c) Epistemanous (d) None of these

90. When a flower has both functional stamens and pistils is termed as
(a) Incomplete (b) Imperfect
(c) Half perfect (d) Perfect

91. An androecium consists of free stamens it is termed as
(a) Polyandrous (b) Mononandrous
(c) Diandrous (d) None of these

92. Always the roots hairs are
(a) Bicellular (b) Multicellular
(c) Long (d) Unicellular

93. Which termed is used for central region of root or stem
(a) Middle cortex (b) Pith
(c) Endodermis (d) Hypodermics

94. Which one is absent in close type of vascular bundles
(a) Xylem (b) Chlorenchyma
(c) Phloem (d) Medullary rays

95. The position of lysigeneous cavity in
    (a) In the pitch (b) Between parenchyma
    (c) Portoxylem (d) Beneath metaxylem
96. The function of lateral meristems in
    (a) Increase length of root (b) Increase thickness of stem
    (c) Increase the size of leaf (d) Increase in root of branches
97. In which of the following conjoint collateral and open type of vascular bundles occur
    (a) Monocot stem (b) Leaf sheath
    (c) Rhizome (d) Dicot root
98. The portoxylem in leaf is directed towards
    (a) Endodermis (b) Cuticle
    (c) Stomata (d) Middle cortex
99. In which of the following passage cells are formed
    (a) Endodermis (b) Pericycle
    (c) Hypodermic (d) Epidermis
100. Which is the location of sieve plates & sieve pores?
    (a) Lateral walls of sieve cells
    (b) Walls of companion cells
    (c) End walls of sieve tube
    (d) End wall of sieve cells
101. When the vascular tissue consists of phloem surrounded to central xylem is described as
    (a) Amphicribral vascular bundle
    (b) Radial vascular bundle
    (c) Both a and b
    (d) None of these

Answer key: ANATOMY - I

1. (c) 2. (a) 3. (c) 4. (a) 5. (a) 6. (a) 7. (a) 8. (c) 9. (a) 10. (a) 11. (a) 12. (d) 13. (a) 14. (b) 15. (c) 16. (b) 17. (c) 18. (d) 19. (b) 20. (a) 21. (b) 22. (a) 23. (c) 24. (a) 25. (c) 26. (a) 27. (b) 28. (a) 29. (b) 30. (c) 31. (a) 32. (b) 33. (a) 34. (a) 35. (c) 36. (a) 37. (b) 38. (a) 39. (b) 40. (a) 41. (b) 42. (b) 43. (d) 44. (d) 45. (b) 46. (b) 47. (b) 48. (d) 49. (d) 50. (b) 51. (d) 52. (b) 53. (a) 54. (a) 55. (b) 56. (a) 57. (d) 58. (b) 59. (c) 60. (b) 61. (d) 62. (b) 63. (a) 64. (a) 65. (c) 66. (d) 67. (b) 68. (c) 69. (c) 70. (b) 71. (c) 72. (b) 73. (b) 74. (c) 75. (b) 76. (b) 77. (a) 78. (a) 79. (d) 80. (a) 81. (a) 82. (a) 83. (a) 84. (a) 85. (d) 86. (a) 87. (a) 88. (a) 89. (b) 90. (d) 91. (a) 92. (d) 93. (b) 94. (c) 95. (d) 96. (c) 97. (a) 98. (c) 99. (b) 100. (b) 101. (a)

ANATOMY - II

1. The pericycle is made up of
   (a) Sclerenchyma (b) Parenchyma
   (c) Spongy tissue (d) Xylem elements
2. The opening & closing of stomata is regulated by
   (a) Passage cells (b) Guard cells
   (c) companion cells (d) Epidermal cells
3. Always the location of pericycle is
   (a) Epidermis (b) Inside endodermis
   (c) Hypodermis (d) Lower epidermis
4. In which of the following sclerenchymatous hypodermis occurs
   (a) Dicot root (b) Monocot leaf
   (c) Dicot stem (d) Monocot stem
5. Which cells are living but without nucleus
   (a) Epidermal cells (b) Companion cells
   (c) Sieve tube (d) guard cells
6. Chemically casperian strip is
   (a) Cutin n lignin (b) Lignin & cellulose
   (c) Lignin n suberin (d) Cutin n suberin
7. Which one is the living structure?
   (a) Sclerenchyma (b) Parenchyma
   (c) Xylem vessel (d) Trachids
8. The corners of Chlorenchyma cells made up of
   (a) Pectin (b) Suberin
   (c) Lignin (d) Resin
9. Age of tree can be calculated by counting
   (a) Total branches of tree (b) Diameter and height of tree
   (c) Annual rings (d) None of these
10. Which one is the lateral meristems?
    (a) Pitch (b) Cambium
    (c) Xylem (d) Cortex
11. The apical meristems develops into
    (a) Endodermis (b) Vascular tissue
    (c) Pericycle (d) None of these
12. Hydathodes are concern with
    (a) Vascular tissue system (b) Epidermal tissue
    (c) Guard tissue (d) Cortex tissue system

13. An anatomist Marcello Malpighi published "Anatomia Plantarum" in
    (a) 1471 (b) 1571
    (c) 1271 (d) 1671
14. The tissue that appears in the cortical region during secondary growth is termed as
    (a) Cork cambium (b) Phellogen
    (c) Phelloderm d) Epidermis
15. When a cork cambium becomes active & forms new tissue in the outer cortical region some pores appear in epidermis that are called as
    (a) Lenticels (b) Hydathodes
    (c) Stomata (d) Pore
16. In presence of cambium the vascular bundle is called as
    (a) Close (b) Open
    (c) Radial (d) Conjoint
17. The location of phloem is collateral vascular bundle is
    (a) Inside the xylem (b) Lateral side of xylem
    (c) On the both side of xylem (d) Outside the xylem
18. The age of plant can be determined by counting
    (a) Annual rings (b) Length of seedling
    (c) Number of branches (d) Height in inches
19. The secondary wood which does not take part in water conduction but gives mechanical support is termed as
    (a) Heart wood (b) Autumn wood
    (c) Simple wood (d) Spring wood
20. The raphides are made up of
    (a) Calcium oxalates (b) Calcium carbonate
    (c) Magnesium sulphate (d) Zinc
21. Bulliform cells occur in
    (a) Bundle sheath (b) Mesophyll tissue
    (c)Vascular bundle (d) Epidermis
22. The main function of phloem is transportation of
    (a) Food (b) Mineral
    (c) Water (d) Light
23. Presence casparian strips is the distinct feature of
    (a) Cortex (b) Endodermis
    (c) Pericycle (d) Pitch
24. The cork cambium & vascular cambium are the examples of
    (a) Apical meristems (b) Lateral meristems
    (c) Intercalary meristems (d) Permanent tissue

25. Secondary xylem remains functional up to
(a) Less than one year
(b) For two months
(c) For one year
(d) As long as plant survives
26. Xylem of stained section of stem appear
(a) Red
(b) Green
(c) Pink
(d) Orange
27. The root cap develops from
(a) Dermatogen
(b) Root hairs
(c) Vascular cambium
(d) Wood cambium
28. The companion cells are associated with
(a) Trachids
(b) Female gamete
(c) Trachids
(d) Guard cell
29. Cork cambium accumulates
(a) Resin
(b) Suberin
(c) Starch
(d) Tannin
30. A characteristics feature of collenchymas is
(a) Rectangular cells with thickening at the corners
(b) Elongated cells with thickening at the corners
(c) Round cells with thickening at the corners
(d) None of these
31. Which is the waxy substance associated with cork
(a) Suberin
(b) Wax
(c) Lignin
(d) Silica deposits
32. In which lignin is absent
(a) Parenchyma
(b) Collenchymas
(c) Sclerenchyma
(d) All of these
33. Which type of vascular bundle occur in dicot stem
(a) Open, collateral endarch
(b) Open
(c) Open collateral exarch
(d) Conjoint collateral
34. In which abnormal secondary growth occurs
(a) Dracaena
(b) Asparagus
(c) Aloe
(d) Agave
35. Which is the externally protective tissue occur in plants
(a) Epidermis and cork
(b) Hypodermis
(c) Endodermis
(d) Both a & b
36. A distinct annual rings occur in plants which grow in
(a) Temperate region
(b) Subtropical region
(c) Wet banks of water
(d) Marshy places

37. The secondary meristems get activated from
    (a) Primary meristems (b) Mature meristems tissue
    (c) Apical meristems (d) Intercalary meristems
38. Which type of vascular bundles occur in dicot leaves
    (a) Open (b) Close
    (c) Closed (d) Radial closed
39. Which is true in case of companion cells?
    (a) Living and non-nucleated (b) Dead cells
    (c) Dead but nucleated (d) Living & nucleated
40. The location of last produced secondary xylem is near
    (a) Cortex (b) Hypodermis
    (c) Cambium ring (d) Inner cortex
41. Which one is absent in the phloem of monocot plants
    (a) Companion cells (b) Phloem parenchyma
    (c) Sieve cells (d) Phloem sclerenchyma
42. In grass the arrangement of vascular bundle is
    (a) In a ring (b) Scattered irregular
    (c) Arranged in two rings (d) Scattered but smaller
43. The transverse section of trachids looks
    (a) Elongated (b) Round
    (c) Rectangle (d) Oval
44. In which lignin is absent
    (a) Collenchyma (b) Sclerenchyma
    (c) Parenchyma (d) Chlorenchyma
45. In which of the following abnormal secondary growth occurs?
    (a) Maize (b) Sugarcane
    (c) Dracaena (d) None of these
46. The diameter of portoxylem in comparison to metaxylem are
    (a) Larger (b) Smaller
    (c) Broader (d) Angular
47. The end region of trenched is
    (a) Projected (b) Flat
    (c) Perforated (d) Walls less
48. The normal appearance of stone cells is
    (a) Hexagonal (b) Round
    (c) Iso-diametric (d) Oval

49. Always the roots has
    (a) Endarch xylem (b) Tetrarch stele
    (c) Exarch xylem (d) Polyarch stele
50. The growth rings are produced due to activity of
    (a) Extrastellar cambium (b) Interstellar cambium
    (c) Interstellar phloem (d) Both b & c both
51. Companion cells regulates the activity of
    (a) Sieve cells (b) Sieve elements
    (c) Sieve tube (d) Sieve plates
52. Phelloderm is made up of
    (a) Phellem +phellogen
    (b) Periderm +phellogen
    (c) Phellem periderm
    (d) Periderm phellogen & phellem
53. Which type of tissue gives mechanical strength to the plant?
    (a) Phloem parenchyma (b) Meristematic tissue
    (c) Cambium (d) Sclerenchyma
54. Which one never occurs in roots?
    (a) Cortex (b) Sieve tube
    (c) Meristematic tissue (d) Chlorenchyma
55. Which of the following tissue do not occur in monocot?
    (a) Root hairs (b) Trachids
    (c) Collenchyma (d) Phloem parenchyma
56. Which is the simple permanent tissue made up of dead cells?
    (a) Sieve cells (b) Sclerenchyma
    (c) Arenchyma (d) merismatic tissue
57. Stele in enveloped by
    (a) Vascular tissue (b) Cortex
    (c) Pith (d) Hypodermics
58. Length of plants increases due to
    (a) Internodes (b) apical meristems
    (c) Nodal buds (d) Phloem parenchyma
59. Which element of phloem is dead?
    (a) Sieve cells (b) Companion cells
    (c) Sieve tube (d) Phloem fibers
60. Which cells is responsible to regulate function of sieve tube
    (a) Guard cells (b) Pitch cells
    (c) Companion cells (d) Endodermal cells

61. Arrangement of xylem in stem is
(a) Diarch (b) Endarch
(c) Polyarch (d) None of these
62. Arrangements of vascular bundles in monocot stem is
(a) Arranged in a ring (b) inside a ring
(c) Scattered (d) In cortex
63. The layers of tissue situated below the epidermis is termed as
(a) Cortex (b) Endodermis
(c) Xylem (d) Phloem
64. Always endodermis is absent in
(a) Xerophytic (b) Floating root
(c) Monocot stem (d) None of these
65. Which is the following is a living mechanical tissue
(a) Parenchyma (b) Cambium
(c) Vessels (d) Xylem
66. Which one is associated with collenchymas?
(a) Pectin (b) Resin
(c) Suberin (d) Lignin
67. Tissue of which type of show disposition outside the cells
(a) Vascular tissue (b) Collenchymas
(c) Glandular tissue (d) Endodermis
68. In which of the following lignin is absent
(a) Pith cells (b) Collenchymas cells
(c) Sieve tubes (d) Sieve cells
69. In which of the following bulliform cells occurs in leaves
(a) Sunflower (b) Catharanthus
(c) Maize (d) Aloe
70. Casparian strips occurs on cells walls of
(a) Inner cortex (b) Endodermis
(c) Cortex (d) Portoxylem
71. When ends walls are absent in xylem it is called as
(a) Protoxylem (b) Trachids
(c) Metaxylem (d) Both a and c
72. Which type of thickenings occur in protoxylem
(a) Dotted (b) Pitted
(c) Spiral (d) Sclariform

73. Characteristic feature of sieve tube is
(a) Presence of lignin (b) Absence of nucleus
(c) Absence of cytoplasm (d) Presence of pectin

74. The highest activity of cambium occurs during
(a) Spring (b) Automan
(c) Winter (d) Summer

75. In which of the following radical vascular bundles occur
(a) Leaf (b) Flower
(c) Stem (d) Root

76. Which takes part in food synthesis?
(a) Chlorenchyma (b) Sclerenchyma
(c) Pith (d) Endodermis

77. Which type of vascular bundle occur in cucurbit
(a) Conjoint (b) Radial
(c) Collateral (d) Bi-collateral

78. In sorghum leaf the mesophyll consists of
(a) Arenchyma
(b) Only spongy
(c) Only palisade
(d) Palisade & spongy parenchyma

79. The companion cell is
(a) Dead (b) Enucleated
(c) Living & thick (d) Nucleated

80. The internal secretory structure is
(a) Guard cells (b) Gum cavity
(c) Resin duct (d) Stone cell

81. In case of root the lateral roots originate from
(a) Inner cortex (b) Stele
(c) Epidermis (d) Pitch

82. Which one of the protective layer of epidermis
(a) Cuticle (b) Cortex
(c) Endodermis (d) Pericycle

83. The endodermis is a part of
(a) Vascular bundle (b) Outer cortex
(c) Stele (d) Pericycle

84. In maize leaf the hygroscopic cells are laterally covered by
(a) Wax (b) Hairs
(c) Stone cell (d) Companion cells

85. Which one is not a zone of cortex?
(a) Epidermis (b) Main cortex
(c) Hypodermis (d) Endodermis

86. Which is the nonliving part of cell in plants?
(a) Cell wall (b) Nucleus
(c) Plasma membrane (d) Mitochondria

87. In plants the cell wall is secreted by?
(a) Cytoplasm (b) Protoplasm
(c) Cell wall (d) None of these

88. How many layers occur in cell wall of plants?
(a) Two (b) Four
(c) Five (d) Three

89. Which layer of plant cell wall composed of pure cellulose?
(a) Secondary wall (b) Primary wall
(c) Middle lamella (d) None of these

90. Which of the following occur in cell wall of all plant?
(a) Cellulose (b) Suberin
(c) Cutin (d) Pectin

91. A tough, hard and chemically complex substance which occur in woody tissue of plants is
(a) Suberin (b) Hemi cellulose
(c) Cutin (d) Lignin

92. The plant cell wall which consists of wax and fatty acids is termed as
(a) Cutin (b) Lignin
(c) Cellulose (d) Pectin

93. When a layer of plant cell wall consists of many types of fatty substance & it is found on the wall of cork cells it is termed as
(a) Cutin (b) Lignin
(c) Suberin (d) None of these

94. The middle lamella of plant cell wall consists of
(a) Pectin (b) Cellulose
(c) Hemicelluloses (d) Lignin

95. Which of the following is cementing substance of plant cell wall & helps in the attachment of cells?
(a) Cutin (b) Mucilage
(c) Pectin (d) Mineral substances

96. The protoplasmic strands in certain cells helps to communicate with adjacent cell is termed as
    (a) Plasmodesmata (b) Pits
    (c) Simple pits (d) Bordered pits
97. In certain cells a small tubular canals present which are termed as
    (a) Canals (b) Cytoplasmic strand
    (c) Plasmodesmata (d) Pits
98. The pits are present in cell wall of
    (a) Xylem trachids (b) Companion cells
    (c) Phloem parenchyma (d) Sieve tubes
99. The slightly swollen centre of pit membrane of plant cell is termed as
    (a) Border (b) Torus
    (c) Rim (d) Simple pit
100. The tissue which has the ability of division is termed as
    (a) Meristematic tissue (b) Sclerenchyma
    (c) Collenchymas (d) None of these

Answer key: ANATOMY - II

1. (b) 2. (b) 3. (c) 4. (c) 5. (c) 6. (d) 7. (b) 8. (a) 9. (c) 10. (b) 11. (d) 12. (b) 13. (d) 14. (a) 15. (a) 16. (c) 17. (a) 18. (a) 19. (a) 20. (b) 21. (d) 22. (a) 23. (c) 24. (b) 25. (c) 26. (a) 27. (d) 28. (d) 29. (a) 30. (b) 31. (a) 32. (b) 33. (a) 34. (a) 35. (a) 36. (a) 37. (c) 38. (d) 39. (d) 40. (c) 41. (c) 42. (d) 43. (b) 44. (a) 45. (c) 46. (d) 47. (c) 48. (d) 49. (c) 50. (b) 51. (d) 52. (d) 53. (d) 54. (d) 55. (c) 56. (b) 57. (b) 58. (b) 59. (d) 60. (c) 61. (b) 62. (a) 63. (a) 64. (c) 65. (a) 66. (a) 67. (b) 68. (d) 69. (c) 70. (b) 71. (b) 72. (c) 73. (b) 74. (a) 75. (d) 76. (a) 77. (d) 78. (d) 79. (b) 80. (d) 81. (c) 82. (a) 83. (c) 84. (d) 85. (d) 86. (a) 87. (b) 88. (d) 89. (a) 90. (a) 91. (d) 92. (a) 93. (c) 94. (a) 95. (c) 96. (a) 97. (d) 98. (a) 99. (b) 100. (a)

ANATOMY - III

1. Which type of tissue found at the tip of root and stem.
    (a) Primary meristems (b) Cork cambium
    (c) Sclerenchyma (d) Interfascicular cambium
2. Which one occurs in cambium of root?
    (a) Secondary meristems (b) Pro-meristems
    (c) Cark (d) None of these
3. Which one occur only in gymnosperms and dicot plants
    (a) Promeristems (b) Lateral meristems
    (c) Intercalary meristems (d) Sclerenchyma

4. The lateral meristematic tissue composed of
   (a) Cambium and phellogen tissue (b) Elongation of stem
   (c) Primary permanent tissue (d) Apical tissue
5. Which one occurs in apical meristems of stem?
   (a) Dermatogen, Periblem, Plerome
   (b) Dermatogen, Periblem, Cambium
   (c) Dermatogen, Periblem, Intercalary meristems
   (d) Dermatogen, Periblem, Lateral meristems
6. The epidermis of any plant is produced from the cells of
   (a) Calyptorgen (b) Periblem
   (c) Plerome (d) Dermatogen
7. Which of the following produce cortex, endodermis and hypodermis of stem?
   (a) Periblem (b) Plerome
   (c) Epiblema (d) dermatogens
8. Which one is the protective part of dicot roots
   (a) Root hair (b) Root cambium
   (c) Root cap (d) Root fibers
9. Which one is the simple tissue?
   (a) Collenchymas (b) Trachids
   (c) Xylem (d) Phloem
10. Which of the following tissue consists of chlorophyll?
    (a) Aerenchyma (b) Chlorenchyma
    (c) Xylem (d) Sieve tubes
11. Which of the following tissue occur in most of the hydrophytic plant?
    (a) Aerenchyma (b) Gums cells
    (c) Cambium (d) Cork cells
12. Which of the following is dead tissue?
    (a) Sclerenchyma (b) Collenchymas
    (c) Chlorenchyma (d) Parenchyma
13. Which of the following tissue is derived from meristems?
    (a) Primary xylem (b) Collenchymas
    (c) Cambium (d) Secondary xylem
14. Which tissue is supposed to be a tissue of mechanical support?
    (a) Sclerenchyma (b) Meristematic tissue
    (c) Aerenchyma (d) Chlorenchyma

15. Which type of tissue consists of lignified cells?
    (a) Chlorenchyma (b) Cortex cells
    (c) Parenchyma (d) Sclerenchyma
16. Which type of tissue occur in fibers of plants
    (a) Sclerenchyma (b) Meristem
    (c) Simple tissue (d) Collenchyma
17. The fibrous tissue of plants is mostly originated by
    (a) Pro-cambium (b) Apical meristems
    (c) Stem meristems (d) Root meristems
18. Which of the following is economic fiber?
    (a) Gram (b) Hemp
    (c) Fenugreek (d) Cajanus
19. Space left between vertically arranged sclerenchyma tissues is termed as
    (a) Lumen (b) Pit
    (c) Cavity (d) Space
20. Xylem fibers which possesses thick wall and simple pits are termed as
    (a) Libriform fibers (b) Sieve parenchyma
    (c) Sieve tube (d) Simple fibers
21. The xylem fibers which has thin wall with bordered pits are termed as
    (a) Phloem parenchyma (b) Trachids fibers
    (c) Sieve tubes (d) None of these
22. The another name of special sclerenchymatous cells is
    (a) Stone cells (b) Mucilage ducts
    (c) Gland cells (d) Resin ducts
23. The complex tissue is
    (a) Collenchyma (b) Meristem
    (c) Parenchyma (d) Xylem
24. In which groups of plants digestive glands are present
    (a) Insectivorous plants (b) Angiospermic plants
    (c) Shady plants (d) Pteridophytes
25. In which part of plant nectarines are found
    (a) Stem (b) Flowers
    (c) Fruit (d) Root
26. When epidermal cell modifies in to a hair like structure, it is called as
    (a) Trichome (b) Tendril
    (c) Cilia (d) Twig

27. A very long coiled flexible hair of plant part is termed as
    (a) Cilia (b) Trichome
    (c) Tendril (d) Stem
28. The stomata without guard cells which exudates water is termed as
    (a) Hydathodes (b) Stomata
    (c) Lentil cells (d) Pore
29. The special ducts which secrete fragrance in floral part is termed as
    (a) Nectarines (b) Osmophores
    (c) Hydathodes (d) Oil glands
30. The latex secreting cells of plant are termed as
    (a) Laticiferous tissue (b) Resin ducts
    (c) Gum ducts (d) Oil ducts
31. In which of the following latex ducts occur
    (a) Gram (b) Radish
    (c) Coriander (d) Nerium
32. The plants of which family consists of latex vessels
    (a) Euphorbiaceae (b) Annonaceae
    (c) Labiatae (d) Papilionaceae
33. Which of the following is an example of dicot plant?
    (a) Bajra (b) Sorghum
    (c) Sunflower (d) Maize
34. Where is the position of endodermis in plants?
    (a) Below the cortex (b) Above the cortex
    (c) Below the cuticle (d) At the centre of stem

Answer key: ANATOMY - III

1. (a) 2. (a) 3. (b) 4. (a) 5. (a) 6. (d) 7. (a) 8. (c) 9. (a) 10. (b) 11. (a) 12. (a) 13. (b) 14. (a) 15. (d) 16. (a) 17. (a) 18. (b) 19. (a) 20. (a) 21. (b) 22. (a) 23. (d) 24. (a) 25. (b) 26. (a) 27. (c) 28. (a) 29. (b) 30. (a) 31. (d) 32. (a) 33. (c) 34. (a)

ANATOMY - IV

1. In dicot stem, patch of sclerenchyma associated with phloem of vascular bundle is termed as
   (a) Hard blast (b) Meristem
   (c) Sieve tubes (d) Root cap
2. In which group of plants the vascular bundles are arranged in a ring form
   (a) Pteridophytes (b) Bryophytes
   (c) Monocot plants (d) Dicot plants

3. Which of the following gives rise to secondary growth?
   (a) Cambium (b) Xylem
   (c) Phloem (d) Sieve tubes
4. The stem increases in thickness due to activity of
   (a) Parenchyma (b) Cambium
   (c) Protoxylem (d) Meristematic tissue
5. When metaxylem occurs towards periphery & protoxylem towards center of stem, the condition is termed as
   (a) Exarch (b) Middle
   (c) Endarch (d) None of these
6. When metaxylem occurs towards center and protoxylem towards peripheral region, the condition is termed as
   (a) Exarch (b) Endarch
   (c) Mesarch (d) None of these
7. The central region of dicot stem consist of
   (a) Pericycle (b) Hypodermis
   (c) Cortex (d) Pith
8. The parenchymatous cells which occur between two vascular bundles of dicot stem are termed as
   (a) Medullary rays (b) Sieve tubes
   (c) Cambium (d) Companion cells
9. What is the function of pith?
   (a) Enzyme secretion (b) Storage of food
   (c) Resin secretion (d) Storage of minerals
10. In which group of plants the vascular bundles are randomly scattered?
    (a) Monocot (b) Dicot
    (c) Pteridophytes (d) Bryophytes
11. Which cell is arranged by living intercellular spaces?
    (a) Parenchymatous cells (b) Xylem
    (c) Sclerenchymatous cells (d) Cambium
12. In which plant stem pith is absent
    (a) Acacia (b) Maize
    (c) Sunflower (d) Groundnut
13. In the vascular bundle of monocot stem there is a water cavity at the lower side of protoxylem which is termed as
    (a) Lysigeneous cavity (b) Resin cavity
    (c) Both a and b (d) None of these

14. How is the outline of xylem vessels of xylem of dicot root?
    (a) Pyriform (b) Triangular
    (c) Circular (d) Rectangular
15. In case of isobilateral leaf, some leaf in epidermis some groups of bigger cells found that are termed as
    (a) Bulliform cells (b) Stomata
    (c) Hydathodes (d) Lenticels
16. In which of the following bulliform cells are absent
    (a) Maize (b) Sunflower
    (c) Sugarcane (d) Bamboo
17. When the cambium situated between phloem and xylem it is termed as
    (a) Interfascicular (b) Cambium
    (c) Fascicular cambium (d) None of these
18. The newly formed cambium which occur between vascular bundles in known as
    (a) Interfascicular cambium (b) Intrafascicular cambium
    (c) Outer cambium (d) None of these
19. Tracheids and vessels are the elements of
    (a) Phloem (b) Parenchyma
    (c) Collenchyma (d) Xylem
20. Who is the father of plant anatomy of Indian origin?
    (a) P. Jayaraman (b) B.G.L. Swamy
    (c) R.M. Pai (d) None of these
21. Where is the Plant Anatomy Research centre in India?
    (a) Mumbai (b) Chennai
    (c) Kolkata (d) Bangalore
22. Which of the following produces numerous root hairs?
    (a) Piliferous layer (b) Root base
    (b) Hypodermis (d) Root cap

Answer key: ANATOMY - IV

1. (a) 2. (d) 3. (a) 4. (b) 5. (c) 6. (a) 7. (d) 8. (a) 9. (b) 10. (a) 11. (a) 12. (b) 13. (a) 14. (c) 15. (a) 16. (b) 17. (c) 18. (a) 19. (d) 20. (a) 21. (b) 22. (a)

Bibliography

1. Aisha Saleem Khan, (2017). Flowering Plants: Structure and Industrial Products, Published by John Wiley & Sons Ltd. , ISBN: 9781119262770.
2. Akhil Baruah, (2005). Advanced Morphology of Angiosperms, Pointer Publisher, Jaipur.
3. Akhil, Baraah, (2013). Plant Taxonomy, Published by Eastarn Book House, Guwahati, ISBN: 9789380261935.
4. Andrian, D. Bell and Alan Bryan, (1991). Plant Form, Published by Oxford University Press, ISBN: 9780198542193.
5. Annie Ragland and V. Kumaresan, (2018). Morphology of Angiosperms, Taxonomy and Botany, Saras Publication, Edition-I, pp. 386.
6. Annie Ragland (2018). Plant Anatomy and Microtechniques, Saras Publication, ISBN: 9789384826000, pp. 388.
7. Aslam Khan (2001). Plant Anatomy and Physiology, Gaurav Book Centre, ISBN: 9788178350493, pp. 334.
8. Esau Katherine, (2002). Anatomy of Seed Plants, Wiley India Pvt. Ltd., ISBN: 9788126508204, pp. 572.
9. Gurucharan Singh, (1999). Plant Systmatics, Science Publisher, US.
10. Meenakshi, C. Mahajan and Sumia Fatima (2014). Families of Angiosperms Vol. I & II, LAP Publishing House, Germany, pp. 354.
11. Michael Hickey & Clive King (1981). 100 Families of Flowering Plants, Published by Cambridge University Press, New York, USA, pp. 567.
12. Mishra, S.R., (2004). Morphology of Plants, Discovery Publishing House Pvt. Ltd., New Delhi, pp. 253.
13. Mondol, A.K. (2016). Advance Plant Taxonomy, Published by New Central Agency, (NCBA), 1st Edition, ISBN: 8173814910.
14. Naik, V.N. (1998). Flora of Marathwada, Vol. I & II, Amrut Prakashan, Aurangabad.
15. Pandey, S.N. (1993). A Text Book of Botany: Anatomy and Economic Botany, Published by Vikas Publication House Delhi, pp. 644.

16. Pareek and Trivedi, (2019). Plant Morphology and Anatomy, RBD Publication, India.
17. Ratikanta Maiti, (2012). Crop Plant Anatomy, Published by Vibha Agrotec. Ltd. Hyderabad, ISBN: 9781780640198, pp. 328.
18. Roy, (2010). Plant Anatomy, Published by New Central Agency, Delhi, ISBN: 9788173815133, pp. 594.
19. Sambamurty. A.V.S.S. (2005). Taxonomy of Angiosperms. I.K. International Pvt. Ltd. New Delhi, India, pp.892.
20. Sanjay Kumar Singh, (2006). Text Book of Plant Anatomy, Campus Book International, ISBN: 9788180300844, pp. 186.
21. Sharma, O.P. (2017). Plant Raxonomy, Mc Grow Hill Education, Edi.-II, ISBN: 9780070141599, pp. 587.
22. Shukla, P. and S.P. Misra, (1979). An Introduction of Taxonomy of Angiosperms, Vikas Publishing House, New Delhi, India, pp. 546.
23. Sinha, R.K., (2010). Practical Taxonomy of Angiosperms, I.K. International Publishing House, pp. 416.
24. Sivarajan, V.V., (1991). Introduction to the Principals of Plant Taxonomy, IInd Edition, Cambridge University Press, New York, USA, ISBN: 9780521356794.
25. Sumia Fatima, (2018). Plant Morphology Published by, Discovery Publishing House Pvt. Ltd., New Delhi, ISBN: 9789350568927.
26. Suniti Sharan, (2011). Plant Morphology, Published by Pacific Books International, ISBN: 9380472374.